Improving Safety Culture

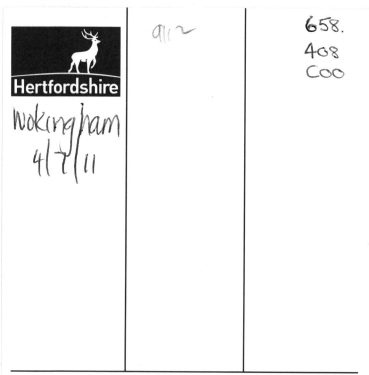

Improving Safety Culture

A Practical Guide

DOMINIC COOPER

JOHN WILEY & SONS

Chichester • New York • Weinheim • Brisbane • Singapore • Toronto

Other Wiley Editorial Offices

John Wiley & Sons, Inc., 605 Third Avenue,
New York, NY 10158-0012, USA

WILEY-VCH Verlag GmbH, Pappelallee 3,
D-69469 Weinheim, Germany

Jacaranda Wiley Ltd, 33 Park Road, Milton,
Queensland 4064, Australia

John Wiley & Sons (Asia) Pte Ltd, 2 Clementi Loop #02-01,
Jin Xing Distripark, Singapore 129809

John Wiley & Sons (Canada) Ltd, 22 Worcester Road,
Rexdale, Ontario M9W 1L1, Canada

Library of Congress Cataloging-in-Publication Data

Cooper, Dominic.
    Improving safety culture : a practical guide / Dominic Cooper.
        p.   cm.
    Includes index.
    ISBN 0-471-95821-2 (paper)
    1. Industrial safety—Management.   I. Title.
T55.C664   1997
658.4'08—dc21   97–25693
                                                                       CIP

British Library Cataloguing in Publication Data

A catalogue record for this book is available from the British Library

ISBN 0-471-95821-2

Typeset in 11/13pt Palatino from the author's disks
by Mayhew Typesetting, Rhayader, Powys
Printed and bound in Great Britain by Bookcraft Ltd, Midsomer Norton, Somerset

This book is printed on acid-free paper responsibly manufactured from sustainable
forestation, for which at least two trees are planted for each one used for paper production.

To my wife and children

Contents

Preface

In recent years companies have begun to recognise the important contribution that an effective safety culture can make to the control of their ongoing operational costs and the efficiency of their ongoing operations. Much of this is due to the recent introduction of EC goal-setting legislation that places the onus on organisations to identify and properly manage the risks created by their activities. Many organisations have realised that this provides the perfect opportunity for them to streamline their operational processes and optimise the associated management and control systems. In practice, it has also meant that responsibility for health, safety and environmental issues has become firmly established as an integral part of the line management function, rather than being the sole domain of the safety officer (or safety department as has traditionally been the case). Therefore, now more than ever before, all levels of line management need to possess a much greater knowledge of how to develop and implement high quality safety management systems. They also need to know how to manage safety on a day to day basis throughout their areas of responsibility.

The traditional 'policing' role of the safety practitioner has also changed. No longer a mere safety officer, the safety practitioner's role is now that of a high-level internal consultant. They are expected to offer independent advice to senior management on the development of the organisation's safety policies and their short, medium and long term strategic objectives for creating and maintaining a positive safety culture. In addition, they are expected to advise line-managers on both the development and implementation of appropriate control and monitoring systems and the review of ongoing safety performance, while at the same time conducting independent reviews of the whole safety management system. To fulfil these functions in an effective manner, it is self-evident that safety practitioners must be authoritative all rounders. While possessing an awareness of all aspects of safety *per se*, he or she will also need to:

- have an up-to-date and in-depth appreciation of all aspects of management and management systems
- be experienced in problem-solving and decision-making

- be highly aware of the effects organisational change and development issues (e.g. project management, team-working, downsizing, contracting out, etc.) exert on safety.

Only when they are armed with all this knowledge will safety practitioners be in a position to recognise the need for change, and be able to positively influence unfolding events to help create an optimal safety culture through-out the organisation. Thus, because of their new consulting role, and the need to ensure that their recommendations accord with business needs, modern safety practitioners must be as familiar with all aspects of management as those practitioners from other disciplines (such as finance, human resources, production, etc.) who comprise the senior management team. Although, the safety profession is making great strides to address these issues, it is still too often the case that many safety practitioners lack knowledge of the most basic management tools and techniques and, therefore, lack an understanding of how they might be used to good effect.

It is also true to say that many people who work in the field of safety do not really know what a 'safety culture' is. Perhaps this is not surprising given that, with very few exceptions, many of us who write or talk about safety culture tend to wave the phrase around like a well worn slogan that is passed its sell-by date. Recent writings, for example, have berated successful real-life attempts to improve safety, and have then gone on to say that what is needed is a 'Safety Culture'. Not only does this create the impression that a safety culture can be pulled out of thin air or poured from a packet of cornflakes, but it also creates obvious difficulties for busy managers.

These managers have often asked of me 'What *does* an identifiable safety culture look like?' My replies used to paraphrase the working definition of safety culture written in the ACSNI report (published by the Health and Safety Commission in 1993) by saying 'that it is the product of people's values and beliefs, their behaviour, and their commitment to your health and safety programmes. This will be evident in people trusting what you have to say, sharing your perceptions of the importance of safety, and having confidence in the effectiveness of your preventative measures'. After scratching their heads, they would reply, 'Yes, but *what does* an identifiable safety culture *look like*?' This set me to thinking that, although those of us who write about safety culture in the academic literature *might* understand what we are all on about, the lay person does not. He or she needs much more concrete evidence than confusing academic definitions that appear to lack substance. In essence, the lay person needs to be able to easily identify certain characteristics, the presence of which would indicate that the company has a good safety culture. Adopting a three level strategy for developing a positive safety culture (i.e. immediate, intermediate and ultimate) this book attempts to highlight some of the most important identifiable characteristics, while also providing the reader with the necessary tools to bring them about.

The 'immediate' level of effort is concerned with developing strategic plans, converting these into action plans, and implementing these so that the organisation can fully integrate safety into all of its systems. The first pointer to look for is the quality of safety leadership demonstrated by the organisation's chief executive officer (CEO) and senior management team. The presence of measurable short, medium and long term strategic objectives to fully integrate safety into all of an organisation's systems (including finance, human resources, marketing, legal, purchasing and supply), which are known to all, demonstrates only one aspect of the required leadership. The regular active monitoring and review of line management's implementation of these strategic plans by the senior management team demonstrates the most vital aspect of good safety leadership. Without this, the possibility of creating a positive safety culture will become little more than an illusion. Importantly, the findings of these reviews should be communicated to every person in the organisation on a regular basis. In other words it is not sufficient to develop strategic plans which are then left dormant. They must be implemented, monitored and reviewed on a regular basis, with information about ongoing progress being made readily available to *all* employees. Thus high quality, demonstrable safety leadership is an easily identifiable and important indicator of a positive safety culture.

Another easily identifiable characteristic of a safety culture is the presence and quality of the organisation's risk control systems. If risk assessments have been conducted on all the organisation's activities, and the appropriate control measures have been fully implemented, it is probable that safety is being actively controlled at the operational level. However, the extent to which risk assessments have been conducted can only be determined if such assessments and the appropriate control measures have been properly recorded. Thus, the presence and quality of recorded risk assessments that cover all of the organisation's activities provides a partial indicator of a positive safety culture. Given that these are supposed to be 'living' documents, the presence of a properly planned review schedule that fully involves the personnel who actually undertake the operational activities provides the other part of this indicator of a positive safety culture.

The 'intermediate' level of effort provides the second part of the three-level strategy, and is concerned with

- developing management information systems to facilitate organisational learning
- developing audit systems by which the whole safety management system can be reviewed.

Thus the next visible characteristic of a positive safety culture is the presence and quality of an organisation's safety management information system. This is because an information system is a sub system of a control system, which in and of itself is a sub system of a management system and is therefore *de facto* the nerve centre of the organisation's prevailing safety culture. Not only does it provide the means by which the organisation can evaluate its ongoing safety activities, it also helps the organisation to measure its effectiveness at controlling safety, as well as providing the knowledge required to facilitate error correction, problem-solving, decision-making and forward planning.

A closely related indicator of a positive safety culture is the extent to which an organisation's safety management systems are reviewed. Because this can only be achieved by conducting regular, planned safety management system audits throughout the whole organisation, the frequency with which these are done provides an easily recognisable indicator of a positive safety culture. Organisations which do not conduct regular safety management system audits could be said to be unconcerned about creating and maintaining a positive safety culture. However, this is only part of the story. The organisation also has to act upon and implement any recommendations for action. Thus, the extent to which an organisation provides the necessary resources and implements the findings of a safety management system audit provides the other part of this safety culture indicator.

The 'ultimate' level of effort is the final part of the three-level strategy. It is concerned with winning people's hearts and minds to the organisation's safety cause by:

- the development of high quality safety training programs
- seeking and acting upon employees' views
- empowering them to become actively involved with safety on a daily basis.

Thus a relatively simple indicator of a positive safety culture is the extent to which every employee has received *high quality* integrated job and safety training. If people have merely been exposed to the odd half-hour video showing people getting hurt from doing the wrong things, it can be said that they have not received the appropriate safety training, as this type of training is a total waste of everybody's time and effort. Examples of high quality safety training include ensuring that *every* manager and supervisor has been trained in safety management to National Examination Board in Occupational Safety & Health (NEBOSH) Diploma standards. Indeed, there is a very strong case for this qualification to become an integral part of every type of management degree course. Similarly, *every* employee should be trained to NEBOSH Certificate level, which suggests that this qualification should be *explicitly* included in all trade courses and National Vocational Qualifications (NVQs). Because the idea of every employee possessing some form of safety qualification represents the ideal, it is not likely to be the case in reality. Therefore, the evidence required is that a planned, integrated series of safety training events (relevant to the target audience), are being conducted on a rolling basis for all employees. In addition, the extent to which an organisation actually changes its systems and management practices to support the safety training provided will also provide a useful indicator of a positive safety culture.

One of the better indicators of a positive safety culture is a good safety climate. Although, 'safety climate' is often mistaken for 'safety culture', as they are both inextricably linked, they are distinctly separate entities. Safety culture is much broader than safety climate as it refers to the whole, whereas safety climate refers solely to people's perceptions of, and attitudes towards, safety. As such, safety climate provides an indicator of how the organisation's membership views the current effectiveness of the organisation's safety improvement efforts. Safety climate is measured via *proven* psychometric surveys, that cover various dimensions thought to be important to safety, on an annual or bi-annual basis. Nonetheless, the very fact that an organisation is willing to actively consult and act upon its membership's views provides a very good indicator of a positive safety culture. Similarly, what the organisation does to address the findings of such surveys provides another indicator through which the prevailing safety culture can be assessed.

Probably the most important indicator of a positive safety culture is the extent to which employees are actively involved in safety on a daily basis. If there is very little involvement, with safety solely dependent upon line-management and a sprinkling of safety representatives, it can be said that the organisation has failed to win people over to the safety effort and, therefore, they do not have a very good safety culture. Conversely, where safety issues are identified and acted upon by all employees as a part of their normal working day, the organisation can be said to have won over people's hearts and minds to the safety cause, and therefore has a living, breathing, pro-active safety culture.

Although not an issue specifically addressed within this book, the status accorded to the safety practitioner also provides a visible and important indicator of a positive safety culture. Given their new consulting role, the modern safety practitioners' status can be determined by looking at their position in an organisation's hierarchy, particularly as the remainder of the organisation will take their cue from the status accorded to the safety practitioner by the CEO. If the safety practitioner has direct, independent and unimpeded access to the CEO, it can be said that the organisation actively recognises the important contribution that the safety function offers to all aspects of its business. If safety practitioners are merely on a par with other functions, and are forced to go through *any* reporting relationships before gaining access to the CEO, then their status is less than adequate.

Although the above provides eight highly important and visible indicators of a positive safety culture, it is much easier to talk about them than it is to put them in place. The difficulty for many managers and safety practitioners is knowing what tools are available and how they can be put to use, so that they can successfully bring about a positive safety culture. Based on my academic research background in industrial, occupational and organisational psychology, and as a result of the consultancy experience gained while applying these disciplines to the field of safety in different sectors of the economy, this book attempts to provide the reader with the practical knowledge required to put these safety culture characteristics in place, in plain, everyday language. How well I have succeeded in these attempts can only be judged by you, the reader.

Dominic Cooper

Acknowledgements

Several people have helped in the preparation of this book by offering practical advice, providing up-to-date research evidence, reading various chapters and providing constructive feedback. Special thanks are due to Martin Slater, the safety manager of Joseph Mason Paints in Derby; Fred Madders, the safety manager of McVities Prepared Foods in Okehampton, Devon, Robin Phillips of the Dept of Building Engineering, UMIST, Manchester; and 'Fats' Van den Raad and Vince Meekin, safety consultants who undertake work for Applied Behavioural Sciences Ltd, Hull. Professor Peter Waterhouse & Glen Davies, Group Safety Manager, United Biscuits Frozen & Chilled Foods Ltd are thanked for reading drafts of the completed manuscript and imparting valuable insights and advice. Any errors remaining are entirely my responsibility.

The patience of the publishers in waiting for the manuscript also deserves particular thanks, especially Claire Plimmer, the publishing editor for Business and Management, whose professionalism and hard work were invaluable in producing the book in its present form. Finally, I am extremely grateful to my wife and children for tolerating my efforts to write this book at the expense of devoting any time to them over the many months that it has taken to complete.

1

The Concept of Safety Culture

INTRODUCTION

The 'culture' of an organisation can be defined as 'the way we do things around here'. As such, culture provides a context for action which binds together the different components of an organisational system in the pursuit of corporate goals. Successful organisations tend to have strong cultures which dominate and permeate the structure and associated systems. Within these organisations nothing is too trivial or too much trouble. Every effort is made by every member to ensure that all activities are done the 'right' way. Thus the prevailing organisational culture serves as a powerful lever in guiding the behaviour of its members in their everyday work.

The more that members repeatedly behave or act in ways that appear to them to be natural, obvious and unquestionable, the more dominant the culture becomes. Although there is a danger that the culture could become static and stagnate, in successful organisations, it tends to be dynamic and take on a life of its own, influencing, and in some cases determining, an organisation's ongoing strategies and policies. An organisation's culture, therefore, impinges upon and influences most aspects of work activity, affecting both individual and group behaviour at all levels in the workplace.

Unless safety is the dominating characteristic of an organisation's culture, which arguably it should be in high risk industries, safety culture can be viewed as that sub component of organisational culture which alludes to individual, job and organisational features affecting and influencing health and safety. The prevailing organisational culture therefore will exert a considerable influence on safety. For example, those organisations that genuinely strive to achieve a quality culture by involving all employees in each step of the process will probably have a greater impact on building a positive safety culture. Organisations that use the idea of a 'quality' culture merely as a marketing device (i.e. achieving BS5750 or IS9000 solely by paper trails) or an excuse for cost-cutting exercises are more likely to ignore safety issues. In the former, the importance of safety as a performance criterion is likely to be accepted by all and may well be integrated into every aspect of the quality process. In the latter, because safety is more likely to be seen as a 'bolt-on extra', adding to overheads and production costs with little payback, it is likely to be rejected as a business performance indicator. A good safety culture, however, is believed to positively impact upon an organisation's quality, reliability, competitiveness and profitability.

The Impact of Safety Culture on Quality

An evaluation of the impact of safety culture on quality in 626 US organisations revealed that better work methods and reduced absenteeism had contributed to improved organisational performance, while also impacting on product quality. Similarly, construction industry studies have shown that projects driven by safety are more likely to be on schedule and within budget. The safety culture of Shell, for example, was shown to have had a significant effect on the progress and completion of a new natural gas liquid plant at Mossmorran, Scotland. Major investments in safety in the British Steel industry not only resulted in significant reductions in accidents with corresponding increases in productivity, but also led to increasingly positive attitudes about quality and safety.

The Impact of Safety Culture on Reliability

The impact of safety culture on the reliability of technological systems is thought to be indirect via organisational structures and processes: partly because the reliability of complex technical systems (e.g. manufacturing plant) is dependent on the quality of its structural components and sub systems; partly because human reliability is dependent on the variability of human error probabilities; and, partly because of the interaction between them. Nonetheless, reliability has been reported to improve by a factor of three, and sometimes by as much as a factor of ten, when quality improvements are initiated. It is likely, however, that some of these improvements are related to the use of better monitoring and feedback systems, both of which are vital safety culture features, and as a result of streamlining production processes.

The Impact of Safety Culture on Competitiveness

A good safety culture can also contribute to competitiveness in many ways. For example, it may make the difference between winning or losing a contract (e.g. many operating companies in the off-shore oil industry only select and award work to contractors with a positive safety culture); it may affect people's way of thinking and lead to the development of safety features for some products which are then used as marketing devices (e.g. air bags in motor vehicles to protect occupants during a collision); and it positively impacts on employees' commitment and loyalty to the organisation, resulting in greater job satisfaction, productivity and reduced absenteeism.

The Impact of Safety Culture on Profitability

Although a focus on safety has often been seen as non-productive expenditure demanded by law, it can also contribute to profit by minimising loss and adding to the capital value of an organisation. For example, construction industry research has shown that an investment of 2.5% of direct labour costs in an effective safety program should, at a conservative estimate, produce a gross saving of 6.5% (4.0% net) of direct labour costs. Similarly, an 82% decrease in lost-time accidents which resulted from a behavioural safety programme saved a manufacturing company an estimated £180,000 to £360,000 in compensation costs in just one year. These figures were considered conservative, as the estimated savings did not reflect those associated with a 55% decrease in minor injuries. In the normal course of events, generating this level of profit might require an extra 30% to 40% of production capacity. As the latter illustrates, the costs of accidents can be considerable. Previous estimates by the Confederation of British Industry (CBI) in 1990 suggested that the minimum non-recoverable cost of each accident was £1,500, whether investigated or not. Similarly, in 1993, based on research in six industries, the Health and Safety Executive's (HSE) Accident Prevention Advisory Unit (APAU) estimated that only £1 in £11 lost as a result of workplace accidents is covered by insurance. Indeed the typical costs associated with accidents include:

- lost production caused by:
  - time away from job by injured person and co-worker(s) in attendance
  - time spent by first-aider attending injured person
  - possible downtime of production process
  - possible damage to product, plant and equipment
- time and costs due to repair of plant and equipment
- increased insurance premiums
- legal costs
- medical expenses

- compensation costs to injured employees
- absenteeism
- lower morale of employees leading to poor performance and productivity
- unsatisfactory employee relations
- low levels of motivation.

As a whole, therefore, the available evidence indicates that an effective safety culture is an essential element of any business strategy, as it has so many positive effects on other areas of business performance. It also illustrates the point that safety culture does not operate in a vacuum: it affects, and in turn is affected by, other operational processes or organisational systems.

THE EVOLUTION OF THE CONCEPT OF SAFETY CULTURE

Traditionally, attempts to identify the most effective methods for preventing accidents have typically addressed two fundamental issues:

- Whether or not employees should be provided with the maximum protection possible
- Whether or not employees should be trained to recognise potentially hazardous situations and take the most appropriate actions.

Implicitly recognising that the potential for an accident is always present, the first approach is based on the fundamental belief that protecting an individual from the potential for harm, either by statutory means or via physical barriers, is the best way to proceed. The second approach is predicated on the fundamental belief that, if the individual possesses the relevant knowledge and skills, accidents will be avoided. Traditionally, attempts to improve safety in the workplace have addressed these issues via legislation, engineering solutions, safety campaigns or safety training. However, as a result of inquiries investigating large-scale disasters such as Chernobyl, the Kings Cross fire, Piper Alpha, Clapham Junction, etc., more recent moves to improve workplace safety have focused on the concept of an identifiable safety culture. Whilst incorporating all the traditional routes to improve safety, the concept of safety culture goes much further by focusing on the presence of good quality safety management control systems.

Legislative Attempts to Improve Safety

Legislative approaches to improving safety have their roots in the industrial revolution of the 18th and 19th centuries. Due to radical changes in technology and the development of new industries, many employees were exposed to all manner of hazards in factories and mines. During this period, the rising number of deaths and injuries led to immense public pressure for parliamentary regulation. Initial parliamentary reluctance, and much opposition from factory and mine owners, led to large chunks of this early legislation being repealed and then reintroduced as deficiencies became apparent. Importantly, however, this legislation introduced the notion of inspectorates for factories (1833), for mines (1842) and for the railways (1840), albeit that the inspectorates' authority was fairly limited. Over the next 100 years a steady stream of legislation followed that further empowered these different inspectorates while also establishing many important principles, such as the mandatory reporting of fatal accidents, the provision of guards for moving machinery and the requirement to provide first-aid facilities. In 1972 the Robens Committee investigated the many shortcomings in safety management of the time, and made various recommendations that subsequently formed the basis of the Health and Safety at Work Act 1974. This Act placed the responsibility for all the previous Health and Safety Inspectorates under the auspices of the Health and Safety Commission (HSC) to bring about changes in safety management practices. The central idea was that the HSC would promote proactive self-regulatory safety management practices by influencing attitudes and creating an optimal framework for the organisation of health and safety. Unfortunately, this proved more difficult in practice than envisaged: partly because of the pervading influence of traditional accident causation models; partly because of 'get out' clauses provided by such qualifiers as 'as far as is reasonably practicable'; and, partly because many employers had real difficulty in understanding what they were required to do in practice. Moreover, legislation can only be effective if it is adequately resourced and policed. This has not always proven possible as, traditionally, the number of inspectors available has been relatively small compared to the number of premises covered by the legislation. In the UK construction industry, for example, at the beginning of the 1990s, there were only 90 or so inspectors to police approximately 100,000 sites, not all of which had been notified to the appropriate authorities. In practice, this meant that many companies could openly flout the 1974 Act with little chance of prosecution. Indeed, many of them implemented safety improvement initiatives only when forced to do so by inspectors.

As a result of recent European directives, the legislative focus has now firmly shifted to proactive management of safety rather than an inspection of sites/premises approach (i.e. the Management of Health and Safety at Work

Regulations 1992 (MHSWR). Accompanied by an Approved Code of Practice (ACOP) issued by the HSC, these regulations came into effect in January 1993. One of the most important features of the new regulations is that the majority of the requirements are of an absolute nature, designated by the term 'shall', rather than 'so far as is reasonably practicable'. Similarly, the emphasis has switched to the *process* of safety management rather than the *outcomes*: employers are now required to take steps to identify and manage hazards by undertaking formal assessments of risk. Thereafter they must plan, organise, implement, control, monitor and review their preventative and protective measures. These measures must be documented and fully integrated with other types of management systems (e.g. finance, personnel, production, etc.). In some high-risk industries (e.g. offshore energy extraction, mining and rail transport) companies are also required to submit a 'safety case' detailing precisely how they intend to put the regulations into effect. Although some may view the new regulations as draconian, much of the underlying rationale is derived from management theory and multi-disciplinary scientific research examining accident causation factors.

ACCIDENT CAUSATION MODELS

During the 19th and early 20th centuries many safety practitioners and factory inspectorates took the view that preventative physical measures such as machine guarding, housekeeping and hazard inspections were the best way to prevent accidents. This view was predicated on the belief that controlling physical work conditions would prevent the majority of accidents. Despite these types of precaution, however, accidents continued to increase at an alarming rate in British factories during and after the First World War. This led to the commissioning of government committees to examine whether accidents were caused by physical working conditions (situational factors) or individual characteristics (person factors). This differentiation was partly based on the hereditary versus environment debate brought about by Darwin's radical theory of evolution, and partly because in-depth knowledge about the causes of accidents could lead to the appropriate countermeasures being applied.

Accident Proneness Models

In 1919, at the behest of these government committees, Greenwood and Woods from the Industrial Fatigue Research Board statistically examined accident rates in a munitions factory. Based on the notion that all munitions workers were exposed to the same levels of risk, they examined three propositions to try to identify the most worthwhile preventative measures. These were that:

- accidents were a result of pure chance, and could happen to anyone at any time
- having already experienced an accident, a person's propensity for further incidents would be reduced (burnt fingers hypothesis) or increased (contagious hypothesis)
- some people were more likely to suffer an accident than others.

If the first proposition were correct, and no differences in accident rates were found for particular types of people, prevention could be focused solely on environmental demands and conditions. If the second proposition were correct, remedial actions could be concentrated upon only those individuals who had previously suffered an accident. If the third proposition were correct, people with low accident liability could be selected for jobs, while those who experienced multiple accidents could be asked to leave.

An analysis of accident records divided into successive three month periods appeared to suggest that some people were consistently more involved in accidents than others, thereby supporting the third proposition. Despite the obvious fact that not all people are exposed to the same levels of risk in their work, these results and those of other studies led to the 'Accident proneness' model which dominated safety thinking and research for almost 50 years. In practice, the pervading influence of this approach meant that most accidents were blamed solely on employees rather than the work processes, poor management practices or a combination of all three, a response that can still be found in some organisations. Typically, investigations to discover the underlying causal factors were felt unnecessary and/or too costly with the result that little attention was paid to how accidents *actually* happened. Thus many companies felt they had little to do in the way of accident prevention other than select the right employees and weed out or re-educate those involved in more than one accident. Importantly, the findings of these types of study placed greater emphasis on the fallibility of people than on the interaction between working conditions and people, and this led to many companies inadvertently neglecting their real safety responsibilities.

Heinrich's Domino Theory

Despite recognition by early researchers of the role that managerial and organisational factors played in the accident causation chain, most practitioners focused almost exclusively on the prominence of employee's unsafe acts. To some extent this prominence, expressed in accident triangles to this

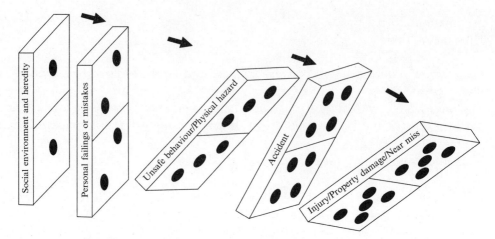

Figure 1.1   Heinrich's Domino Model of Accident Causation — Adapted from H. Heinrich, D. Peterson and N. Roos (1980) Industrial Accident Prevention *(5th Ed.) New York: McGraw-Hill. Reprinted by permission*

day, reinforced the prevailing view about 'accident prone' people. This research led to Heinrich's seminal work 'Industrial Accident Prevention', published in 1931. Heinrich postulated that accidents were caused by either an unsafe act, an unsafe condition, or both. Termed the 'Domino' theory, this work provided the first sequential theory of the accident causation process. Not only was safety behaviour demonstrated to play a greater role than previously thought (see Figure 1.1: *Heinrich's Domino Model of Accident Causation*), but it also brought the interaction between behaviour and conditions (situation) into sharper focus for the first time.

In essence, the Domino theory asserted that accidents were caused by a sequence of events which encompassed five discrete stages. This began with a person's heredity and environment which predisposed that person to behave in certain ways (such as being an accident prone person), and which led to either an unsafe act or the creation of an unsafe condition. In turn, either of these caused an accident which resulted in an injury. Heinrich asserted that each stage of the accident process was analogous to a row of dominos in line with each other. If one fell, it automatically knocked down all the other dominos. Neutralising any one of the first four would prevent the fifth: the injury. Heinrich concluded that the key domino was that pertaining to unsafe acts. This perhaps reflected his findings that approximately 80% of accidents were *triggered* by unsafe acts, with the remaining 20% being caused by unsafe conditions (known as the 80:20 rule).

Although designers, engineers and the statutory bodies addressed many of the unsafe conditions by guarding against or legislating for the control of technological hazards, Heinrich thought that unsafe acts were caused by poor attitudes, a lack of knowledge and skill, physical unsuitability and an

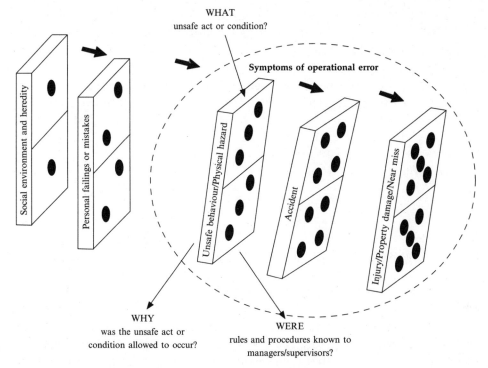

WHAT
unsafe act or condition?

Symptoms of operational error

Social environment and heredity

Personal failings or mistakes

Unsafe behaviour/Physical hazard

Accident

Injury/Property damage/Near miss

WHY
was the unsafe act or
condition allowed to occur?

WERE
rules and procedures known to
managers/supervisors?

Figure 1.2   *Weaver's Domino Model of Accident Causation — Adapted from D. Weaver, 'Symptoms of Operational Error',* Professional Safety, *Oct 1971, (Asse). Reprinted by permission*

unsafe environment. This view led to much training and propaganda in attempts to change attitudes, the effectiveness of which was, and still is, questionable. Heinrich summarised his theory in terms of ten axioms of industrial safety that at the time were considered to be somewhat revolutionary, with the result that they tended to be ignored. Although some were relatively simplistic, the underlying rationale has become influential in current safety management practices. For example, axiom 7 which states '. . . the methods of most value in accident prevention are analogous with the methods for the control of quality, cost and quantity of production', is not too dissimilar in intent to the Total Quality Management (TQM) techniques encompassed by, and advocated in, the current MHSWR 1992.

Weaver's Domino Theory

Other theorists used Heinrich's domino theory as the starting point for their own work. For example, in 1971 Weaver modified the original theory to propose that the last three dominos in the sequence were caused by management omissions. Expressed as symptoms of operational error (see Figure 1.2:

Weaver's Domino Model of Accident Causation) that interact with unsafe acts and/or conditions, Weaver drew on the notion of multiple causality due to underlying organisational factors. Although the unsafe act or condition was still the immediate cause, Weaver suggested that the underlying causes of operational error could be discovered by asking 'What was the unsafe act? Why was it allowed to occur?' and, 'Were the rules and procedures known to all concerned?'. In essence, Weaver's model placed the immediate responsibility for accidents squarely on the shoulders of poor supervision and line management, while also implicitly recognising the interaction between management systems and accidents.

Adams' Domino Theory

Building on Weaver's adaptation of Heinrich's basic model from an industrial engineering systems perspective, in 1976 Adams changed the emphasis of the first three dominos to reflect organisational rather than person features (see Figure 1.3: *Adams' Domino Model of Accident Causation*). By doing so, he was one of the first theorists to move away from the discredited accident proneness approach. Importantly, Adams also implicitly recognised the notion of a safety culture by stating that the personality of an organisation was reflected in its stable operational elements. With reference to this organisational 'personality', Adams proposed that operational errors were caused: by the

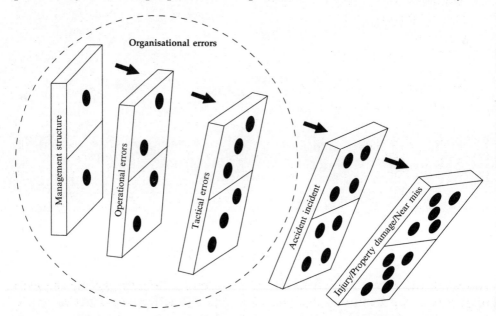

Figure 1.3   Adams' Domino Model of Accident Causation — Adapted from E. Adams (1976) 'Accident causation & the Management systems', Professional Safety, Oct, (Asse). Reprinted by permission

management structure; the organisation's objectives; the organisation of the workflow system; and how operations were planned and executed. In turn these operational errors caused 'tactical errors' (unsafe acts or conditions). The essential difference here is that Adams explicitly recognised that tactical errors were the result of higher management's strategic errors. Thus, Adams was one of the first safety theorists to specifically highlight the multiple interactions between organisational structures, systems and sub systems, and unsafe conditions and/or employees' safety behaviour. Indeed, Adams' work is reflected in Johnson's Management Oversight and Risk Tree (MORT) published in 1975 which is an analytical tool set out in a logical-fault tree format that provides a systematic basis for detailed accident investigations. Although the scale and complexity of MORT has limited its practical application, it has proven to be of immense value for building theories of accident causation. This is partly because it recognises the interactions between physical (job), procedural (organisational) and personal elements, and partly because it has helped to discover that a number of parallel accident sequences develop over a period of time, prior to the various causation elements coinciding and interacting to produce an incident. This latter point, and others, was picked up and developed further by James Reason in 1993.

Bird and Loftus' Domino Theory

In parallel with these developments by Adams from the perspective of management theory and total loss control, Bird and Loftus adapted Heinrich's Domino theory to reflect the influence of management in the accident causation process (see Figure 1.4: *Bird and Loftus' Domino Model of Accident Causation*). This model takes the view that poor management control creates either poor personal factors (e.g. lack of appropriate training) or poor job factors (e.g. unguarded machinery). In combination, these two factors lead to either unsafe acts or unsafe conditions. In turn these cause an incident, which leads to losses related to people, property or operational processes. This model in particular has exerted a great influence on safety practices in some industries (e.g. chemicals and mining) by virtue of its subsequent development into an auditing tool (i.e. the International Safety Rating System (ISRS)) and its emphasis on cost savings and financial return.

Reason's Pathogen Model

Although the above models have proved useful in identifying the sequence of events in the accident causation chain, they have largely failed to specify *how* and under what conditions each of the sequential elements might interact to produce accidents. Many practitioners have continued to blame

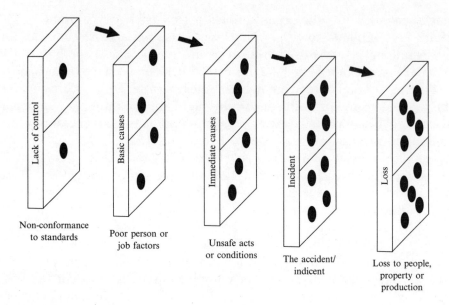

Non-conformance
to standards

Poor person or
job factors

Unsafe acts
or conditions

The accident/
indicent

Loss to people,
property or
production

Figure 1.4   Bird and Loftus' Domino Model of Accident Causation — Adapted from Bird, F.E. and Loftus, R.G. (1976) Loss Control Management, *Institute Press, Loganville, Georgia. Reprinted by permission*

the individual for the unsafe act, or merely identify and rectify the immediate unsafe conditions, rather than examining how and why the unsafe act occurred, or how the unsafe condition was created. A more recent causation model by Professor James Reason has largely overcome these shortcomings. Initially based on an analysis of the Chernobyl disaster in 1987, Reason likened the accident causation process to 'resident pathogens' in the human body. Similar in concept to physiological immune systems, Reason argued that all organisational systems carry the seeds of their own demise in the form of these pathogens. In 1988 Reason termed these resident pathogens as 'latent' failures. In much the same way as Johnson had identified that accident sequences develop over a period of time, Reason suggested that the 'latent' failures lie dormant, accumulate and subsequently combine with other latent failures which are then triggered by 'active' failures (e.g. unsafe acts) to overcome the system's defences and cause accidents. Reason proposed that 'active' failures were caused by poor collective attitudes or by unintentionally choosing the 'wrong' behavioural response in a given situation, both of which may result in a breach of the system.

In later works, Reason recognised the limitations of his original resident pathogen model and, in conjunction with Wreathall, identified how and where latent and active failures might be introduced into an organisational system. This modified model suggests that pathogens are introduced into the system by two routes.

- Latent failures caused by organisational or managerial factors (e.g. top-level decision-making).
- Active failures caused by individuals (e.g. psychological or behavioural precursors).

Illustrated in Figure 1.5: *Reason's Pathogen Model of Accident Causation*, Reason's model is based on the notion that all types of productive systems incorporate five basic elements.

- High-level decision-making.
- Line management co-ordination of operational activities.
- Preconditions in the form of technology, manpower and resources.
- Productive activities that require the synchronisation of people, materials and technology.
- Defences of some form or another to minimise the effects of potentially hazardous circumstances.

Reason suggested that each particular element of the production model is associated with its own particular form of latent or active failure. Importantly, the principle pathogens emanate from the higher echelons and are spread throughout the system by the various strands of line management as they implement strategic decisions. These notions come across clearly through his description of the two ways in which system failures, or systemic pathogens, are introduced: types and tokens. 'Types' refer to general organisational and managerial failings, whereas 'tokens' are more specific failings relating to individuals. However, two different forms of types exist.

- *Source* types which are associated with senior management's strategic decisions.
- *Function* types which are associated with line management's implementation of senior management's fallible strategic decisions.

Analogous to Adam's tactical errors, tokens also divide into condition tokens which comprise the situational (man-machine interface, workload, etc.) or psychological (attention, attitudes, motivation, etc.) precursors of unsafe acts; and unsafe act tokens that are further classified on the basis of whether they are caused by:

- slips and lapses (skill-based errors)
- mistakes (rule-based and/or knowledge-based errors)
- volitions (deliberate infringements of safe working practices).

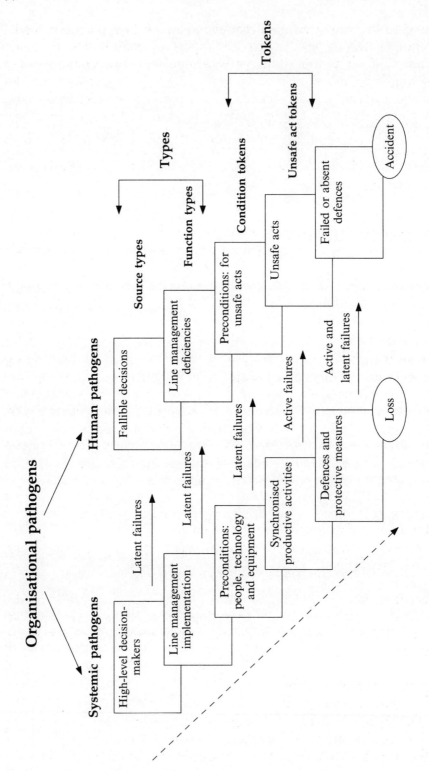

Figure 1.5 Reason's Pathogen Model of Accident Causation – Adapted from 'Reason, J. 'Managing the Management Risk: New approaches to Organisational Safety', in B. Wilpert and T. Qvale Reliability & Safety in Hazardous Work Systems. LEA Hove (UK). Reprinted by permission of Psychology Press Ltd, Hove, UK

Compared to previous causation models, Reason's 1993 pathogen model is fairly comprehensive, and makes an important contribution to safety management in so far as it identifies and distinguishes between the types of error that might be made, and where they might be introduced into an organisational system. It also stresses the importance of identifying and rooting out possible latent failures before they can be triggered by active failures. Like Adams before him, therefore, Reason shifts the main focus of accident prevention away from the operator's unsafe acts and more onto the organisation's overall management system, particularly in relation to the implementation of the organisation's strategic decisions.

ORGANISATIONAL CHARACTERISTICS OF A GOOD SAFETY CULTURE

In parallel with the development of the accident causation models outlined above, researchers attempted to identify certain organisational characteristics thought to distinguish low accident companies from high accident companies. Conducted in the USA during the early 1960s to the end of the 1970s across a wide variety of industries, this research discovered the following consistent features:

- Strong senior management commitment, leadership and involvement in safety
- Closer contact and better communications between all organisational levels
- Greater hazard control and better housekeeping
- A mature, stable workforce
- Good personnel selection, job placement and promotion procedures
- Good induction and follow-up safety training
- Ongoing safety schemes reinforcing the importance of safety, including 'near miss' reporting.

More recent research conducted in the UK at the end of the 1980s by the CBI revealed similar features. However, by incorporating lessons learnt from implementing TQM initiatives they also highlighted other essential features that included:

- Accepting that the promotion of a safety culture is a long term strategy which requires sustained effort and interest
- Adopting a formal health and safety policy, supported by adequate codes of practice and safety standards
- Stressing that health and safety is equal to other business objectives

- Thoroughly investigating all accidents and near misses
- Regularly auditing safety systems to provide information feedback with a view to developing ideas for continuous improvement.

Importantly, all the above features were also identified in a report produced in the early 1990s by the Advisory Committee on the Safety of Nuclear Installations (ACSNI) Study Group on Human Factors, indicating broad agreement about the specific factors that positively impact on safety performance. Although most of the features identified allude to the presence of organisational systems and modes of organisational behaviour, the ACSNI group also highlighted the importance of various psychological attributes that exert their influence on safety *per se*. These include perceptions about and attitudes towards accident causation, risk and job-induced stress caused by conflicting role demands and poor working conditions. The prominence of these psychological factors was also highlighted in a study at British Nuclear Fuels Ltd (BNFL), which showed that only 20% of the root causes of accidents were attributable to inadequacies of equipment and plant, with the remaining 80% being caused by people-based factors such as poor managerial control, worker competencies and breaches of rules. Based on this accumulated body of evidence the ACSNI Study Group suggested that for practical purposes, safety culture could be defined as:

> *'. . . the product of individual and group values, attitudes, competencies, and patterns of behaviour that determine the commitment to, and the style and proficiency of, an organisation's health and safety programmes.*
>
> *Organisations with a positive safety culture are characterised by communications founded on mutual trust, by shared perceptions of the importance of safety, and by confidence in the efficacy of preventative measures.'*

TOWARDS A MODEL OF SAFETY CULTURE

To a greater or lesser degree, each of the accident causation models described above recognises the presence of an interactive or reciprocal relationship between psychological, situational and behavioural factors. Heinrich, for example, identified the interactive relationship between behaviour, situations and person factors at operator levels, while his 80:20% rule implicitly recognised that the strength of someone's behaviour, or the situation (e.g. workflow process) may exert different effects at different moments in time. The interactive relationship between management systems and managerial behaviour was also recognised by Weaver when he stated that accidents were symptoms of operational error. However, Adams' far-reaching insights recognised the mutually interactive nature of the relationship between all three factors, *and* the time-related causal relationship between high level strategic decisions and tactical operational errors. Similarly, Reason's pathogen model recognises that person, situational and behavioural factors are the immediate precursors of unsafe acts; that the strength of each may differ; and that it may take time for one element to exert its effects on the other two elements (e.g. the temporal relationships between latent (managerial) and active (operational) failures). Importantly, the work carried out to identify the organisational characteristics of a positive safety culture also emphasised the interaction between organisational systems, modes of organisational behaviour and people's psychological attributes. Clearly, therefore, this interactive relationship between psychological, situational and behavioural factors is applicable to the accident causation chain at all levels of an organisation. Consequently, it can be cogently argued that culture is actually:

'The product of multiple goal-directed interactions between people (psychological), jobs (behavioural) and the organisation (situational)'.

Viewed from this perspective, an organisation's prevailing safety culture is reflected in the dynamic inter-relationships between members' perceptions about, and attitudes towards, organisational safety goals; members' day-to-day goal-directed safety behaviour; and the presence and quality of organisational safety systems to support goal-directed behaviour.

Consistent with the idea that culture can best be described as *'the way we do things around here'*, the potency of this interactive model for analysing 'safety culture' resides in the explicit recognition that the relative strength of each source may be different in any given situation: e.g. the design of a production system may exert stronger effects on someone's work-related safety behaviour than that person's safety attitudes. Similarly, the interactive influence of each source may not occur simultaneously: e.g. it may take time for a change in safety behaviour to exert an influence on and activate the relationship with the workflow system and/or work-related safety attitudes.

Thinking of safety culture in these terms, therefore, provides an organising framework to assist in ongoing practical assessments and analyses. As such, given the appropriate measuring instruments, the relative influence of each component can be determined in any given situation, so allowing either highly focused remedial actions or forward planning to take place.

Indeed, the merits of this interactive framework for analysing safety culture become apparent if we separate the ACSNI Study Group's working definition of safety culture into its component parts. For example, 'individual and group values and attitudes' refers to members perceptions about and attitudes towards safety goals; 'patterns of behaviour' refers to members'

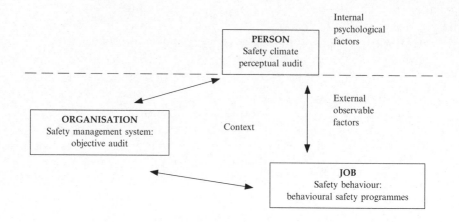

Figure 1.6   Cooper's Reciprocal Safety Culture Model

day-to-day goal-directed safety behaviour; and, the 'style and proficiency of an organisation's health and safety programmes' indirectly refers to the presence and quality of organisational safety systems to support goal-directed safety behaviour. Moreover, the second section implicitly recognises the 'reciprocal' relationship between each of these elements, acknowledged in paragraph 80 of the ACSNI report which states '. . . the whole is more than the sum of the parts. The many separate practices interact to give a much larger effect'. It becomes clear that this working definition of safety culture alludes to the reciprocal relationship between an organisation's safety management system(s) (SMS), the prevailing safety climate (perceptions and attitudes), and daily goal-directed safety behaviour (see Figure 1.6: *Cooper's Reciprocal Safety Culture Model*). Since each of these safety culture components can be directly measured in their own right or in combination, it is possible to quantify safety culture in a meaningful way at many different organisational levels, which hitherto has been somewhat difficult. Accordingly, the organising framework also has the potential to provide organisations with a common frame of reference for the development of benchmarking partnerships with other business units or organisations. This latter point may be particularly important to industries where there is substantial use of specialist sub-contractors (e.g. construction and offshore), as people from different organisations will be able to communicate in the same language. Additionally, it provides a means by which the prevailing safety culture of different departments can be compared usefully.

The practical utility of the interactive framework is further enhanced by the fact that the model can be applied to each individual component (see Figure 1.7: *Cooper's Reciprocal Safety Culture Model Applied to Each Element*). For example, because we can measure people's perceptions and attitudes

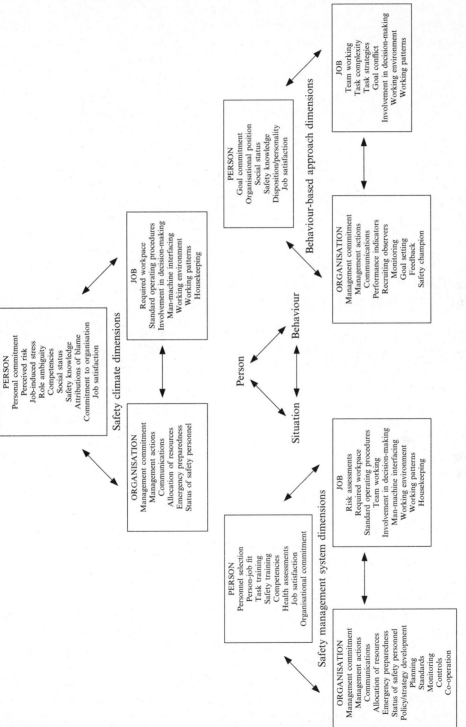

Figure 1.7 Cooper's Reciprocal Safety Culture Model Applied to Each Element

about the prevailing safety climate via psychometric questionnaires, it is feasible that we could discover that a work group's levels of perceived risk (i.e. person factors) is determined by their perceptions of the required workpace (i.e. job factors) and management's commitment to safety (i.e. organisational factors). Similarly, we might discover that the implementation of motivational strategies to improve employees' levels of safety behaviour is affected by the levels of commitment (i.e. person factors), competing goals (job factors) and quality of communications (i.e. organisational factors). These relationships also apply to safety management systems where person factors (e.g. safety training) will interact with job factors (e.g. man-machine interfacing) and organisational factors (e.g. allocation of resources).

In recent years, many of these relationships have been empirically examined in a wide variety of industries by the author and found to hold true, providing support to the notion that safety culture can be meaningfully analysed by using the model to focus on its constituent components: i.e. safety management systems (situational), safety climate (perceptual) and goal-directed safety behaviour (behavioural).

Safety Management Systems

Safety management systems are integrated organisational mechanisms designed to control health and safety risks, ongoing and future health and safety performance, and compliance to legislation. In principle, a good safety management system mirrors that for quality management systems, in that it should be a fully integrated and cohesive system centred around policies, strategies and procedures that provide internal consistency and harmonisation. The development of such a system should be seen as a practical way of creating the awareness, understanding, motivation and commitment of all personnel, while also optimising an organisation's health and safety performance *per se*. In this way safety becomes everyone's responsibility. Nevertheless, because safety management is dependent upon many organisational activities, this diffusion of responsibility requires every activity to be reviewed and integrated into a holistic process. Although this may pose considerable challenges that have resource implications, the evidence suggests that the benefits will tend to more than outweigh the costs. The main challenges are more than likely to be associated with changes to spans of control (i.e. management systems), communication systems (i.e. organisation structure), co-operation (e.g. management styles), and competencies (i.e. training). Each of these are central features of the MHSWR 1992 which place a statutory duty on organisations to actively manage safety, and as such are clearly related to the development of a safety culture.

Management Control Systems

Managing safety is in many respects exactly the same as managing productivity, quality or other functional areas of operations. Ironically, however, one of the primary causes of accidents is poor managerial control. Accordingly, it makes good sense for organisations to have clearly stated and measurable safety objectives, monitoring procedures and regular feedback so that deviations in safety performance can be instantly recognised and rapidly dealt with. Because these issues relate to both individuals and organisations, there is a need for the same types of supporting structural systems and sub system that are used for TQM. Commonly termed 'management by objectives' when applied to organisations, and 'goal-setting' when applied to individuals or workgroups, the process of setting a specific goal or objective is known to exert a strong influence on performance. In essence, goals work by focusing people's attention and actions on the achievement of a desired end or target. For example, a corporate philosophy encapsulated within a 'vision statement' such as

'Safety is THE number one priority. We firmly believe it must take precedence over all other business activities'

specifies the direction and actions a company wishes to take. Goals therefore pose challenges that serve to mobilise people's effort, boost their determination and motivate them to search for better and safer ways of doing things. However, people also require the means to monitor and measure their progress to ensure that the goals are being reached. In the same way that TQM systems might utilise statistical process control (SPC) or 'just in time' (JIT) inventory controls, the monitoring of safety performance can be conducted by a variety of methods at many different levels in an organisation. This may be carried out by some form of organisation-wide safety management system audit that compares actual safety management practices with those laid down in the organisation's safety policies, rules and procedures. Similarly, highly visible features such as accident rates, compensation costs, or number of days since the last lost-time accident may be used as gross, ongoing safety performance indicators. Irrespective of the particular safety system features being monitored, the main purpose is to provide information feedback by which the organisation can compare existing practices with advocated procedures, and take any necessary remedial actions. Performance feedback is a particularly important component of the functioning of any system as it prevents decay and facilitates change. The supply of rapid and easily understood feedback is known to encourage error correction, problem-solving and organisational learning. It also serves to positively affect people's motivation by signalling the boundaries of what the organisation considers to be proper performance. Organisations, however, are not automatically self-correcting. Therefore, the process of attending to, interpreting and acting on performance feedback becomes especially critical when it relates to safety. There is no point, for example, in asking the workforce to report near misses (feedback) if the issues raised are not addressed immediately or within a reasonably short time span. All too often the credibility of near miss systems is fatally damaged either because of management failures to act or because the systems and sub systems become overloaded.

Communication Systems and Organisational Structure

Ensuring that information feedback is available to the right people at the right time means that an effective communications system needs to be in place. Inevitably, the system will be judged by how well it can cope with bi-directional horizontal and vertical flows of information that emanate either from within the organisation or from external sources such as suppliers or statutory bodies such as the HSE. In some instances, changes in the structure of an organisation may be necessary simply because safety management involves a greater flow of information outside the normal vertical lines of communication. In much the same way as cross-functional management is crucial to the success of TQM, safety management may require the formalisation of horizontal arrangements for organised communication between departments, or business units. Similar to the principle of internal markets, examples of horizontal activity might include each organisational sub-unit being both a customer and supplier of safety-related information. For example, as a customer, the maintenance department receives 'products' from purchasing (the supplier). These products are then regularly monitored *in situ* by maintenance personnel. Each time a problem or 'failure' arises with the product the maintenance department becomes the supplier, by routinely sending information back to the purchasing department (who has now become the customer). As this scenario illustrates, the more direct and shorter the communication link the more effective the system is likely to be, as delays and duplication of effort are avoided.

One of the many types of organisational arrangement known to improve co-ordination and communication is a matrix design where the normal vertical hierarchy is overlaid with horizontal communication channels (see Figure 1.8: *Example of an Organisational Matrix Design*). A matrix-type design results in people communicating more on the basis of who has relevant information rather than who reports to whom. In turn, this leads to reduced information processing demands from a tighter coupling of the communication system. Other advantages reside in the design's ability to be applied to the whole organisation and/or individual functional departments, and to

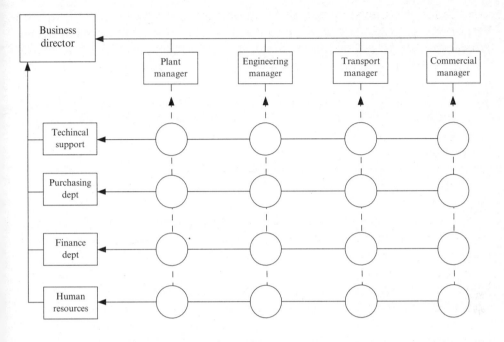

Figure 1.8   Example of an Organisational Matrix Design

reduce organisational or operational segmentalism while explicitly linking the whole structure with external factors and technological change. Importantly, this type of structure lends itself to the vertical and horizontal auditing of the system's effectiveness in controlling risks advocated by the HSE. Moreover, because flexibility is the essence of a matrix design, it allows dynamic responses to unforeseen events by incorporating the conflicting requirements of both uniformity and diversity pressures. It therefore simultaneously overcomes problems associated with tight functional coupling and brings about the internal coupling of managerial responses to systems activity. Matrix structures are also thought to release top management's time from problems of operational co-ordination, thereby allowing them more time for strategic planning. From a safety management perspective this should enable chief executive officers (CEOs) and other top management to 'walk the talk' amongst personnel, which many tend to claim is difficult because of time constraints.

Co-operation and Management Styles

By its very nature an organisational matrix design requires the use of multidisciplinary work teams where members pool their different knowledge and expertise. Consequently, co-operation and communication between functional departments is significantly improved in a way that allows for much greater control of risks (for example, the impact on safety of a particular course of action in many operational areas can be assessed prior to implementation). Thus, the possibility of introducing latent failures via organisational decision-making may be drastically reduced as safety management becomes routinely integrated with everyday operational management. It is also possible, and desirable, for these teams to develop localised safety policies, standards and procedures that take into account the inter-relationships between relevant functional departments or operational areas. Because involvement in decision-making is one of the best ways to achieve ownership of safety, membership of these teams should be flexible and relevant and, where practicable, ought to reflect all hierarchical levels. Even though some may argue that lower level personnel should not be involved in policy development or planning, the delegation of some authority to these levels can provide a motivational spur that may have beneficial spin-offs in other operational areas. For example, the effect of exposing people to situations where they need to take account of other viewpoints offers the advantage of broadening their outlook and encouraging their self-development. These issues may be particularly salient for junior management, given their crucial role in implementing company policies. Giving people the opportunity to influence critical decisions serves only to improve such people's overall effectiveness for the good of the organisation.

Recognising and managing resistance to change. Introducing effective cross-functional management teams is not, however, a simple matter. For smooth transitions to proceed, the potential for conflict will need to be identified and addressed, otherwise there is a danger that the developing safety culture will be threatened or stifled. This adds a political dimension to safety culture, as changes in an organisation's structure will almost inevitably affect the distribution of authority as well as functional relationships between different work groups within the overall workflow system. Because change often involves the unknown it may be perceived as a threat to existing power bases or jobs. For example, many supervisors or managers may become demotivated if they view the changes as a de-skilling exercise that threatens their power or authority. As in TQM systems, however, middle management play a crucial pivotal role, as they stand at the crossroads of the vertical and horizontal planes in a matrix design and are able to orchestrate strategy development. In general, their status tends to be significantly enhanced as more of their time is spent co-ordinating work groups, developing the skills and abilities of their work group membership, taking part in recruitment, and in dealing with important technical problems rather than continually being sucked into day-to-day crisis management. Significantly, they will also be seen to be fully involved in setting safety standards, devising safe systems of work, assisting in risk assessments, etc., which has the effect of visibly demonstrating their commitment to safety as well as their care and concern for personnel.

Similarly, tightly controlled hierarchical organisational structures tend to propagate hostility among functional departments as each tries to protect and enlarge their spheres of influence. Attempts to change these functional inter-relationships will, therefore, almost certainly encounter resistance, particularly if different units operate under very different safety cultures. For example, operational or production functions will perhaps attach greater significance to safety *per se* than support functions such as finance, pur-chasing or marketing, simply because of their differing work demands. Nonetheless, support functions play a vital role in developing an organisa-tional safety culture, either because of their roles in monitoring, allocating and distributing operational resources, or because of their effects on production generally. For example, an increase in sales orders may impact on the required workpace and the amount of work, as deadlines will have to be met. By necessity, therefore, every function and business unit must have an equal say in the overall process if balanced and reflective changes are to be achieved. If this is made clear to all concerned at the outset, less overall resistance and conflict should result, particularly if change does not merely degenerate into cost-cutting, productivity improvement or empire building exercises that lose sight of the main objective: namely that of developing a proactive safety culture. However, should any resistance be encountered it may be overcome by joint discussions of the problems, particularly if these are conducted in a spirit of co-operation and flexibility.

Many other potential pitfalls can also be avoided if a slow and iterative process is adopted. Although this could lead to possible criticisms of increased time, cost and effort a reflective, universal and broad based approach is much more likely to result in the development of a safety culture that will hold. This approach is supported by TQM researchers who state

'. . . *Experience suggests that small incremental changes are the best means of facilitating culture change and holding the gains made'.*

Competencies

As many organisations will have already discovered when implementing TQM, the development of a safety culture must be paralleled by a systematic training process to develop people's job and safety-related competencies. For example, although specific safety management training (such as NEBOSH)

and safety training in general are necessary, in themselves they are insufficient. All personnel will also need specific general management training that focuses upon problem-solving, decision-making, goal-setting, communication skills, leadership and group processes. This type of training should be seen as an investment adding to competitive advantage rather than a cost, as the beneficial effects will impact on operational areas beyond the original focus on safety. However, it will also be necessary to install or optimise the use of existing support systems such as recruitment and selection, training needs analyses, health monitoring, publicity, etc. The human resource function is probably best placed to provide the necessary supporting systems. As the guardians of key organisational processes, they exert a large influence on the development of organisational culture via selection, placement, appraisal procedures and reward systems, and would therefore be expected to exert a significant impact on the development of a safety culture. The strategic safety role of the human resource function has been more fully developed by Ian Glendon and Eugene McKenna in their book *Human Safety and Risk Management*, and is often implicitly recognised in companies where the human resource function has joint responsibility for human resource practices, training and safety.

Safety Climate

Inevitably, changes made to either organisational structures or safety management systems will impact upon people's perceptions about and attitudes towards safety as well as their daily safety-related behaviour. This illustrates the point that, because safety culture is a dynamic entity that is continuously changing, there is a need for reliable measuring instruments so that the effectiveness of improvement programmes can be properly assessed and evaluated. Psychometric measures focused on perceptions about, and attitudes towards, safety are commonly used to assess the prevailing 'safety climate'. Although many assert that attitudes, values, beliefs and norms form the core of safety culture, research evidence shows that climate differs from culture in many important ways. In a review of this evidence, Denise Rousseau highlighted the distinctions between the two. In essence, she showed that climate is more specific as it refers to people's descriptions about their everyday experiences, whereas culture largely reflects the prevailing social group norms (i.e. 'the way we do things around here'). For example, the statement 'I do not wear a hard hat on scaffolds because I am always knocking my head on the transoms' describes why an individual does not wear a hard hat (i.e. climate), whereas 'this is a hard hat site' reflects a site-wide behavioural norm (i.e. culture). Thus, although the two are clearly related, culture alludes to the prevailing behavioural norms for a particular work group, whereas climate is more concerned with the way a person describes their perceptions of these behavioural norms. As these perceptual climates serve as a person's frame of reference or anchor point, they are known to affect various work outcomes (e.g. accident rates), by shaping attitudes and behaviours.

The Relationship Between Perceptions and Attitudes

Perceptions are based on complex interactions between a multitude of physiological, psychological and environmental influences. Risk perception research conducted in the workplace, for example, has revealed that a person's ability to determine the risks of perceived hazards is influenced by the ease with which they can recall similar past instances; how confident they are about their own task skills; the manner in which hazards are presented in communications (e.g. safety films); their beliefs about the causes of accidents; and the amount of control they feel they have over any hazards. Although this is not an exhaustive list of risk perception factors, they do illustrate how a person's description of events or hazards will be subjected to many biases, both real and imagined. Added to this is the fact that perceptions are intertwined with people's attitudes, causing them to affect perceptions and vice versa. For example, research conducted by the author in the chemical industry revealed a negative relationship between process workers' perceived levels of risk and their expressed commitment (attitude) towards safety: i.e. the riskier a job was perceived to be, the higher people's commitment to safety tended to be. Conversely, the greater these people's commitment to safety, the more they perceived their jobs to be risky. Moreover, the intensity of this commitment tended to determine both an individual's acceptance of company safety initiatives and their personal safety behaviour. Even though these relationships are very complex, there is still a need to know what safety-related perceptions and attitudes people hold if a proactive safety culture is to be developed.

Psychometric Surveys

Identifying people's perceptions and attitudes is often achieved by surveying the workforce about their views on specific work-related characteristics that affect safety. Their views may be related to management commitment and actions, the required work pace, the effects of job-induced stress, de-manning, etc. The essential point is that, in combination, these types of characteristic prompt people to construct a perceived image of risk, danger and safety in the organisation that is self-sustaining. Two approaches commonly used to survey the workforce are structured interviewing of a random sample selected from the workforce, and the distribution of a questionnaire to the whole workforce. Based on how closely people agree in the way they describe their everyday working environment, the results of either one of these are aggregated to produce meaningful scores with which to direct remedial actions. These scores are often validated against some measure of safety performance (e.g. accident rates) to establish those perceptions or attitudes which predict changes in accident rates. For example, the surveys might reveal that, as a result of an expansion in sales, temporary increases in the required work pace are affecting accident rates because people experience high levels of stress and anxiety that cause them to make many more errors. Thus, the usefulness of such surveys is immense. For example, they allow people to describe elements of safety in terms that have particular meaning to them, while at the same time forcing them to confront their own views on safety. Similarly, the results confront the organisation itself with particular work-related factors that are affecting safety. This allows management to direct their attention to such things as poor communications, weaknesses in safety procedures, gaps in training, etc., of which they may not have been aware. They can also be used to assess and evaluate the effectiveness of safety improvement programmes in improving the safety climate of an organisation. For example, the results of surveys conducted by the author have shown that behavioural safety initiatives improve personnel's perceptions about, and attitudes towards, many work-related safety features. These surveys are therefore extremely useful diagnostic tools for management in focusing safety improvement efforts prior to implementation, as well as in determining the impact of safety awareness campaigns, safety training and behavioural safety initiatives—a task which in the past has been very difficult.

Safety Behaviour

For many years safety professionals have been aware that the majority of workplace accidents are triggered by unsafe behaviours, and that their control is one of the keys to successful accident prevention. However, many organisations, even those companies with low accident rates have been frustrated by their inability to control unsafe acts. Traditional approaches have tended to focus on raising the safety awareness of employees through publicity campaigns, safety training or disciplinary actions in an attempt to change both behaviour and attitudes. Although each of these approaches has its place, they are not in themselves efficient methods for managing change in either attitudes or unsafe behaviours.

Motivational Strategies

The fact that changing behaviour leads to a change in attitudes enables management to focus attention on these behaviours, utilising techniques of goal-setting and performance feedback, which result in significant and lasting improvements. The combination of goal-setting and performance feedback is a powerful management tool that has previously been used to good effect to improve a whole host of safety performance factors. By harnessing these motivational forces, behavioural safety approaches offer an effective alternative to traditional methods such as safety training or safety information campaigns, because they have to take into account the inter-relationships between the organisation, the job and the individual. Thus behavioural safety initiatives meet the needs of both the individual and the organisation, while also positively impacting on safety culture. Since these behavioural approaches also emphasise continuous improvement and incorporate the principles and philosophies of TQM, the two tend to reinforce and gain strength from each other when they are simultaneously implemented in the workplace.

Over many years, regardless of the industrial sector, scientific evaluations have typically found that implementing a behavioural safety initiative leads to:

- improved levels of safety performance
- significant reductions in accident rates and associated costs
- improvements in co-operation, involvement and communication between management and the workforce
- improvements in safety climate
- ongoing improvements to safety management systems
- ownership of safety by the workforce
- enhanced acceptance of responsibility for safety
- better understandings of the relationship between safe behaviour and accidents.

Clearly, these motivational techniques are central to the improvement of safety culture as they impact upon behaviour, perceptions and attitudes, and on safety management systems. Nonetheless, the degree to which they are successful is dependent upon many factors, such as the mechanisms used to set goals, how committed people are to reaching the goals, how confident people are in their abilities, whether or not safety goals conflict with other goals, the methods used to deliver feedback, the prevailing safety climate, and the current status of the safety management system. As the astute reader may have already surmised, many of these features are reciprocally related, and so paying attention to them is likely to produce long lasting effects.

Management Commitment

As in so many organisational endeavours, one of the most salient features that affects people's motivation is the totality of commitment of senior management and line management. This feature in particular has been shown to account for much of the variation in safety performance at many different levels in an organisation. Because the development of a proactive safety culture is an empowering process that aims to win people's hearts and minds, it is absolutely vital that senior company management actively demonstrate their commitment by providing the necessary leadership and resources to implement any improvement strategies. The minimum required of senior management to demonstrate the requisite commitment is for them to:

- develop and actively transmit a corporate safety vision
- establish the prime importance of safety so that it is actively incorporated into all methods of working
- set key safety objectives and devise safety policies by which the organisation can conduct and control itself
- stimulate the involvement of staff in the planning and implementation of safety improvement strategies
- become a role model for others to follow
- provide sufficient time and financial resources to implement all the necessary actions.

Unfortunately, inconsistency between the typical vision statements issued by organisations which state that 'safety is a top priority' and actual managerial practices is all too commonplace. In the author's experience, it is not unknown for safety personnel to try to promote a positive safety culture according to stated company policy, while senior managers are merely concerned with satisfying the minimum of legislative requirements. Often this is due to senior managers focusing their attention on other competing organisational goals such as cost-cutting exercises, organisational 'downsizing' (i.e. compulsory redundancies) or productivity maximisation. Ironically, the net effect is often a demotivated, confused and/or fearful workforce who pay lip service to safety. In turn, this tends to result in increases in operating and accident costs, which in turn decreases profits. Because the development of a proactive safety culture requires the strongest possible commitment from senior management, it is incumbent upon them to ensure that the aims expressed in vision statements are put into effect and adhered to, at all levels. For example, one way of achieving this may be to chair a steering committee of senior managers that allocates responsibility to subsidiary units for the attainment of corporate safety policy, which meets regularly to determine the procedures to be employed, and which monitors outcomes. An integrated network of similar committees that report to the local senior management in subsidiary units could also be set up. However, other highly visible actions may also need to be taken that reinforce the importance of safety, for example, by regularly emphasising the importance of safety and/or promoting safety advisors to senior levels within the organisations hierarchy to enhance their individual status and that of safety in general. The essential point is for senior management to promote a collective commitment of care and concern that is expressed in behavioural norms across the whole organisation. The role of CEOs and other senior management in achieving these aims is that of continual demonstration of their care and concern by ensuring that the organisation adopts sound technical, ergonomic and organisational practices that have been shown to improve safety.

HOW TO READ THIS BOOK

The organising framework of the safety culture model described above is used to provide a basis for the plan of this book. Chapter 2 outlines a strategic direction for creating a positive safety culture by mapping the three components of the safety culture model onto three levels of effort, while also providing practical guidance on problem-solving, decision-making and managing resistance to change. Chapter 3 is concerned with practical methods for evaluating and integrating organisational systems, covering topics such as workflow analyses, job-design, work group communication analyses, job analyses and work safety analyses. Chapter 4 focuses on risk assessments and the associated risk control measures. Chapter 5 is concerned with integrating management information systems to help facilitate organisational learning, by focusing on management control mechanisms, information systems and system structures. Chapter 6 covers strategies and best practice for reviewing the adequacy of safety management systems. Chapter 7 focuses on winning hearts and minds via safety information campaigns and safety training. Chapter 8 describes the measurement of safety climate, and how this can be achieved, while Chapter 9 focuses on how to implement a behavioural safety initiative by offering a step by step guide.

SUMMARY

In recent years, in conjunction with the challenge of reducing accident costs, the results of inquiries into large scale disasters has highlighted the important role of a proactive approach to safety management. This has led to many companies assigning high priority to improving an organisation's safety culture. However, scientific models of human behaviour suggest that any attempts at improving an organisation's safety culture should take into account the interactive relationship between how people behave, the attitudes and perceptions that people hold, and the situation or environment that people work in. Many TQM initiatives have failed because this relationship has been ignored or overlooked when organisations attempt cultural changes. Accordingly, it makes good commercial sense to simultaneously focus on the relationship between safety management systems, safety climate and safety behaviour when attempting to promote a positive and identifiable safety culture. Efficient safety management systems that enhance organisational control, communication, co-operation and people's competencies need to be developed, implemented, monitored and reviewed. This will require an understanding of personnel's perceptions about, and attitudes towards, safety so that management can direct their attention and actions in the most effective manner. Similarly, attention needs to be paid to implementing motivational strategies so that people willingly behave safely in a consistent manner. All of this will require strong leadership and commitment from the very top of the organisation to ensure that a strong safety culture permeates the whole organisation. If successful, the business rewards in terms of competitive advantage, quality, reliability and profitability can be immense.

Because every company faces different circumstances, it is not practicable to offer precise solutions to the myriad of problems associated with the development of a proactive safety culture. Nonetheless, the reader is offered an organising framework that enables constructive analyses of these problems and a strategic direction that draws attention to the different options that are available, whether the organisation is already well on the road, or just starting out. Similarly, because many cultural change initiatives tend to falter due to a lack of managerial know-how, additional practical advice is offered on general management issues to facilitate the required cultural change.

Section One

The immediate level of effort

2

Effective Leadership for Developing a Safety Culture

INTRODUCTION

Effective leadership from senior management is a key feature of a positive safety culture as it determines how everybody else in the organisation will view and act upon safety issues. Unfortunately, safety management is not a field that excites many senior managers and executives. Attending to safety issues tends to be seen as something that is required by the legislature, is boring and has little 'glamour' attached to it, rather than as something that will be seen to contribute to profit and competitiveness. Perhaps because of safety's perceived dowdy image, corporate safety initiatives are all too often delegated to middle and junior managers, with the result that senior managers tend to become even less involved in the management of safety (i.e. *'I have successfully washed my hands of that problem!'*). Inevitably, this abdication of responsibility tends to result in safety management becoming too narrowly focused, with strategic direction being lost in the process as middle and junior management concern themselves with the 'how' of safety, rather than with the 'what' and 'why'. In turn, this tends to result in specialist departments, groups or committees being set up to advise middle and junior managers about how safety might be improved. The use of external consultants also becomes much more widespread as they begin to fulfil middle or junior managers' safety responsibilities for them (e.g. conducting safety management system audits), further adding to operational costs.

LEADERSHIP

At this juncture, before exploring a strategic approach to safety management, it is worth examining what is meant by leadership. Although difficult to pin down, leadership is generally viewed as *the* key determinant of organisational success in all its various endeavours. To some people, a leader is a charismatic individual who by sheer force of personality is able to influence what others do. To others a leader is someone who holds a position of formal authority that grants them power and influence over others. The essential point is that a leader is seen as someone who influences other people's behaviour to achieve certain goals. In this context the terms of leader and manager are synonymous: they are both concerned with determining goals and objectives; taking decisions about what needs to be done; and, motivating others to do what is required. As such both are judged by what they *do*, not by what they *say*. This latter point is extremely important, given that safety culture is best described as 'the way we *do* things around here'. By way of example, if a CEO issues vision and mission statements proclaiming the importance of safety, but does not match the rhetoric with the necessary resources, he or she would soon lose the confidence and commitment of the workforce, which in turn would exert knock-on effects in other operational areas.

Leadership Factors

In principle, the factors that contribute to effective leadership and management of safety are exactly the same as those for other operational areas such as quality and productivity. Researchers have identified two factors of extreme importance to effective leadership: caring and controlling behaviours. Caring behaviour refers to being concerned with:

- people's well-being
- assisting people when necessary
- establishing a good rapport with subordinates
- establishing good two-way communications by explaining things
- being generally available.

Controlling refers to:

- the setting of targets
- maintaining performance standards
- clarifying people's job-roles, expectations and responsibilities
- motivating people to follow rules and procedures.

The Effects of a Lack of Balance between these Leadership Factors

The degree to which a leader is either caring or controlling will almost certainly influence people's reactions to organisational initiatives (both safety or others). Leaders who are more caring than controlling tend to be anxious about being liked by their subordinates, often at the expense of getting the job done. In turn, this could lessen their influence as they may be seen as 'a soft touch', too easy-going, and/or unable to make decisions. For example, when attempting to discover and sort out safety-related problems, they may 'bend with the wind' and agree with two completely opposing views from two different individuals so as not to upset anybody. Inevitably, this type of behaviour will affect their credibility with their subordinates, to the extent that the leader's authority is largely ignored as people attempt to rectify any safety-related problems themselves. Although laudable in some instances, the danger is that this type of 'unauthorised' problem-solving could lead to dangerous practices that result in people being injured, maimed or killed.

At the other end of the spectrum, those who are more concerned with controlling people than caring about them tend to create an 'us and them' adversarial approach to organisational life. Although this latter type of leader often cannot understand why there is an 'us and them' divide, over a period of time it tends to become much greater as it is mutually reinforced by both sides of the divide: by the leader through frustration that he or she feels obliged to continually tell people what to do; by the subordinates through frustration and resentment at being continually told what to do. In practice, such leaders may find that safety-related or other problems are not brought to their attention as they have alienated themselves from their subordinates: It is a natural reaction for people subjected to extreme control to adopt the stance of only doing just enough to keep themselves out of trouble. In relation to safety, the net effect of being overly concerned about controlling people is that knowledge of near misses and dangerous practices is kept suppressed as people try to avoid placing themselves in the line of fire. Because of a fear of discipline or sanctions, there is once again a danger that people will engage in 'unauthorised' problem-solving which could result in someone being injured, maimed or killed.

Effective Leadership

The most effective leaders are those who are both highly caring and highly controlling. These leaders tend to believe strongly that the two are mutually inclusive. They explain problems and agree decisions with people to ensure high levels of commitment to particular courses of action. In parallel, this tends to lead to a team approach to problem-solving where the issues can be fully explored, decisions made and acted upon in a co-operative spirit. Such an effective leader demonstrates that he or she is both caring and controlling by:

- communicating to subordinates the path by which the organisation's goals can be achieved
- specifying the time frame for the goals to be achieved
- helping people along this path by providing all the necessary resources
- removing any organisational obstacles that will prevent the organisation's goals being reached within the allotted time span.

In essence, therefore, effective leadership of safety requires that senior managers develop and implement a strategic plan for safety that captures the hearts and minds of the organisation's employees, personally demonstrate excitement and enthusiasm for the changes and model the behaviours that others are expected to follow, while also maximising the use of the organisation's resources to deliver a productive but safe working environment.

STRATEGIC PLANNING

Developing a strategic plan for cultivating an optimal safety culture requires senior managers to develop corporate safety objectives which, unlike rhetorical vision or mission statements, are precise statements of intent. In turn these must be measurable in one form or another, so that it is possible to confirm whether or not the objectives have been met at some predetermined point in time. Many leadership researchers have commented that the real genius of leadership is demonstrated by asking probing questions rather than pretending to have all the answers (which, given the complexity of modern organisations, is virtually impossible). Thus, developing corporate safety objectives that are right for the organisation requires senior managers to commit their intellect, energy and authority to asking some very searching questions of themselves and their management team. In general terms these will be concerned with the why, the what, the how, the where, and the when of safety. Although these questions may sound simple and superficial they do force senior management to focus their attention on the safety issues affecting their organisation, and on the interactions between safety and other operational areas of the organisation's operations. It is also important to recognise that every level of management within an organisation should ask these types of question of themselves on a regular basis if a positive safety culture is to be developed and maintained throughout the whole organisation.

Establishing the Purpose of the Organisation's Safety Culture

The first question that should be asked is 'Why are we trying to develop a positive safety culture?' This question is designed to focus senior management's attention on the real purpose of their effort, and what level of safety performance they want to achieve. As such it examines whether they know why they are doing what they currently do, and whether these efforts will achieve their purpose. For example, many organisation's safety efforts are merely designed to comply with legislative requirements, with the creation of a positive safety culture being a possible by-product. Other organisations are more concerned to focus on the number of lost time accident (LTA) statistics so that they are below their industry average, which is simultaneously expected to promote a positive safety culture and a caring public image. These organisations tend to be more concerned with the management of accident statistics than promoting the actual well-being of people. Although satisfying legislative requirements and reducing the number of LTAs are both important *outcomes* of safety initiatives, in the author's view the real purpose of establishing a positive safety culture is to make health and safety a truly dynamic and continuous concern for the well-being of every person who comes into contact with the organisation, be they employees, contractors, customers or suppliers. In other words it is more than just preventing accidents or satisfying legislative requirements, it is about ensuring that every aspect of people's well-being is catered for in the pursuit of the organisation's goals.

Establishing what an Identifiable Safety Culture Actually Means to the Organisation

Making safety a dynamic and continuous concern for the well-being of people requires the senior management team to ask themselves the seemingly simple question 'What do we believe is a positive safety culture?' the answer to which will provide the necessary direction for the next question, which asks 'How can we achieve a positive safety culture? The 'what' is not an easy question to answer since safety culture is not a physical entity that can instantly be bought or made. It is an elusive phenomenon made up of the way that the organisation's systems and sub systems are developed, aligned and synthesised to assist everybody in the organisation to *think about and actively pursue the well-being and safety of people*. This is not only consistent with the view that 'safety culture is the product of multiple goal-directed interactions between individuals, jobs and organisations', but it also leads to the inescapable conclusion that a positive safety culture can only come about by optimising and aligning *all of the organisation's systems* to achieve the goal of people's well-being, *not just specific safety systems*. Thus the goal becomes one of integrating all the organisation's systems to achieve a balanced risk-reducing interaction between people, the production processes and the working environment within a specified period of time. In practical terms, *how* this achieved is dependent upon the extent to which each of these elements is fully examined as a separate entity, and as a whole, so that the inter-relationships between each can be identified and harmonised.

Establishing how the Organisation Intends to Develop a Safety Culture

Achieving such a balanced integrated system inevitably leads to the question 'Where should we best focus our efforts to achieve a positive safety culture?' Although this is a key issue that again defies easy answers simply because each organisation has a different starting point, this question can be broken down into two related issues. The first is concerned with identifying what kinds of effort are needed, while the second is concerned with ensuring that the organisation's resources are used to their best effect to maximise the return on investment. To satisfy both these issues, it may prove useful to design a strategy around three levels of effort, respectively termed immediate, intermediate and ultimate levels. Each of these levels of effort addresses a separate set of issues in sequential order at different points in time, which when combined result in vast incremental benefits. Moreover, each of these levels of effort broadly corresponds with one of the components of the safety culture model presented in Chapter 1 i.e. safety management systems, safety behaviour and safety climate.

The Immediate Level of Effort

In principle, the *immediate* level focuses upon an examination of workflow processes and their supportive functions (which may possibly lead to the redefining of organisational structures so that the overall functioning of the organisation is synthesised into a streamlined whole), developing control systems, establishing accountability, and codifying rules and procedures. In practice, this examination is usually achieved by undertaking task, job and workflow analyses (see Chapter 3), which explicitly incorporate risk-assessments (see Chapter 4). Termed the immediate level because of its immediate practical and conspicuous implications, the advantages of focusing the initial effort at this level are that senior management visibly demonstrate that they are truly committed to improving people's safety and well-being, as well as also providing a solid foundation upon which to build the intermediate and ultimate levels of effort. However, it is important to note that if such an exercise is conducted, people's expectations about particular safety problems being resolved will be raised. If the resources to address these problems do not follow, management's credibility will be seriously undermined, which in turn will make it more difficult for them to implement any other types of improvement initiatives in the future. Over a period of time it would be expected that the benefits of all these undertakings would begin to diminish in terms of its returns (e.g. accident rates may begin to plateau). As a result, proactive leaders recognise that more effort will be needed *before* the benefits begin to diminish, and move straight into the *intermediate* level of effort.

The Intermediate Level of Effort

The *intermediate* level of effort is concerned with developing feedback and monitoring systems to facilitate organisational learning, error correction, problem-solving and forward planning. Thus, it is more about the analyses and correction of deviations, which will obviously require the allocation of financial and time resources to develop reporting systems and safety management information systems (see Chapter 5). However, for these to function as intended, it is extremely important to simultaneously develop a no-blame philosophy throughout the whole of the organisation. The advantages offered by a no-blame philosophy are that it facilitates both the gathering of useful information in an atmosphere that is psychologically 'safe', while also enabling the organisation to look beyond the human component of any deviations so that any systemic pathogens can be identified and addressed before causing any further harm to either people or production systems (see Chapter 6).

The Ultimate Level of Effort

Having developed dynamic, living control and feedback systems, the senior management team should direct their attention to the ultimate level of effort. Termed the *ultimate* level because it is perhaps the most difficult aspect of the strategic plan, this is more concerned with specifically capturing people's hearts and minds in relation to safety. The difficulties arise simply because people's hearts and minds are not under the direct control of the organisation. Thus, the ultimate level of effort is employed to ensure that everybody receives the appropriate safety training for their jobs, while organisation-wide safety information campaigns are also put into effect in attempts to get people thinking about the safety issues involved in their jobs, and what it means to them personally (see Chapter 7). With the use of appropriate measuring instruments it is possible to discover what perceptions and attitudes people actually hold in regard to a company's safety efforts (see

Chapter 8). The results of these can be used to focus remedial attention and effort on those features of an organisation's functioning thought to affect safety negatively. (These measuring instruments can also be used by the senior management team to help them focus on where best to start improving their safety culture.) Similarly, proven strategies that harness group processes can be brought to bear to motivate people to behave safely (see Chapter 9) and help each work group to positively redefine their safety-related norms.

It is important to recognise that, *de facto*, winning people's hearts and minds begins when the first level of effort is implemented. This is achieved in part by developing and transmitting a corporate safety vision that establishes the primary importance of safety to the organisation. In addition, the whole management team, led by senior managers, need to set an example and become a role model for others to follow if people are to be persuaded that safety is important to the organisation. In many instances, this may require the whole management team to undergo formal training in safety management to a specified standard (e.g. NEBOSH certificate level) so that everybody is able to solve problems and communicate in a common language within a common framework. This formal training could and should be extended to all employees over a period of time.

Warning Comments on the Three Levels of Effort

The three levels of effort outlined above provide a broad framework for senior management to identify where their organisation currently is in relation to developing a positive safety culture, and act accordingly. However, in light of the strategic levels of effort outlined above it is also possible to comment upon the fact that many organisations attempting to develop a positive safety culture often focus most of their initial efforts on the ultimate level in an attempt to capture the hearts and minds of their employees by trying to change their attitudes via safety information campaigns or safety training, while ignoring the front-end work (for whatever reason) required at the immediate and intermediate levels of effort. Such attempts generally fail, simply because these organisations hold unrealistic expectations of what safety training and safety information campaigns can deliver (see Chapter 7).

Converting Strategic Plans into Action Plans

Having determined where best to focus their efforts, the next question the senior management team should focus upon is 'When should we begin to implement the strategy, and by when should our objectives be met?' In other words, the senior management team need to think about developing an action plan that implements the strategic plan. Because an action plan is concerned with turning vision statements and corporate intentions into action, they are by their very nature linked to the use of resources. They may, for example, show how many people are to be involved in a particular activity, the types of skills and qualifications thought to be important to assisting the effort, and what each person is to be responsible and held accountable for. Thus, the action plan will specify the start date in light of an organisation's current circumstances, the accounting period when capital expenditures might best be used in relation to tax advantages, the availability of human resources, and the amount and types of equipment, etc. In essence, therefore, action plans are used to establish and specify guidelines for all the various activities involved in the implementation effort. These are then translated into detailed plans by individual business units or functioning departments within a specified time scale for completion.

The importance of setting a time scale for the implementation of a company's objectives cannot be underestimated as it focuses line management's attention and mobilises their efforts. In the chemical industry, for example, a well known multi-national company set a two-year time scale on the completion of their safety objectives for each of their business units back in the early 1990s. At the end of the two-year period a 55% rate of improvement had been achieved in the company's incident rate, compared to the objective of a 60% reduction. Subsequently, on the basis of such achievements, the board set new three-year occupational health objectives for each business unit. This illustrates the point that it is incumbent upon the senior management team to monitor and review both the strategic plan, and the implementation of the action plan at frequent intervals to assess progress, and set further objectives, or realign their plans in light of the progress achieved.

Transmitting Management's Intentions for Developing a Safety Culture

On the basis of the types of searching questions outlined above it may prove useful to develop a vision or mission statement that encapsulates senior management's intentions in relation to developing a safety culture. Unlike most vision or mission statements it should not be long on rhetoric, but should be constructed in such a way that it actually guides the in-depth formulation and implementation of the strategic plan, i.e. what the strategic direction is and how the organisation is going to achieve it. An example might be:

'Our intention is to make Health and Safety a truly dynamic concern for the well-being of every person who comes into contact with our organisation, by integrating all of our systems to achieve a balanced risk-reducing interaction between people, our production processes and the working environment'.

In essence, therefore, the purpose of this type of vision or mission statement is to serve as a guiding principle or 'frame of reference'. As such it should specify the ultimate objective and state how this will be achieved.

PROBLEM-SOLVING

Converting a strategic plan into an action plan is not as easy as it sounds because it involves both problem-solving and decision-making, both of which can be difficult because of a variety of factors related to individual, group and organisational characteristics, as well as uncertainties caused by economic, social, political, technological and other changes. However, once completed, the action plan could form the basis for the organisation's health and safety policy (in one sense, *if operationalised* a company's health and safety policy is an action plan). It is recognised that the vast majority of companies may have already developed their health and safety policy to comply with the Health and Safety at Work Act 1974 section 2(3). Not surprisingly, however, these policies have tended to be written by safety managers and subsequently 'signed off' by senior managers. They are often written in such a way that they emphasise compliance to legislation rather than reflecting the organisation's strategy for developing a positive safety culture. However, given that these are intended to be 'living' documents that need to be reviewed periodically, developing an action plan to align the organisation's overall objectives for developing a positive safety culture with their existing health and safety policy provides such a review opportunity.

Systematic Problem-Solving

Systematic problem-solving and decision-making is a process consisting of the following steps, represented by the easily remembered acronym IDEAL:

I = Identify the problem
D = Define and represent the problem
E = Explore possible solutions
A = Act on the solutions
L = Look back and evaluate the effects of these solutions

Identifying and Defining the Problem

In relation to safety culture, the first step involves identifying the scope of the problem. In a sense the searching questions the senior management team have already asked itself should have defined the scope of the problem and led to a strategic plan. As such the translation of the strategic plan into an action plan is the point at which the problem is defined and represented in its entirety. In the current context, representation refers to identifying and outlining all the appropriate elements that may impact upon the development of a safety culture. For example, the existing health and safety policy, legislative requirements, the organisation's current health and safety strategies and their effects, the structure of the organisation, the availability of human and economic resources, other current corporate objectives (e.g. market aims, increasing return on investment, etc.), and defining the organisation's most appropriate 'level of effort' in light of the organisation's particular circumstances (i.e. immediate, intermediate or ultimate) may all prove to be important factors to consider.

Exploring Solutions

Once the scope of the problem has been identified and represented within some form of overall picture, an appropriate problem-solving strategy needs to be adopted in order to bring everything together into a coherent whole so that the appropriate decisions can be made. As such the next step involves the exploration of possible solutions, using an appropriate problem-solving strategy in light of an organisation's particular circumstances. Numerous methods for systematically solving problems are available and include the use of decision matrices, decision trees, Ishikawa (fishbone or cause effect) diagrams, force field analyses, etc. In essence, each of these attempts to provide structure to the problem aids in the decision-making process, by breaking down the problem into its component parts to provide a focused analysis of the key factors contributing to the problem. However, different types of problem-solving methods may only be appropriate in certain circumstances as they may not be effective in all situations.

Problem-solving tools. One type of problem-solving tool, decision trees, begin with the actual problem (e.g. how do we synthesise and align all of our systems to produce a positive safety culture?) and are used by problem solvers to work their way directly towards the desired end-state (i.e. a positive safety culture) by specifying the various steps to be taken. Decision trees, therefore, work on the assumption that the problem solver has sufficient in-depth knowledge and understanding of the problem to solve it. In other words they require expert knowledge. In many instances, however,

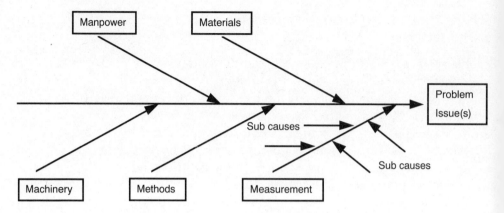

Figure 2.1   Ishikawa Diagram — Adapted from Ishikawa, K. (1984) What is Total Quality Control the Japanese way? *Prentice-Hall. Reprinted by permission*

this expert knowledge is not readily available. Therefore, a different strategy will be required. Ishikawa diagrams were originally developed for use in TQM to identify the fundamental root causes of problems, the relative importance of each of these causes and the potential relationships between each of them. Illustrated in Figure 2.1: *Ishikawa Diagram*, the diagram begins on the right hand side with the issue(s) facing the problem solver, such as the senior management team. The major factors contributing to the problem are then identified and labelled as causes, each of which can be further broken down into sub causes, and so on, until all the possible causes have been identified. The five major factors commonly considered are:

- manpower (e.g. staffing, management styles, competences, communications, training, etc.)
- materials (e.g. economic resources, corporate objectives, etc.)
- machinery (e.g. plant, equipment, computers, vehicles, etc.)
- methods (work practices, health and safety initiatives, risk assessments, etc.)
- measurement (safety audits, accident investigations, safety training results, etc.).

As these diagrams work backwards from the specified problem, they are ideal for converting strategic plans into action plans simply because all the factors contributing to a problem can more easily be identified. Seemingly simple, when used in the right way they are deceptively powerful tools to aid decision-making. Although they do not require the use of expert knowledge, analyses of the causes are usually best conducted in teams, since most of the activities or factors contributing to each of the causes and sub causes involve groups of people. In the context of aligning and synthesising all of the organisation's systems to develop a positive safety culture, it may prove useful to use one of these diagrams to visually represent each operational area or organisational system (e.g. safety, quality, production, support functions, etc.). This enables them to be compared with each other to identify where the commonalities and differences between the various systems reside. Having identified the commonalities, the senior management team can give due consideration as to whether or not it is possible to integrate any of the systems together, bearing in mind the number of differences and their relative importance. If it is possible, the management team should then consider whether or not it is desirable in light of their particular circumstances.

Similarly, these types of diagram could be used to examine an organisation's existing health and safety policy to identify which elements have been operationalised to good effect, and which elements are weak or non-existent in practice. In this way it is possible to work backwards from the existing policy and tie it in with the various elements of any strategic plans.

Identifying Obstacles to Implementing Solutions

The two problem-solving methods previously discussed focus primarily on generating and evaluating alternative solutions. An essential part of the management decision-making process, however, is the need to know whether or not these alternatives will actually work in practice, and whether or not they will have the desired effect. A technique known as 'forcefield' analysis can help management to focus on any obstacles to successful implementation. Forcefield analysis considers the effects of two mutually opposed forces: driving forces that support or encourage implementation, and restraining forces that resist implementation. The general aim of the forcefield analysis is to identify, *in advance* of implementation, the critical forces that will assist or hinder the implementation effort. Once identified, the strength of the resisting forces can be minimised or totally eliminated, whereas the driving forces can be further strengthened. As a general principle, it is best simultaneously to weaken the resisting forces while strengthening the driving forces in any given circumstance, although it is recognised that this may not always be possible.

As shown in Figure 2.2: *Forcefield Analyses Overview* the current status is indicated by the heavy black line, whereas the desired state (e.g. end goal) is indicated by the dotted line. It is between the current and end states that the restraining forces lie. Conversely, the driving forces supporting the implementation are on the other side of the black line, pushing against the restraining forces. It is important to identify and label each individual driving and restraining force, and assess the relative strength of each, i.e. some driving forces will be stronger than others, while some restraining

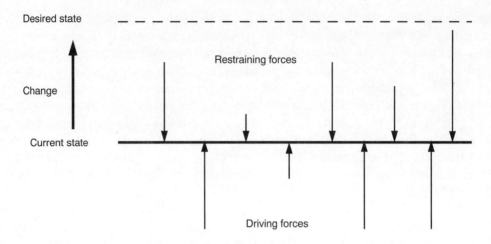

Figure 2.2   Forcefield Analyses Overview – Adapted from Lewin, K. (1951) Field Theory in Social Science. *Harper, New York. Reprinted by permission*

forces will be stronger than others. A simple mechanism to demonstrate the strength of a restraining or driving force is to use the length of the arrowed line as an indicator: the longer the line, the stronger the force.

An example to demonstrate the utility of forcefield analysis might be a national company which had taken on board the notion of safety culture. They bought in external consultants to put an effective safety management system in place, train all managerial levels in safety management auditing techniques and risk assessments, and set up a series of safety committees. In addition, a number of initiatives were instigated to publicise and communicate the importance of safety (e.g. monthly in-house safety newsletters). All of these are driving forces as illustrated in Figure 2.3: *Example Forcefield Analyses*. After two years, the number of accidents had decreased by only 12% per annum, 2% more than that before implementation. During the third year the number of accidents had begun to rise significantly. In addition, a cost–benefit analysis revealed that the consultants' fees still significantly exceeded what was saved by the reduced accident costs, two and a half years on. Senior managers began to question why the intended results had not met expectations. They met with each of the work groups and held discussions to find out what was happening 'on the ground'. With some vigour, the senior management team were informed about problems that they had not previously considered. The first of these was the resentment felt by everybody that external consultants had been used to impose their 'proprietary' brand of safety management on people, which was primarily top-down driven and predicated on the use of discipline and fear. This resentment was further compounded by the scale of the consultants' fees, which the work groups contrasted with the need for a de-manning exercise

Desired end state (i.e. a positive safety culture)

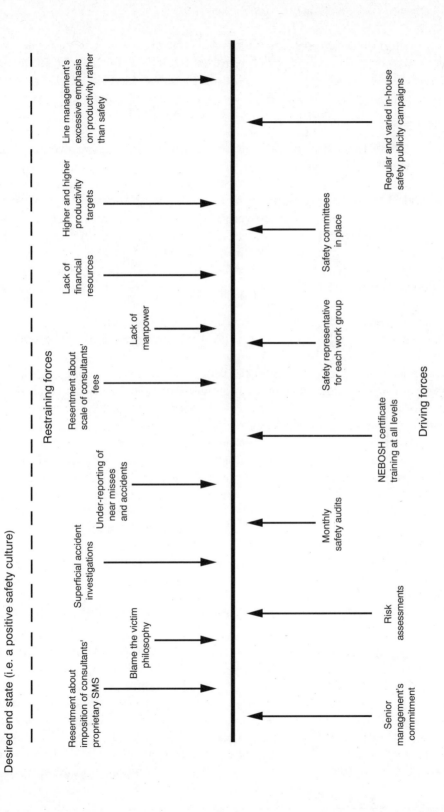

Restraining forces

Line management's excessive emphasis on productivity rather than safety

Higher and higher productivity targets

Lack of financial resources

Lack of manpower

Resentment about scale of consultants' fees

Under-reporting of near misses and accidents

Superficial accident investigations

Blame the victim philosophy

Resentment about imposition of consultants' proprietary SMS

Driving forces

Regular and varied in-house safety publicity campaigns

Safety committees in place

Safety representative for each work group

NEBOSH certificate training at all levels

Monthly safety audits

Risk assessments

Senior management's commitment

Figure 2.3   Example Forcefield Analyses

that had taken place to reduce fixed labour costs. Similarly, whenever a safety problem had been identified which required capital expenditure, the funding was never forthcoming, even though ever-increasing targets set for production had always been met. Indeed, the general concern to meet the production targets had resulted in superficial accident investigations, which tended to result in the accident victim being blamed and disciplined, with the corresponding effect that employees no longer reported near misses or accidents unless it was totally unavoidable. Similarly, middle and junior management's attendance at the safety committee meetings diminished, as did the monthly safety audits they were required to carry out, simply because they were so hard pressed for time to deal with production issues, let alone safety issues. The senior management team laid out each of these restraining forces on the forcefield analysis sheet. Each individual restraining force identified was further examined with other forcefield analyses to identify how they might be weakened or eliminated. On the basis of these analyses, management focused their remedial efforts and changed much of the character of the previous approach to developing their safety culture to good effect.

Thus forcefield analysis is a useful tool that can be used to identify all the salient issues involved in the implementation of an organisation's strategic approach to developing a safety culture, *prior to actually doing so*. As the above example indicates, the senior management team were very committed to developing a safety culture but, even though they had spent a six figure budget, they had not considered all the salient issues before implementation. It also illustrates the point that someone else's safety culture cannot be bought and imposed on people: it must be developed over a period of time by the people in the organisation themselves, so that it is in accordance with their own values and beliefs. In this way the organisation's 'citizens' will feel 'ownership' which in turn will increase their commitment to it. This is not to say that organisations cannot, or should not, learn from each other about the way they approach things, just simply that buying in and imposing an alien culture on an organisation will often not work out as planned.

INCREASING PEOPLE'S COMMITMENT TO A DECISION

Much of what has been discussed in relation to problem-solving and decision-making has referred to tools and techniques used to identify the major factors involved in developing a strategic action plan for promoting a positive safety culture. However, a significant human element also needs to be taken into account if people are to commit themselves to carrying out any strategic action plans. Typically, people engage in three types of decision-making, each of which is susceptible to different psychological phenomena. These are: individual decision-making, two-person decision-making, and group decision-making. Regardless of the type, a good decision is one that will achieve its objectives and which people will be prepared to implement to the best of their ability. In the first instance, this will be dependent upon the 'technical' quality of the decision-making. For example, is the decision specific and realistic? Will it achieve its objectives? Questions to be considered in relation to the decision's acceptability to those who have to carry it out include: Will people 'buy in' to the decision? Will they be prepared to implement it willingly? The more acceptable it is to people, the more committed they will be to its implementation. Thus the more people are involved in the decision-making process, the more likely they are to be committed to carrying out the decision and reaching the original objectives (e.g. integrating all of the organisation's systems to develop a positive safety culture).

Individual Decision-making

When people make decisions on their own, they often do so on both an emotional and rational basis. This can sometimes be detected in such statements as:

> *'We know that we sometimes behave unsafely, and shouldn't. But so what! We haven't been hurt, and anyway, management care more about productivity than safety. We have asked them for years to improve our working environment, but they won't. If they won't do that, why should we bother to change the way we do things?'*

In this, example, although the emotional component is exerting the greatest influence on this person's decision and subsequent behaviour, it is also based on a rational assessment of the situation. Many people feel that decision-making should be made only on the basis of rational thought, and that they should suppress their emotions and feelings. However, although the resulting decision may be logical, this can lead to decisions being made that people do not actually like, which in turn will affect their commitment to carrying them out. This lack of commitment is likely to show itself in situations where the person has to support the decision, or carry it out in the face of some resistance.

This can be illustrated by the case of two scaffolders who were working alone in an isolated area of an old plant that was being prepared for dismantling. The offices and main working complex were some two miles away and they had been taken to the area in the scaffold lorry. During the course of their work it became apparent that they were going to run out of materials, so the driver went to the stores area to collect what was needed. During his absence, one of the scaffolders fell off the building and landed on a concrete pad containing six inch protruding tips of old steel reinforcing bars. This resulted in the scaffolder breaking both his legs and puncturing a lung. Although his companion knew that he should immediately go for assistance, he also knew he would have to leave his injured colleague who was begging him to stay and help. He therefore allowed his emotions to guide his decision-making and stayed with his companion in the hope that the driver would soon return. Unfortunately, his colleague died during the two hours it took for the driver to return. This case illustrates that a decision may be made solely on the basis of emotion or 'gut feel'. Although the person may be highly committed to his or her decision, it may be a poor decision because it has not been fully thought through and may not achieve its objectives. In the example, had the decision-making scaffolder been guided by logic and run for help, it is likely that his injured colleague would have received assistance within 30 minutes, thereby increasing his chances of survival.

The Motivational Element

The emotional component often reflects the motivation of the decision-maker. In many instances, for example, the primary cause of indecisiveness is a lack of internal motivation to actually make a decision. This can be illustrated aptly by the case of an operator working in a mandatory Personal Protective Equipment (PPE) area. His manager often entered the area without wearing the necessary PPE to read a gauge. However, this same manager often disciplined the operators who entered the area without wearing their PPE. The operator's colleagues often put pressure on him to report the manager, so that he could be disciplined. Thus when the manager entered the operators' area without PPE, the operator was faced with the dilemma of either ignoring the fact that his manager was not wearing the appropriate PPE and face the teasing of his colleagues, or else reporting him so that he would be disciplined, but having to face the manager's wrath at some later stage. In the event the operator decided not to decide. He waited for the situation to resolve itself, which it did when the manager, without wearing the appropriate PPE, eventually slipped and fell into a product bath severely burning his arm in the acidic solution.

Conversely, being overly motivated to decide on something could lead to decisions being made before the person has fully evaluated all the alternatives. This can be illustrated by an analysis of the Chernobyl disaster conducted by Professor James Reason in 1987. The Chernobyl 'experiments' were being conducted to test a modified device that would help to prevent a system melt-down. To do this they needed to operate the plant at 25% of its normal operating power levels, which gave a 5% built-in margin of error as the safety rules expressly stated that the minimum power levels at which the plant could be operated were 20%. The experiment was originally intended to start at 13.00 hrs, but at 14.00 hours the plant was requested to supply the national grid, by which time it was operating at 50% power. Nine hours later, at 23.10, the plant was released from the grid. This considerably reduced the 'time frame' within which to conduct the experiments, and the operators were anxious to get started. One hour and 18 minutes into the experiment, the power levels had fallen to a very dangerous low of 1%. Within the next 32 minutes the operators manually struggled to raise the power levels to somewhere near its minimum 20% safe operating level, and did in fact achieve stabilisation at 7% of power. At this point the whole experiment should have been abandoned.

At 01.03, however, in an attempt to simulate the load of the Emergency Core Cooling System they started all eight 'cooling' pumps, instead of the maximum six stipulated in the safety regulations. They used four of the pumps for the simulation and the other four to provide safer core cooling as they continued the experiment. Attempting to cope with falling steam and water levels at 01.19, they increased the feedwater flow threefold. However, this caused even less steam to pass through the core, causing some more control rods to be withdrawn (in other words the brakes were being taken off!). At 01.22 the remaining number of core rods were checked. Only six or eight were still thought to be operating, less than the absolute minimum of 12. *Remarkably the shift supervisor decided to carry on with the experiment.* At 01.23 the steam lines to the turbine generators were closed to establish the necessary experimental conditions for repeat testing. However, this also disconnected the automatic safety trips. At 01.24 the 'experimenters' finally realised that they had made some wrong decisions and attempted to correct the situation by driving home the emergency shut-off rods. This did not work because the emergency rods jammed in warped tubes. Two explosions then occurred that blew the reactor roof off. Although there were many factors involved in this incident, the reduced time frame almost certainly led to both the operators and experimenters being overly motivated to make decisions about continuing the experiment, without fully evaluating other alternative courses of action throughout its various stages (i.e. stopping the experiment).

Information Availability

In some instances people do not have all the information they need to predict the outcomes of different courses of action. The potentially disastrous consequences of this can be illustrated by the case of an explosion in pipework caused by the use of a wrong type of coupler. Because of the nature of the product, the pipework was joined by special couplings instead of flanges. These couplings needed particular bonding arrangements to prevent the build-up of electrostatic energy. However, during maintenance a standard rubber sleeve had been used to replace one of the special couplings. Subsequently, the section of the pipework with the rubber sleeve was ignited by a static electricity charge. Although nobody was injured the consequences could have been much more serious. Investigations revealed that the fitter had not been informed about the importance of the particular bonding arrangements, and had made a decision about the choice of a rubber sleeve based on his previous experience. A similar example is provided by the *Herald of Free Enterprise* disaster. Because no one person had been allocated responsibility for monitoring the status of the bow doors, information about previous 'open door' incidents was not readily available. This meant that the potential risks of leaving port with open bow doors had not been taken into consideration when the company were devising and implementing their safety systems. It also illustrates the point that in many organisations the only safety information available to decision-makers is limited to that gained from accident and near miss reports. In turn, this over-reliance on such reports means that useful information about the impact of previous safety-related decisions also tends to be limited (see Chapter 5).

Competing Alternatives

Too many competing alternatives can also cause problems for anyone struggling to select the best alternative. In essence, the decision-maker has to judge the relative merits of each and prioritise them according to how well they fit with the decision's objectives based on the perceived costs and benefits of all possible outcomes. However, difficulties often arise when people try to assess the alternatives because they may not be easily compared. This leads to a tendency for people to try to reduce the available alternatives into a common framework. When done systematically the resulting decision is usually the optimal one (e.g. using cause/effect diagrams, etc.). More often than not, however, decision-makers faced with large amounts of competing information merely tend to select and focus on those pieces of information that confirm what the person already believes is the right course of action while ignoring the alternatives, thus arriving at a satisfactory rather than optimal solution.

Sometimes none of the alternatives being considered is viable, and the person blindly goes round in circles trying to decide which alternative to accept, without recognising the fact. Often this is due to the person just making comparisons between all alternatives, rather than taking into account the practicality of each in a given situation. This illustrates the point that viability and acceptability problems are often linked to specific situational constraints. For example, 'I can't behave safely when undoing valves, simply because they are ten foot above the floor level, and the only way to reach them quickly is to climb on the handrail'. Thus, both the practicalities of the situation and the task to be achieved will exert a large influence on a person's decision-making processes.

Two-person Decision-making

All the features previously outlined will also apply to two-person decision-making, except that two new elements will influence the quality of any decisions. These are related to whether or not the decisions are to be made in a competitive or co-operative spirit.

Competitive Decision-making

If the decisions are being made in a competitive spirit it is likely that the information available will be limited only to that considered politically and/or strategically expedient. The resulting decision(s) may be made on the basis of incomplete information, with all the attendant problems, or solely on an emotional basis. In either event, the quality of the decision is likely to be less than adequate, either because it is unrealistic and will not achieve its aims, or because one of the parties will not be committed to carrying it out to the best of their abilities. Competitive decision-making may also arise when the potential solutions to a problem involve two fundamentally opposing viewpoints. This can be illustrated by a discussion between a manager and safety representative about ways to improve adherence to procedures. The manager fundamentally believed that employees were the cause of accidents. This view was based on his belief that accidents were caused by employees not adhering to the standard operating procedures. He therefore wanted to introduce a disciplinary regime involving 'safety policemen' to ensure the rules were not breached. Conversely, the safety representative fundamentally believed that the existing safety procedures led to conflicts between productivity and safety, to the extent that they got in the way and slowed the job down, which is why people did not always follow them. Rather than see the introduction of 'safety policemen' and a disciplinary approach, the safety representative wanted a review of the standard operating procedures with a view to streamlining them. Although it is within the manager's power to implement his preferred option, when the differences between the viewpoints appear to be so large, a wise person attempts a compromise. This is simply because if either viewpoint were to be imposed at the expense of the other, it is almost certain that the losing party would be less than committed to implementing the winning decision, which in turn could create unnecessary tensions and undesirable knock-on effects.

Co-operative Decision-making

Decision-makers who operate in a co-operative spirit are more likely both to communicate all the available information to each other and to achieve an optimal solution. Even so, they may still be unable to agree the best way

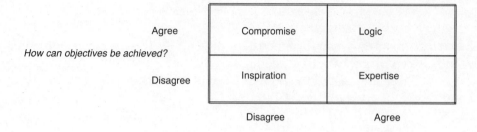

Figure 2.4   Co-operative Decision-Making Model

forward in relation to either the objectives of the decision, or the methods to achieve the objectives, or both. The co-operative model of decision-making illustrated in Figure 2.4: *Co-operative Decision-Making Model* provides a framework by which people can resolve their disagreements in two ways. First, it can help to identify the areas where the parties are in disagreement and, second, it suggests an appropriate mechanism that might be used for finding a solution. If both parties disagree about the objectives of the decision (i.e. what is to be achieved), it shows that some inspiration is needed. This might be achieved via a brain-storming session whereby both parties bounce around various ideas. As they find areas of agreement, these can be noted until such time as a compromise is reached or both are in full agreement. Similarly, if one party is adamant about what is to be achieved while the other disagrees, it may be that a compromise is needed, or that expert advice should be sought. Having come to an agreement about what the objective is, the framework can then be used in the same way to identify areas of agreement or disagreement about how the objectives can be achieved.

By way of example, if we use the co-operative framework to analyse the scenario presented above, it becomes clear that neither party actually differs in their objectives. Both want to increase adherence to procedures. They merely differ as to the methods to be adopted to achieve the objectives: the manager wishes to introduce monitoring and disciplinary procedures, whereas the safety representative wishes to re-examine the existing procedures to make operational adherence more realistic. In this scenario it would make sense for each party to take it in turns to explain the rationale for their preferred option. For example, the manager might explain that each time a procedure was not followed, the probability of someone being injured or the possibility of pathogens being introduced into the organisation's production system was increased. In turn these pathogens could cause someone a serious injury at a later date. The safety representative might explain that because the management's daily emphasis and the organisation's reward systems were heavily geared towards production, the procedures would always be breached because of the perceived conflict between productivity and safety goals. Were the manager to insist on complete compliance to existing procedures, although this may lead to short-term adherence, it might also lead to even greater productivity/safety conflicts, which in the longer term would lead to further violations of the procedures, thus negating what he was trying to achieve in the first place. On the basis of this discussion the two might agree to the following compromise: the safety representative would try to ensure that his fellow employees followed the existing procedures, while also being allowed to review them within a specified time period. In parallel the manager would ensure that the profile of safety was increased by being placed as the first item on the agenda at all management meetings, and that each front line manager's annual performance appraisal would include specific safety objectives. As this example attempts to illustrate, all decision-making should be undertaken in a co-operative spirit so as to minimise resistance, while also increasing ownership of, and commitment to, the improvement process. If difficulties are encountered, the co-operative model of decision-making can be used to identify the areas of disagreement. Thereafter, wherever possible, people should try to be flexible and willing to compromise.

Group Decision-making

Given that most decisions concerning the creation of a positive safety culture will be made in groups (e.g. board meetings, senior management meetings, safety committee meetings, etc.,) the factors surrounding group decision-making are both important and relevant. Decision-making in groups is much more complex than that discussed so far, even though many of the same factors come into play. This is because the process is affected by issues surrounding the social interactions between all the various parties and this tends to affect how decisions are arrived at, as well as the actual topic of the decision-making. Researchers have shown that groups often decide to adopt an action which is most likely to succeed, even though it may not be the best solution to the problem. Out of the 150 strategic decisions studied, 90 appeared to adequately 'satisfy' everybody but actually failed to deliver the expected benefits. In part this was because the proposed solutions appeared 'blindingly' obvious, which meant that the decision-making groups simply did not go on to consider all the alternatives, to the extent that as other issues emerged they were ignored. The 1986 *'Challenger'* US space shuttle disaster provides an example of this. The disaster occurred when a booster 'O-ring' split on lift-off and caused a blow-out which led to the rocket fuel igniting and subsequently exploding. The underlying cause was traced to the faulty decision-making of NASA officials and the principal contractor, Morton

Thiokol. Previous incidents surrounding the failure of the O-rings were well known to both NASA and Morton Thiokol, but because these had not caused any serious incidents, NASA officials decided that these O-ring failures could be tolerated. Perhaps because people have a tendency to continue with a course of action if negative outcomes do not become apparent, NASA officials became 'blinded' to recognition of the associated problems and the potentially disastrous consequences (as has been the case in many major disasters in recent years). This example also serves to illustrate the point that the decisions made by a group will be affected by the beliefs and values held by its membership. Indeed, the underlying causes of many major disasters (e.g. the Kings Cross underground fire, Chernobyl, etc.) can be laid at the door of faulty decision-making based on the senior managers' underlying beliefs and assumptions about the causes of accidents. Many senior managers tend to focus on the immediate and obvious cause (e.g. the operator) rather than the underlying causes (e.g. an accumulation of systemic pathogens), simply because they tend to receive little feedback about the actual causes of accidents from middle and junior managers.

Groupthink

The *Challenger* example also aptly illustrates the point that groups can sometimes become an isolated 'mutual self-reinforcing society': i.e. they often actively display interest only in facts or opinions that support their preferred policy, while simultaneously ignoring views that run counter to the preferred policy. This often occurs when a group becomes too far removed from the daily activities of the organisation. An inward looking group 'culture' tends to form whereby the group members continually seek and receive confirmation and approval from each other for their ideas. Many high-level groups (e.g. company boards, senior management groups, etc.) tend to exhibit this type of behaviour which is termed 'groupthink'. In part, groupthink comes about because the group tends to be made up of like-minded people: i.e. in terms of their thinking they are all clones of each other. They see things in exactly the same way, all the time. Any person who deviates from the groups norm (e.g. challenges the group's view of things) tends to be ostracised or ignored. Thus, groupthink can come about because people fear losing status within the group, and the potential adverse impact this might have for them in terms of their career.

Groupthink can also be created by lower echelons of management who are so concerned to present a rosy picture of what is happening on the ground, that each time information is passed up the organisation's hierarchy the information is filtered, sanitised and embellished to make individual managers look good to their managers, and so on. It is not uncommon, for example, for information about a business unit's safety performance to be changed to focus only on the positive, while simultaneously down playing the negatives as the information gets closer to the top of the organisation. Thus by the time it has reached the boardroom it has become patently false 'positive' information, upon which the executive function is expected to make strategic decisions. The practical effects of this are often felt when middle management's requests for funding of capital projects for safety improvements are refused, simply because the request is totally at odds with the 'rosy picture' already presented to the board. The message from this scenario is that, if middle management wish to secure capital funding from their executive, then they should consistently provide decision-makers with a realistic picture of what is actually happening on the ground.

Overcoming Groupthink

Researchers have shown that 'groupthink' can be avoided simply by ensuring that the membership of a group is made up of people of diverse age, length of service, educational level and functional disciplines. This mix often leads to the group being more:

- receptive to change
- able to seek, accept and integrate new information into existing strategies
- creative and innovative in their decision-making
- willing to pursue different strategies
- effective at implementing strategies.

The body of evidence surrounding this research has also shown that such groups exert a significant effect on their organisation's commercial performance, sometimes by more than 50% (indicating the potential for improving organisational safety performance). Although such a mixed group may sometimes create tensions between members, it does build in and legitimise healthy scepticism and critical evaluation of various options, as people feel free to air their doubts. In turn this forces the group as a whole to consider alternative views and courses of action. Research has also shown that potential tensions could be minimised if the leaders of such groups avoid stating their preferences for a particular course of action at the beginning of discussions, and also actively encourage, or at least tolerate, criticism of their judgements.

STRATEGIC COMMUNICATIONS

Once decisions have been made about how an organisation will implement its strategic plan to develop a positive safety culture, the next stage is to communicate and sell the proposed changes throughout the organisation.

The way this is done will affect people's commitment to the change process, and how well the plan is actually implemented. The purpose of the communication is to transmit information throughout an organisation so that the communicator (e.g. board) and the receiver (e.g. the organisation) share a clear, common understanding of what (if any) actions are required. However, because organisational communications cover such a wide range of activities, the processes involved are complex, pervasive and continually in operation at many different levels within the organisation, embracing both informal mechanisms (such as grapevines and rumour mills) and formal mechanisms (such as safety committee structures and steering committees). To appreciate the complexities involved one only has to consider that communications can be one way, two way, top-down or bottom-up between employees and managers, employees to employees, managers to managers, departments to departments, business unit to business unit, organisation to statutory authorities and vice versa, and so on. To complicate matters further, communications can either be conducted verbally face to face with the attendant problems presented by social and behavioural cues, or presented in written form with the potential problems bought about by too much or too little information and in language that may be familiar to the communicator but totally alien to the receiver. Further complexity is added when the explicit content of the message is at odds with the implicit message presented 'between the lines', or when the message is reinterpreted and communicated onwards to others.

All of this adds up to the fact that even the simplest message can be easily misunderstood or distorted simply because of the complex influences that may be operating on the communication process. It makes sense, therefore, to consider how the communication process can be enhanced so that the opportunities for misunderstandings can be eliminated or at least reduced. In essence there are two main forms of communication, written and verbal, each of which can enhance understanding or create difficulties, depending upon how quickly feedback can be given and received. The more rapid the potential for feedback, the more quickly any errors of interpretation can be corrected.

Verbal Communications

Although most people tend to prefer face-to-face verbal communications simply because the opportunity for feedback is thought to be instant, in practice the type of face-to-face communication used will determine both the opportunity for feedback and the speed with which it can be given and received, and this in turn will affect the degree to which people will become committed to the change process. Len Holden from the Leicester Business School, for example, has shown that although information communicated via formal presentations and mass meetings reach a large audience, the potential for feedback is low, as is the speed with which it can be given or received (See Figure 2.5: *Len Holden's Communication Channel and Feedback Matrix*). This means that if the strategic plan is initially to be presented to the workforce in large groups, it is incumbent upon those who present the message to ensure that it is very clear, unambiguous and consistent with the stated objectives. The exercise should therefore mainly be used to prime people as to the direction the organisation is taking and why, what the objectives of the strategic plan are, how they will be achieved and within what timeframe. Typically this type of one-off presentation is not conducive to enhancing people's commitment to a change process, simply because the audience are passive recipients of information who will probably remember only about 20% of the information presented. In other words it is not enough just to present information and exhort people to follow the strategic plan. Mass audience presentations should be followed up very quickly with a series of departmental meetings and team briefings where the specifics of the strategic plan can be presented and discussed. In this way, because the potential for two-way feedback is very much higher, the opportunities for misunderstandings are correspondingly much reduced, which in turn enhances the potential for harnessing people's commitment. In principle, these meetings should be conducted by the main executive function as it visibly demonstrates their commitment to the strategic plan while also allowing employees directly to express their concerns, rather than allowing the grapevine to spread false rumours and undermine the intended message. This is easier in smaller rather than medium to large organisations, although wherever possible, any strategic plan should be communicated to employees by those who have formulated the plan rather than the task being delegated to others, as the potential for misinterpretation is also avoided (a corporate video may be appropriate here). It also brings any potential implementation problems to the executive's attention, so that they can then focus upon them and resolve them. On logistical grounds alone this could prove difficult and therefore unrealistic in large organisations (e.g. multi-nationals). This means that the executive function of each individual business unit should take on the task of communicating the board's intentions, as this at least demonstrates senior management's commitment to the change process. However, in itself, this will require that *all* the individual business directors are clear about the board's *specific* intentions so that a consistent interpretation of what is required is transmitted to the remainder of the organisation.

Written Communications

In parallel with the verbal communication exercises, written communications should also be used to reinforce the message even though, as shown by Len

Communication type	Communication channel	Feedback potential	Feedback immediacy
Written	Memos	low	low
	Post—internal/external	low	low
	'In-house' company newspapers/journals/newsletters	low	low
	Company reports	low	low
	Bulletins/noticeboards	low	low
	Suggestion schemes	low	low
	Safety book	medium/high	low
Verbal	Formal presentations	low	low
	Mass meetings	low	low
	Departmental meetings	medium	high
	Team briefings	medium	high
	Grapevine	high	high
	Face-to-face	high	high
Behavioural cues	Body language	high	high
Technical	Audio/video tape	low	low
	Television	low	low
	Voice mail	low	low
	E-mail	medium	medium
	Fax	medium	medium
	Telephone/teleconferencing	high	high
	Internet	high	high

Figure 2.5 Len Holden's Communication Channel and Feedback Categories – Adapted from Holden, L. (1995) 'Organisational Communication', in T. Hannagan (1995) Management: Concepts & Practices. Pitman Publishing, pp. 259–291. Reprinted by permission

Holden's work, the opportunities for rapid feedback are limited. One of the most common methods for disseminating strategic information throughout an organisation is via in-house publications such as newsletters, magazines, bulletins, etc. Although many of these vary in their production quality, they can be an extremely useful method for communicating an organisation's strategic direction. Care must be taken however, to ensure that conflicting messages are not inadvertently transmitted within the text, as this can seriously undermine people's commitment to the change process. One recent example seen by the author went as follows:

> 'We have good rules and procedures which are there to protect everyone and ensure we work safely. We MUST comply with them at ALL times, unless a manager issues a written dispensation for a specific job'

The beginning of the paragraph is very clear as it emphatically states that people must comply at all times with the rules and procedures. The conflicting message comes with the caveat that a manager may override this requirement as and when he or she sees fit. Although this may be understandable from a managerial point of view as there may be a requirement for flexibility within given circumstances, in practice the whole workforce took this to mean that the company was only concerned for everybody to follow the safety rules *if it did not interfere with production*. They did not believe that the company concerned actually meant what they said about safety being of prime importance, which meant that the safety initiative to which the communication referred was dead before it had even begun. Another example involved the use of a photograph which showed a group celebrating 1000 days since the last lost time accident in a workshop. On the floor next to their feet was a piece of round metal tubing constituting a trip hazard. Unfortunately 'own goals' of this nature are quite common. This means that those charged with publication should take the time to examine the content of any message and edit out any potential conflicts, as this can go a long way to eliminating the potential causes of resistance to change. Technological communication media could also be used to help transmit the strategic plans. Indeed, those companies that have purchased networked computer systems have a prime communication medium at their disposal in relation to safety *per se*, as they could easily be used for transmitting all types of safety message.

RESISTANCE TO CHANGE

By their very nature the changes dictated by a strategic plan involve replacing the familiar with something unknown. This often causes people to feel uncertain and confused during the period of change. Typical quotations which arise include: 'Does this mean I have to go to more meetings?' 'How much more work do the changes mean?' 'How are we supposed to find the time?' 'Will the necessary resources follow?' and 'Will we have to stop the job if someone says it is unsafe?', etc. Inevitably, such uncertainty will lead to some resistance while people at all levels accept and actively embrace the changes required to develop a positive safety culture. Being able to recognise and deal with such resistance will almost certainly affect the successful introduction of a strategic safety plan into the workplace (or any other type of safety improvement initiative).

The Function of Resistance to Change

Resistance to change is a very natural reaction, and is something that we all tend to engage in at some time or other. The function of resistance is to try to remove the demands for change. Although resistance can take many forms, many people's initial reaction tends to be that they deny the need to change (e.g. 'We have always done things this way, it's only when people are careless that accidents happen') which results in their resisting any changes regardless of the merits, and trying to avoid making the changes when they are introduced. In other words, many people tend to be opposed to the idea of change itself, rather than the purpose of the changes. Why should this be? In the main change is seen as stressful. This stress is often caused by people feeling threatened by the unknown, seeing any changes as an increase in workloads, and/or having to acknowledge that the way things are currently done is not right (e.g. putting production before safety). Because some find the latter hard to accept, they rationalise it to themselves by feeling they are not a part of the problem (e.g. 'We have fewer accidents here than other departments') and therefore offer resistance (by carrying on as before).

Identifying Different Forms of Resistance to Change

In practice the only way that resistance can be adequately dealt with is to identify the actual causes of the resistance while remaining flexible enough to overcome it. By providing the necessary support and encouragement, people will begin to explore the opportunities presented by the change and become committed to the change process.

Resistance to change comes in many shapes and guises, but the main forms are:

- Emotional — The way people feel about the changes or new ideas
- Cognitive — The way people think about the changes
- Social — The way groups of people attempt to cope with the changes
- Behavioural — The way people behave towards the changes
- Organisational — The way departments help or hinder the change process

Emotional Resistance

Emotional resistance often shows itself when people create a situation where they can vent their fears by becoming angry, or ridiculing the change effort in an attempt to embarrass those advocating change. An example of the former can often be found in behavioural safety initiatives, when people who do not want to change their unsafe behaviour start shouting about how management are trying to blame the workforce for the company's safety ills. An example of the latter can be found when the workforce say that focusing on safety behaviour is trivial and a complete waste of time. Instead management should spend money to address the real safety issues (e.g. update production equipment, etc.).

Cognitive Resistance

Cognitive resistance is often revealed when people find ways of reducing the demands for change. For example, saying things like 'We have done things this way for 30 years, why should we do it any differently now?' Other forms might include trying to change the subject or bringing up trivial objections to confuse the situation. The idea is to distract the person from the points he or she was trying to convey. Other instances may include people saying they will do one thing, but then doing something else (e.g. a supervisor saying he will conduct a weekly safety meeting in his department, but not actually doing so). Although this may occur for a number of reasons (e.g. production pressures), typically it is often related to a failure to understand the reasons for the change. Sometimes, however, forgetfulness or deliberate avoidance may play a part.

Social Resistance

Social resistance can be summed up as the use of social relationships to reduce the demand for change by using established friendships as a reason for not doing anything. For example, 'Come on. We've been friends for a long time. Because we have very few accidents here, there does not seem to be much point in wasting more time, money and effort focusing on safety issues, does there?' Social resistance can also manifest itself when those charged with implementing change are deliberately socially isolated from their work group (i.e. they are ignored during tea breaks, etc.) Although this type of resistance is usually confined to companies where the management style is highly autocratic and where there is a history of poor industrial relations, persistence is the key to breaking down this type of activity.

Behavioural Resistance

Behavioural resistance is normally quite passive in the sense that people say they will do something but fail to follow it through. In other words, people are stalling for time. This can take the form of different people continually asking and arguing about the trivial details of the change initiative. Other forms of this include people saying they do not have sufficient time to turn their attention to the change process simply because they are too busy; or saying that it is too difficult to get people together to discuss the changes. In practice, this often occurs because of competing duties. Although this may be true in some instances, these competing duties sometimes provide a convenient excuse for something not to be done (e.g. not holding weekly safety meetings, not conducting safety inspections, etc.). In other instances, behavioural resistance may be more active. For example, the change agent asks for information (e.g. risk assessment records) and the person concerned says that he or she does not have them at the moment, even though they are sitting in a cupboard. In essence, therefore, behavioural resistance takes the form of someone appearing to comply with the change requirements, but not actually doing so.

Organisational Resistance

Resistance may also be encountered from whole departments or work groups who do not see the need for change (e.g. 'We don't have accidents here'), and have made a collective decision not to get involved. It is worth considering the typical sources of this resistance. In the main these are related to:

- group dynamics
- integrated functions
- organisational politics
- organisational systems.

Group dynamics. Collective decisions not to get involved with a change process are difficult to overcome, but not impossible. More often than not a department or work group's rejection of a change process revolves around a dominant person, who may or may not be the formal leader (i.e. the departmental head, or team leader). Sometimes it is due to an informal leader exerting a large influence on collective opinions. Irrespective of who may be responsible, the collective decision tends to become self-reinforcing. Importantly, the longer the period that the collective refusal is allowed to remain the more it also tends to gather strength. If a department or work group does show signs of resistance, it is a good idea to target the opinion makers (formal and informal) and try to win them over to support the changes. If this does not prove possible, it may be better to 'go round to the back door' and appeal to other group members to support the change programme.

Integrated functions.   With the recent moves towards TQM, many organisations have become leaner and less hierarchical. This means that, perhaps more than ever before, an organisation's sub-units (e.g. departments) are more closely aligned and therefore more dependent on each other. Although largely beneficial, this means that resistance to a change process in one department will tend to exert a large influence on other 'non-resisting' departments by affecting their ability to implement change. One example that may demonstrate this concerns a company whose board had recently stressed the need for improved safety performance, and had set extremely stringent accident reduction targets to be met within the next two years. In this company, the maintenance department needed regularly to remove and clean a filter on the production plant. On one occasion, the isolation valves used to isolate the filter prior to removal became blocked and failed to shut off properly due to foreign bodies in the product. This caused the maintenance engineers to be splashed with hot carcinogenic liquid product. Upon investigation, the safety advisor and the maintenance manager came to the view that the only logical and safe way to fix the problem was to shut down the plant and undertake the necessary remedial actions. However, when presented with this option, the production management team forcefully pointed out that it would take at least a week to shut down safely and restart the plant while also incurring enormous costs (through lost production, wages, etc.). Because of the vast amounts of money involved, and the resistance from the production management team the safety advisor was forced to agree to provide the maintenance engineers with PPE until the problem could be fixed during a planned shutdown some two years later.

When difficulties arise between integrated functions, it is a good idea to encourage the leaders (both formal and informal) to attend joint planning sessions. Providing a forum where people can air their views and thrash out the issues will often help to overcome the difficulties as it allows the various parties involved to shape the change process to suit local conditions. In addition, as they begin to provide their own solutions, they are more likely to become actively committed to the change process.

Organisational politics.   Resistance to change from departments and work groups may also emanate from a perceived loss of status, power and influence that will affect their relative standing with other departments. Sometimes this may be due to a faulty change strategy, but more often than not it is related to issues of who is controlling what and who. For example, one of the most recent EC safety directives is concerned with employee consultation on health and safety at work, whereby management are expected to listen, evaluate and, where appropriate, act upon the issues raised by the workforce. Prior to these regulations, it was often the case (and probably still is in some companies), that management teams were reluctant to allow their workforce to become involved in safety matters—not because they wished to see people injured, but more on the basis that devolving power on safety matters would somehow affect their status. The danger of such political activity is that safety becomes a political football that subsequently affects people's safety-related attitudes and motivation and this in turn affects the importance with which the development of a safety culture is viewed and implemented on a daily basis.

Organisational systems.   Change can also be stifled by rigid bureaucratic systems that require complete compliance to existing rules and procedures to get anything done. This can slow down the process to such an extent that people revert back to the old ways of doing things just to achieve their tasks. Other management issues can also exert an important influence on change. This will include the degree of influence that various organisational functions are allowed to exert on the decision-making process and the success of previous change initiatives. In organisations where there has been a history of management failing to follow through change initiatives, people wait until management turn their attentions to other issues, and simply allow the change initiative to fizzle out. This is usually caused by a lack of management commitment to the process. The reasons for this can be quite varied: it is sometimes because the changes have been imposed from above without consultation; sometimes because of a rapid turnover within the management team itself; and sometimes because of extreme work pressures. It is also possible that each of these may have occurred simultaneously. Overcoming difficulties caused by organisational systems is not simple as it may entail some restructuring of the system itself, or of people's job roles (see Chapter 3). Nonetheless, as far as possible, it is a good idea to clarify who is responsible for who and what, the kinds and levels of support and resources required, and to whom they are accountable. Performance should then be periodically monitored and reviewed. In this way, people are far more likely to carry out their roles in a visible and consistent manner, because difficulties with organisational systems, levels of support, resources, etc., can be quickly identified and dealt with. The end result is that the change process is not seen as a passing management fad that will fade away.

Managing Resistance

In principle, the best way to manage resistance is to allow people to become involved and influence the change process. This can best be achieved by those implementing change if they:

- expect resistance
- recognise it for what it is
- are clear about what changes are needed
- explain the need for change
- ask for co-operation, not submission
- encourage discussion
- ask for suggestions and follow them through
- are flexible and willing to negotiate
- are clear about the time limits for change.

3

Methods of Evaluating and Integrating Organisational Systems

INTRODUCTION

Having developed and converted a strategic plan into an action plan which has been communicated throughout the organisation, the next step becomes one of implementation. However, when considering the scale of the task of integrating an organisation's systems and sub systems into a balanced risk-reducing interaction between people, production processes and the working environment, it becomes apparent that the development of a positive safety culture will only be achieved in the longer term. This means that decisions have to be made about where to begin, based upon the status of the organisation's current efforts. Assuming that little has been done, the *immediate* level of effort is the logical starting point, as it provides a solid foundation upon which to build the *intermediate* and *ultimate* levels. The immediate level of effort is primarily concerned with examining the organisation's workflow processes and their supportive functions, and as such mainly addresses the situational elements of the safety culture model presented in Chapter 1. Notwithstanding this, because of the interactive nature between the situational and behavioural elements of the safety culture model, it is important to examine the organisation's systems in conjunction with what people do, how they do it, what tools, plant and machinery they use, how everybody's tasks are structured into an integrated workflow process, what supportive functions are in place, and what risks are associated with each of these factors. The purpose of these examinations is to streamline the overall workflow process to achieve a risk-reducing balance between productivity and safety needs, develop the associated control systems, codify the appropriate rules and procedures, and establish accountability. However, given the complexities involved in examining all these factors, a combination of different analytic methods or tools appropriate to different levels of analysis will be needed. It is important to recognise that a thorough examination of all these factors is not always going to be a simple and straightforward task (e.g. its very nature may induce resistance), and that it can take a considerable length of time. It is essential, therefore, that senior managers continually demonstrate their commitment to the process by providing the necessary time and human and financial resources while also taking a personal interest in the monitoring and reviewing of progress.

IDENTIFYING STRUCTURAL PROBLEMS

A prime reason for focusing on the immediate level of effort is that it can be invaluable in addressing two of the major problems in the management of health and safety:

- poor communications
- poor management control.

In part, these sorts of problem often arise from the way various activities in a business unit or department are structured and organised: communication networks are often disjointed and overloaded, resulting in confusion and duplication of effort, while management's operational goals (e.g. productivity versus safety) are often at odds with each other. In other words, the day-to-day quality of managerial and communicative *behaviour* is often dependent upon *situational* features determined by organisational structure. Common signs of structural problems include:

- poor motivation and morale because of a high workload caused by poor support systems, a lack of clarity about people's job roles and a lack of adequate manpower
- people being subjected to competing pressures from different sources within the organisation which emanates from a lack of clearly defined priorities
- decision-making is poor because of a lack of the right information at the right time, because mechanisms to co-ordinate the decisions emanating from different functions are inadequate, or because decision-makers fail to delegate properly, causing them to become overloaded with work
- conflicts and a lack of co-ordination caused by competing goals, and/or a lack of formal mechanisms to allow liaison between functional departments, and/or a lack of involvement in planning

- rising costs caused by a high ratio of 'chiefs' to 'Indians', and an excess of meetings, paperwork and procedures which distracts people from their main duties
- informal patterns of communication which differ considerably from, and are used more than, the intended formal communication networks.

Although the above list is not exhaustive, it illustrates some of the common structural problems often found in organisations which, on their own or collectively, impact upon the day-to-day management of health and safety. Organisations experiencing these types of problem would benefit from an objective examination of the entire workflow process, as this is likely to reveal structural deficiencies in the way that work is done, in communications systems, in management systems, and spans of control. In turn, this allows an organisation to address both its safety and productivity problems simultaneously.

Although it is recognised that organisations differ in size and the way they are structured, the principles of workflow analysis are exactly the same for every organisation, except that the scale of the exercise may be much greater for some organisations than others. As with most things, the larger the scale of the exercise, the more likely that things can be achieved by breaking the exercise down into smaller, easily managed elements. In larger organisations, therefore, it is often more appropriate to begin at the level of each individual business unit.

USING WORKFLOW ANALYSIS TO IDENTIFY SPECIFIC INFORMATION-SHARING PROBLEMS

Workflow analysis is primarily a method for *systematically* identifying the intensity of information-sharing between an organisation's functional areas. As such it helps decision-makers to optimise communications by aligning or re-aligning various functional activities so as to avoid duplication of effort, while at the same time creating meaningful clusters of activity that are more amenable to managerial control. Importantly, the degree and frequency with which information is shared has many practical implications. For example:

- the frequency at which information is shared between an engineering manager and production manager in relation to prioritising particular safety problems may affect the speed with which remedial works are carried out
- the number of people from different functions involved in discussing and analysing complex information about a new production process may speed up or delay its commissioning

- decisions about the best way of sharing limited resources may be affected by a lack of attendance at formal meetings
- the control of safety standards may be affected by a lack of regular information from the safety advisor.

Step One—An Initial Review

In the first instance, before conducting a formal workflow analysis, judgements have to be made about how well the current systems are operating. The more evidence there is of the structural problems already mentioned the more likely that a thorough review is warranted. As a first step, this will involve systematically plotting all the main activity areas (e.g. production, engineering, despatch, marketing, purchasing, finance, etc.,) and the flows of materials and information between each. Identifying the main operational and supportive functions is normally a relatively easy task as most organisations already represent them in organograms (organisation charts). Some of these also include information about the task functions involved and the staff to whom responsibility is allocated for the area. Within the context of workflow analyses, the combination of task functions and the associated staffing comprise an activity area. Therefore, should the tasks and staffing not be represented by the organogram, the analyst will need to identify each of these by other means (e.g. talking to or interviewing people in each work area). Once identified, each of these activity areas are laid out horizontally *and* vertically to form a matrix (see Figure 3.1: *Workflow Analysis Matrix*).

Step Two—Identifying the Intensity of Workflow Relationships

Consideration needs to be given to the intensity of relationships between activity areas and the workflow process so that informed judgements can be made about the scale of change required (if any). The second step therefore consists of identifying the relationships between the activity areas and the workflow process by considering:

- how functionally dependent each activity area is on other activity areas (e.g. production and despatch)
- how frequently communications take place between each activity area (e.g. engineering and production)
- what the common sources of information, materials, etc., are for each activity area (e.g. safety, purchasing and supply, human resources, etc.)

Activity	1 Engineer maintenance	2 Process operations	3 Quality control	4 Finance admin	5 Purchasing and supply	Etc.
2 Process operations	1 1 / 1 1					
3 Quality control	3 2 / 1 1	1 1 / 1 1				
4 Finance admin	3 5 / 4 3	2 5 / 4 3	7 6 / 3 3			
5 Purchasing and supply	1 4 / 1 1	1 4 / 1 1	1 1 / 1 1	1 1 / 1 1		
Etc.						

Box key:

Reasons for linkage	Required closeness
Type of communication	Risks of failure

Linkage key:
1: Co-ordination required
2: Sharing of information
3: Transfer of information
4: Sharing of equipment
5: Sharing control mechanisms
6: Sharing geographical location
7: None required

Closeness key:
1: Absolutely necessary
2: Especially important
3: Important
4: Ordinary closeness
5: Unimportant
6: Not desirable

Communication key:
1: All forms below
2: Face to face
3: Telephone/radio
4: Computerised
5: Written
6: Formal meetings
7: None

Risk key:
1: High
2: Medium
3: Low

Figure 3.1 Activity Relationship Matrix – Adapted from J. Child (1984) Organisation: A Guide to problems and practice, (2nd ed.). Harper & Row. Reprinted by permission

- how decisions made by one activity area affect other activity areas (e.g. how a successful sales drive will affect production, purchasing and despatch activities)
- how these relationships might impact upon people's safety.

Step Three—Evaluating the Intensity of Workflow Relationships

The third step involves evaluating the relationships between each of the activity areas by focusing upon four key elements:

- Reasons for linkage
- Required closeness
- Type of communication
- Risks caused by communication failures.

The first key element focuses on *why* the activity areas should be linked. In broad terms, activity areas might be closely aligned because they:

- form one link in a continuous co-ordinated chain (e.g. market research—sales—purchasing and supply—production—despatch)
- are dependent upon the same sources of data (e.g. sales, human resources, safety)
- are dependent upon the sharing of equipment and materials (e.g. computers)
- are dependent upon the same people for control (e.g. production manager)
- share a common geographical location.

The second key element focuses on establishing the importance of the required closeness by asking why they need to be closely aligned. As such it is mainly concerned with examining the frequency of the communication links between the different activity areas and the reasons for the communications, which may be related to the processing and distribution of information, or joint decision-making, etc.

The third key element focuses on the form(s) that the communication takes. For example, whether it is conducted face to face, by telephone or radio, written (e.g. memos, letters, computer), or through formal meetings.

The fourth key element considers the risks associated with a communications failure. Although this latter aspect is often implicit in workflow analyses, it should be made explicit as it allows areas of communication failure and the potential consequences of such a failure to be identified. In turn this helps to ensure that critical communication links between the various activity areas are monitored, reviewed and maintained. The importance of this can be illustrated by the 1974 Flixborough disaster which destroyed the entire site, killed 28 workers, injured 36 on site and also injured several hundred people in the surrounding area. One of the primary causes was the failure to record plant modifications (e.g. installing a temporary reactor bypass), which meant they could not be communicated to maintenance engineers before they started their tasks.

Step Four—Prioritising the Importance of Workflow Relationships

Once all these relationships have been established and evaluated the workflow analyst assigns scores to each of the four elements. Whichever score is assigned to the attributes that make up each element, it avoids confusion if the most important share the same numeral (e.g. the most significant attributes in each element are all signified by a one). These individual scores are then summed to produce an overall score. Used in this way, the lower the score assigned to the communication links between the various activity areas, the more it indicates the importance of the communications. Typical scoring attributes within each element are as follows:

- Reasons for linkage
  1   Co-ordination required
  2   Sharing of information
  3   Transfer of information
  4   Sharing of equipment/materials
  5   Sharing of control mechanisms
  6   Sharing same geographical location
- Required closeness
  1   Vital (continual critical communications)
  2   Very important (frequent critical communications)
  3   Important (less frequent but necessary communications)
  4   Ordinary closeness (non critical communications)
  5   Unimportant (little need for communications)
  6   Not desirable (communications are unnecessary and could be damaging)
- Types of communication
  1   Face to face
  2   Telephone/radio
  3   Computerised
  4   Written
  5   Formal meetings

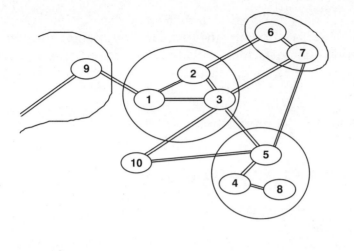

1 = Engineering/maintenance

2 = Process operations

3 = Quality control

4 = Finance

5 = Purchasing and supply

6 = Goods in

7 = Despatch

8 = Human resources

9 = Drawing office

10 = Customer services

Figure 3.2   Clusters of Closely Related Activities — Adapted from J. Child (1984) Organisation: A Guide to problems and practice, *(2nd ed.). Harper & Row. Reprinted by permission*

- Risks arising from communication failure
  1 High (potentially disastrous)
  2 Medium (serious)
  3 Low (unimportant).

Once the scores have been assigned, they are placed on the matrix in a box divided into quadrants (see Figure 3.1). The boxes can be colour-coded to indicate the relative overall importance of the communication links between the activity areas (e.g. red could be used to indicate vital communication links). In this way it is possible to logically identify different clusters of activity areas where co-ordination of effort and communication links are vital (see Figure 3.2: *Clusters of Closely Related Activity Areas*). These clusters could then form the basis for discussions about an objective, non political, realignment of the organisation's activities to bring about enhancements to the functioning of all its communications systems. This should lead to better day-to-day management control by ensuring, for example, that the right information is available at the right time and that formal liaison mechanisms between functional departments are improved.

To minimise resistance to any possible changes while also creating com-mitment to the change process, it is very important to actively involve people at each stage of the analysis, particularly as they may have developed close personal relationships through the existing associations between task activities. Ignoring these factors could seriously damage any subsequent realignment. Encouraging the participation of those affected by the analytic process is very important for any changes to be successfully introduced, particularly as people may disagree with the way the analyst has clustered together different activity groupings.

JOB CHARACTERISTICS ANALYSIS

Achieving a balanced risk-reducing interaction between productivity and safety may also involve the redesign or restructuring of people's jobs. Whereas workflow analyses are primarily concerned about the flow of information within an organisation or business unit as a whole, job characteristics analyses are more concerned with the way particular work groups are structured and the way they operate. This is because the functioning of work activities and systems is usually the result of group activity rather than individuals working independently of others. A number of factors known to affect how well a group performs have important implications for both productivity and safety. As shown in Figure 3.3: *Hackman and Oldham's Job Characteristics Model* these include the degree to which the work requires a number of different activities that allows group members to use a wide range of skills (i.e. skill variety), the extent to which a whole piece of identifiable work is completed by the work group (i.e. task identity), the degree to which a group's tasks impacts upon other groups or people (i.e. task significance), the degree to which the group can operate independently of others, schedule their work, and determine the procedures which can be used to complete their work (i.e. autonomy), and the degree to which the group members can obtain information about the effectiveness of their work (i.e. feedback). Importantly, each of these *situational* job-related features is known to affect people's *perceptions and attitudes* towards their work, as well as their work-related *behaviour*.

Skill Variety

It is widely known that giving people the opportunities (*situation*) to demonstrate a variety of skills enhances their interest and motivation (*attitudes*), while also improving their productivity (*behaviour*). On the other hand, jobs which tend to be repetitive induce role strain. This type of role strain leads to boredom, which in turn leads to apathy, fatigue and depression, which in turn lead to errors and mistakes, which in turn increase the potential

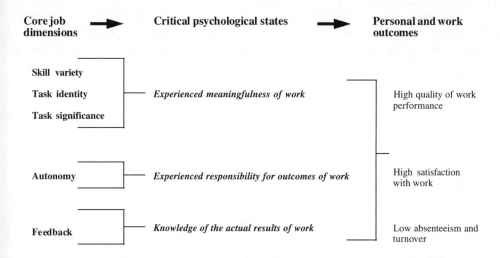

Figure 3.3   Hackman and Oldham's (1975) Job Characteristics Model — Adapted from Hackman, J.R. and Oldham, G.R. (1980) Work Redesign. *Addision-Wesley, Reading, MA. Reprinted by permission*

for both poor quality production and/or accidents. A lack of skill variety could also lead to increases in labour turnover, and/or sickness absenteeism. Higher labour turnover means increased recruitment and training costs, and possible increases in accident rates (those with less than five years' experience in their current jobs tend to be over-represented in accident statistics), while sickness absenteeism is known to increase the activity rate of the remaining group members, which in turn leads to increased accident rates. (In one study conducted by the author, the degree of overlap between sickness absenteeism rates and accident rates was 75%.) Present moves towards multi-skilling, flexible working or total preventative maintenance (TPM) schemes whereby machine operators undertake servicing, maintenance, re-setting of machines, self-checking etc., are welcome developments to stimulate the use of a wide variety of skills amongst the workforce. Nonetheless, such schemes should ensure that personnel are fully trained in at least one core activity, before being trained for other related activities. In this way, people do not become a 'jack of all trades and master of none'. It is also of extreme importance to ensure that any type of multi-skill training also fully incorporates training in the safety aspects of each type of job, so that people are not put at unnecessary risk.

Task Identity

The extent to which a group or an individual identifies with and completes a whole and identifiable piece of work is also related to reduced absenteeism (leading to reduced accident rates), reduced stress, and high quality work performance simply because the work is seen as meaningful and important. In turn this impacts positively on people's self esteem, which tends to induce ownership of, and commitment to, their work. This is in contrast to jobs designed specifically to reduce discretion and responsibility so that people only complete a part of the task. Because these types of job tend to be seen as irrelevant and boring, not only do they create role strain (increasing the potential for accidents), but they also lead to lower productivity and reduced quality. This is because jobs that remove discretion and responsibility ultimately lead to loss of skills, and also tend to lead to learned helplessness where people say things like 'I can't do that because it is not in my job description'. Therefore, redesigning a job so that a group is responsible for the completion of a whole piece of work not only helps to minimise role strain, but also encourages the group members to use a wider range of their skills and abilities for the good of the organisation. Completing a whole piece of work within a particular work group could also reduce communication problems associated with the work while improving the flow of raw materials, etc., which in turn could help to reduce operational costs.

Task Significance

The degree to which a group's task is perceived to impact upon other people determines the significance with which the task is viewed. The more that people feel their job is significant and important, the more they are likely to feel 'ownership' of the task, and the more committed they become to completing it to the best of their abilities. In turn this tends to increase both quality and productivity. A rarely acknowledged aspect of task significance is its implications for health and safety. One example that illustrates this concerned a sales manager who strongly pressurised a plants production manager to produce 200 tonnes of a particular product over the Christmas break instead of shutting down as was normally the case. After much resistance, the plant manager agreed, as the order appeared to be of the utmost importance. However, when it came to despatching the finished goods, the client told the production manager that the order was not meant to be fulfilled until the end of January and that they would not accept it until then. Not only did this mean that people had worked unnecessarily over the Christmas break (for which they were paid triple time) but, because the production company operated a just-in-time policy, they had limited amounts of storage space in the warehouse. This meant that most of the extra 200 tonnes of product had to be stored in the main production area. This caused much of the production area and the associated access routes to become severely blocked, which resulted in an operator suffering a broken leg due to a forklift truck running into him when he stepped out from behind one of the pallet stacks. Other effects included the serious risks presented by the blocking of access routes in the event of an emergency, plus the fact that the company was unable to complete other orders, which ultimately led to the loss of two important customers. In essence, all of this was caused by the sales manager not appreciating the impact that his function was having on other parts of the organisation. This example illustrates the point that it is very important to let people know the impact that their jobs have on others, so that it can at least form a part of their decision-making process when considering different courses of action.

The Interactive Effects of Skill Variety, Task Identity and Task Significance

In combination, the three aspects of jobs outlined above (i.e. skill variety, task identity and task significance) are thought to collectively influence the *experienced meaningfulness* of the work, which leads to high quality work performance. In practical terms, this means that people low in experienced meaningfulness are much less likely to care about their job and less likely to be motivated to produce good quality products or services. Similarly, these people are less likely to be committed to the organisation, and/or take their safety responsibilities seriously. Because of the effects which each of these aspects can exert on people's well-being and on production outcomes, it is a good idea to try to ensure that each one of the above are present in individuals' jobs, and for the work group as a whole: i.e. there should be opportunities to use a wide range of skills, there should be opportunities to complete a whole job, and people should be made aware of the significant impact that their jobs have on others. If this is not possible for one reason or another, the more that any one of these aspects can be catered for, the more it will partially compensate for the lack of the ideal job design conditions in the other two.

Autonomy

Autonomy refers to the amount of independence and freedom that people or work groups have to make their own decisions or influence events (e.g. determine their own work schedules and procedures for carrying out their tasks). In essence, autonomy is concerned with the amount of control people have over their jobs within certain prescribed boundaries, and is defined as 'the opportunity and responsibility for people to actively influence their work outcomes'. Job control is known to be central to the notion of skill, competencies, job-induced stress, coping strategies, perception of risks and/ or hazards, acceptance of the necessity and desirability of safety rules and procedures, and safety culture *per se.* Allowing people the opportunity to exert control over their jobs has important positive implications for many areas of an organisation's functioning, but particularly in relation to health and safety.

This was aptly demonstrated by the author and colleagues in an HSE funded study in the construction industry. On some sites people were asked to determine their own levels of safety performance and to aspire to reach them (control). The levels of safety performance these sites decided upon were imposed upon other sites i.e. they were told what level of safety to aspire to and reach. Based on approximately 1.5 million observations of people's everyday safety behaviour over the course of a year, the overall results showed that on the sites where people were told what level of safety to reach, safety performance declined or stayed the same, whereas the sites where people decided for themselves showed dramatic and consistent improvements in safety performance. Why should this be? Researchers believe it is because autonomy or job control affects people's *experienced responsibility* i.e. the extent to which people feel personally responsible for the outcomes of their performance. For example, a work group or person high on experienced responsibility will be concerned to ensure that people in their work area always work safely and adhere to laid down procedures. Experienced responsibility is thought to affect performance by leading people to become highly satisfied in their work, which in turn positively affects their commitment to their organisation (i.e. accepting the organisation's goals and values, being willing to exert extra effort on behalf of the organisation, and wanting to stay with the organisation). Increased job satisfaction is also related to reduced labour turnover and absenteeism rates (ergo accident rates), as well as leading people to accept the challenges the organisation presents to them (e.g. improve levels of safety performance). Thus, autonomy or control over one's job can exert extremely beneficial effects on both health and safety and the amount and quality of production.

Feedback

Feedback refers to the extent to which people can obtain information about the effectiveness of their behaviour, so that they can modify their subsequent behaviour to attain the desired goals. The most effective feedback is derived directly from the job in hand as it progresses, rather than from an external source such as a supervisor or manager on an occasional basis. This is because immediate feedback allows people to instantly regain control over specific activities that might be causing errors. Thus immediate feedback exerts a much greater effect upon people's behaviour than delayed feedback. Immediate feedback from a job is also known to increase people's satisfaction with their work, increase productivity and the quality of their efforts, while at the same time reducing labour turnover and absenteeism rates.

Although the design of many jobs does not allow the job holder to immediately evaluate the effectiveness of their performance, the presence of immediate feedback from a task has many health and safety implications, particularly in relation to hazard detection. One of the prime reasons, for example, that people do not wear personal protective equipment (PPE) is that it masks or eliminates the potential for feedback from a task. For example, hearing protection reduces the possibility of being able to listen to the whine of a machine to provide an indication of its operating speed, or of correctly hearing what people might be saying (this is not to argue that hearing PPE should not be used). Although people can sometimes obtain feedback cues from the working environment (e.g. certain visual features indicate a slippery floor) some hazards are not so easily detected (e.g. an increase in the temperature of an acetylene gas bottle). When we add to this the fact that a person primarily focuses on the task in hand, and that hazard detection is normally a secondary consideration, it becomes *vital* to ensure that feedback cues which signal potential dangers are present in people's jobs. Wherever possible within any given job, therefore, it is important to ensure that danger warnings (such as visual and audible alerting signals) are present and obvious and that particular prompts which signal danger are taught to jobholders and reinforced by information displayed on or near the potential hazard (for example, lathe operators are taught that a build-up of metal chips might fly off the machine, and this is reinforced with a warning on or near the lathe).

Job Characteristics Questionnaire

Unless undertaken on a formal basis by an organisation, the task of redesigning every job in an organisation is obviously beyond the scope and authority of most people. Nonetheless, every manager or supervisor is able to exert some influence and authority in redesigning the jobs of people under their control. For example, they can decide upon the scope and range of people's duties, allocate certain degrees of responsibility and self control to individuals, decide upon the extent to which subordinates can participate in discussions and decision-making, and decide upon the methods used to supervise or control the group's activities. For many managers or super-visors the key question is on what basis, and how? Fortunately, the ability to assess the degree to which the task attributes of skill variety, task identity and significance, autonomy and feedback are present in people's tasks can be achieved by using a safety-orientated variant of a job characteristics ques-tionnaire developed by Eric Lawler and colleagues (see Figure 3.4: *Safety*

Here are some statements about your job. How much do you agree or disagree about each?

My Job:	Strongly disagree	Disagree	Slightly disagree	Not sure	Slightly agree	Agree	Strongly agree
1] involves a variety of tasks...............................	1	2	3	4	5	6	7
2] allows me to be left on my own to do my work.........	1	2	3	4	5	6	7
3] is arranged so that I often gain satisfaction from seeing jobs through from beginning to end	1	2	3	4	5	6	7
4] provides immediate feedback on how well I am doing, as I work...	1	2	3	4	5	6	7
5] is considered to be important to my organisation.......	1	2	3	4	5	6	7
6] gives me considerable opportunity for choosing how I do my work...	1	2	3	4	5	6	7
7] gives me the opportunity to do a number of different things..	1	2	3	4	5	6	7
8] provides me with immediate knowledge about the danger(s) present in my work.............................	1	2	3	4	5	6	7
9] is viewed by other members of the workforce as being important	1	2	3	4	5	6	7
10] provides an opportunity for independent thought and action...	1	2	3	4	5	6	7
11] has included training for me to safely carry out different aspects of the tasks I am required to do..................	1	2	3	4	5	6	7
12] is arranged so that I have the opportunity to complete the work I start...	1	2	3	4	5	6	7
13] provides me with enough information to know that I am performing my job safely.............................	1	2	3	4	5	6	7
14] is arranged so that I have the chance to do the whole job	1	2	3	4	5	6	7
15] is one where a lot of people's safety can be affected by how well I do my job.....................................	1	2	3	4	5	6	7

Scoring

Skill variety ....Questions 1, 7, 11
Task identity..Questions 3, 12, 14
Task significance ....Questions 5, 9, 15

Experienced meaningfulness = the person's scores for Skill variety + Task identity + Task significance

Autonomy...Questions 2, 6, 10
Feedback..Questions 4, 8, 13

Safety orientated adaptation of E. Lawler *et al's* Job Design Questionnaire: Centre for Effective Organisations. University of Southern California. U$

Figure 3.4   Safety Oriented Adaptation of Job Design Questionnaire

Oriented Adaptation of Job Design Questionnaire). Pertinent to both blue and white collar jobs, the survey is intended to be used to:

- diagnose existing jobs to assist in job redesign
- evaluate the effects of job redesign activities
- evaluate the effects of job redesign on people's motivation and job satisfaction.

A manager could distribute this to members of his or her work group. However, the effectiveness of job redesign schemes is far more successful and longer-lasting when the whole organisation is involved. As far as possible, therefore, the survey should be distributed to every member of an organisation, and they should be asked to rate the various attributes for their own job.

Scoring the Job Characteristics Questionnaire

Scoring each person's job is simply a matter of adding together the responses for each task attribute to derive a total score ranging from 3 (low) to 21 (high). The lower the score for each dimension, the greater the need to consider ways in which the person's job could be enhanced to include the missing attribute (i.e. skill variety, task identity, task significance, autonomy and feedback). The total scores possible for all five attributes will range between 15 and 105. The total scores for *experienced meaningfulness* (i.e. skill variety + task identity + task significance) will range between 9 and 63. The lower the total score, the less motivating the person's job.

A copy of each person's results should also be collated by a central team (perhaps from Human Resources, or from the safety function, or both) with a view to assessing where enhancements are required in various jobs for the organisation as a whole. This can be done on an individual level, a work-group level or for the organisation as a whole simply by adding each individual's scores together for all five job characteristics to produce their total job score, adding everybody's total job scores together and dividing the total by the number of people to produce an average figure. This average figure would fall in one of three bands: Poor (15–45), Average (46–75) and Good (76–105). Individual jobs or work groups scoring in the poor range would indicate that serious attention should be paid to enhancing their job characteristics; those scoring in the average range would need some job redesign attention, while those scoring in the good range would require little attention. At the very least the results would indicate which jobs or work groups are finding their work demotivating. The performance of these work groups could then be compared with other work groups to ascertain whether or not their productivity and/or quality performance is lower than the norm, or whether their turnover, absenteeism levels and accident rates are higher than the norm. Significant differences (in the expected direction) in these types of performance indicators would then signal that urgent attention needs to be paid to redesigning these jobs. Similarly, within each work group the results for different people could be compared so as to prompt discussions among the group members about how to redistribute the workload or introduce the five core job dimensions into individual jobs, particularly if large differences between group members were found. However, several different forms of job redesign change are commonly found, each of which can exert different effects upon people.

Job Enlargement

Job enlargement is one of the most widely known attempts at job redesign. Job enlargement refers to jobs that are expanded horizontally to increase the scope and range of people's duties, i.e. it increases skill variety and task identity without necessarily increasing people's authority or autonomy. Job rotation is another form of job enlargement that caters for increased skill variety by moving people between various tasks at regular intervals. For either of these two methods to be effective, it is important to ensure that there is high quality training for the new skills, and that the procedures and instructions for undertaking the tasks are very clear. Importantly, high quality refresher training is also needed at frequent intervals (e.g. every six months). However, it must be noted that these two forms of job redesign may not actually improve or enhance people's jobs as intended. As one of the founding fathers of job redesign, Frederick Herzberg once said '*Adding one Mickey Mouse job to another Mickey Mouse job doesn't add up to any more than two Mickey Mouse jobs*'. In other words simply adding a number of dreary, repetitive, routine jobs together, or rotating people around them, does not make a job any the more motivating or satisfying (although it may alleviate boredom). What is needed is the addition of discretion so that people can be involved in the decision-making processes.

Job Enrichment

Job enrichment develops a job so that it incorporates skill variety, task identity and task significance and allows people to exert greater control over their day-to-day activities so that they have some discretion and responsibility for planning, executing and evaluating their own work. As the job provides people with an in-built feedback mechanism whereby they are able to regularly monitor, assess and correct their own performance. In essence, therefore, employees undertake some of the duties typically done by their supervisor. Herein also lies the problem with job enrichment as far as many managers and supervisors are concerned, as they believe they are giving up their own authority for which they have had to work hard. Some even believe that the supervisory role will no longer be needed. However, in the main these fears are groundless, as leaderless groups tend not to function very well. In practice therefore, managers and supervisors would be released from the trivial and mundane day-to-day pressures of crisis management, progressing orders and raw materials, or reallocating people to different tasks. Instead they can concentrate on managerial activities (e.g. undertaking safety management system audits), identifying and developing people's training needs, taking a more strategic role in directing their work group, etc. Although the five job characteristics outlined above need to be incorporated into people's individual jobs, it is also important to ensure that the same characteristics are present for the work group as a whole.

Self-Managing Work Groups

A key feature of the successful performance (safety or otherwise) of any work group is its ability to manage and control its own everyday activities. The extent to which a work group is self-managing can be determined by the amount of collective control it exerts over the pace of its work, the degree to which it is able to allocate and distribute the required workload between its membership, the degree to which it can organise and decide upon the timing of rest breaks, and the degree to which group members are involved in recruiting and training new group members. In essence therefore, the work group determines the means to meet the desired performance outcomes by deciding on the details of production and distribution. The wider organisation, however, also needs to play its part in supporting the work groups by ensuring that:

- there are clear goals and objectives to work towards
- the rewards for meeting the goals and objectives are given to the work group as a whole, not just particular individuals
- the work group has free access to suitable and adequate resources
- there is free access to relevant information when required
- there are frequent opportunities for the work group to undertake high quality training.

WORK GROUP COMMUNICATIONS

Poor communications are a reliable indicator of underlying structural problems both in a work group's design, and in poor interpersonal relationships between people (e.g. supervisor and subordinates). A critical safety aspect of work group redesign that is known to exert a great influence on the work group's effectiveness is the style and quality of communications between its members. This is because communications are also an important source of information feedback that helps to determine a group's norms (i.e. their standards and patterns of behaviour). For example, if a manager or supervisor temporarily turns a blind eye to safety to suit productivity needs, but disciplines people for breaching safety rules when things are quiet, the group norm becomes one of only adhering to safety when things are quiet (rather than when it is needed the most). In essence, communication refers to a two-way exchange process that involves the transmission and receipt of information, opinions and ideas. If a communication is not received (a common cause of complaint in organisations) it could be argued that there has not been any communication at all.

Any form of communication has an objective which is translated into a code of some sort (e.g. speech, writing, etc.) and transmitted via some medium (e.g. talking, memoranda, e-mail, etc.). The degree to which a communication is successful depends upon people being able to interpret the message and respond in the way the communicator originally intended. The manner in which the recipient responds provides the communicator with feedback about how successful the communication has been in reaching its objectives. At each stage in any communication process, therefore, potential problems could arise that need to be overcome.

This has important implications for the way in which information is communicated between members of a group. It is often the case, for example, that supervisors pass on instructions to a work group by posting a memo on a noticeboard (which is not read by everybody), rather than talking to people directly and explaining the reasons for, and the importance of, the instructions. Similarly, people often listen to others without knowing what the person is trying to say, simply because the communicator has not thought about the message he or she intended to convey.

Modes of Communication

Communications inside a group serve at least three primary functions. First, they allow the passing of important job-related information between a group's membership; second, they allow group members to monitor each other to check on how things are going; and third, they allow people to discover which kinds of behaviour and beliefs are acceptable to the group.

An examination of group communications reveals that four interacting features are particularly important:

- the mode of communication
- the complexity of the information that has to be transmitted
- the amount of information that has to be processed
- the configuration of the group's communication network.

For example, a manager may write a four-page handwritten memo to warn his or her work group about the occupational exposure limits of a particular substance implicated in an accident and post it on a noticeboard. People attempting to read it may not understand the person's handwriting, and/or what is meant by occupational exposure limits, and/or because it is four pages long, they may lose interest and not read it all. At worst, they may not even know it is on the noticeboard. Thus despite good intentions, the message may not be fully understood or even received by the group members.

In general there are four modes of communication: oral, written, visual and behavioural.

Oral Communication

Speech or oral communication is the simplest and most direct mode that allows instant feedback, with the giving and receiving of task orders being the most common in work groups. Oral communications can also be conducted via the telephone, public address systems, dictaphones or radio. Often, geographical distance will determine which media is used. For example, a maintenance engineer in a chemical plant will often use a radio to keep in contact with the control room, whereas two control room operators will tend to use direct face-to-face conversations (a prime example of the influence the situation exerts on people's behaviour). However, since speech tends to get taken for granted, problems often occur in relation to the language that is used. For example, an engineer may talk in technical terms that are not easily understood by non-engineers. This has important implications for safety, as demonstrated by the number of accidents caused by poor communication. During the years 1986/87 and 1989/90 in UK manufacturing industries, for instance, 38 fatalities occurred due to people misinterpreting instructions. Similarly, because of the pressure of dealing with emergencies in aircraft, native English-speaking flight crews often revert to non-flight language that causes other members of the flight crew to be uncertain about which actions to take. In some instances, such communications have led to major accidents (e.g. the 1977 collision of two aircraft on the runway in Tenerife). In work groups where co-ordination between people is dependent upon good verbal communications, therefore, the employing organisation should expend considerable effort ensuring that people undertake verbal communication training for both normal and emergency situations, until it becomes automatic (i.e. over-learnt). Eliminating the potential for misunderstanding in any work group is dependent on people being very clear and concise. In general this means that people should:

- be very clear about the purpose of the communication, i.e. have a clear objective
- use shorter sentences, as these tend to be more easily understood
- only use terms known and understood by everybody in the work group (this point has implications for new group members, who should be taught these group-specific terms as a part of their induction training)
- communicate important information directly to everybody in the work group, and not assume that telling one person will lead to everybody being told.

Written Communication

The most common types of communication in many organisations tend to be those that are written. This is because:

- information presented in written form tends to be selectively free of ambiguity and errors
- a written communication is more permanent than verbal communication and can be filed away for future reference
- effort is minimised as one communication can be duplicated and sent to numerous people or posted on noticeboards
- electronic transmission (e.g. e-mail, the Internet, etc.) demands it.

However, the same problems that apply to verbal communication also apply to written communication. The objectives of the communication are not always clearly defined, the sentences may be too long, the language can be full of jargon, and it does not always reach the intended audience. For example, many safety communications are posted on noticeboards, which many people do not read, or information presented in written safety communications is not passed on to the appropriate people. The extent to which these two factors were implicated in accidents in the UK construction industry was revealed in a study conducted in 1990 for the HSE by Debbie Lucas and Claire Whittington which examined a random set of 30 serious or fatal accidents. The failure of people to see written communications posted on noticeboards was implicated in three of them (10%), while the failure to communicate written safe systems of work to those doing the work was implicated in 15 of them (50%). In relation to noticeboards, the reason most people do not read (*behaviour*) material presented on them is quite simply that noticeboards tend to blend into the background, as they have merely become a part of the furniture (*situation*). Similarly, information contained in written communications is often not passed on to those undertaking the work (*behaviour*) because of perceived time pressures (*situation*), and/or because supervisors do not deem it necessary for the task in hand as they assume tradespeople know what they are doing (*attitude*). Unfortunately, many safety professionals also tend to rely on noticeboards as communication devices because of pressure of work (e.g. they have many meetings to attend, or they have to compile reports, statistics etc., for their managers). A practical way to ensure that most people actually receive the information (assuming it is important), is to send everybody a copy via the internal mail system. Similarly, if a job or task is important enough to deserve its own written safe system of work, it is just as important to ensure that those conducting the task are made aware of it.

Visual Communication

Visual communication refers to the use of colours, signs, graphs etc. In the main, visual cues are used to convey:

- warnings (e.g. black and yellow striped tapes used to cordon off a hole in a floor)
- instructions (e.g. a picture of a white hard-hat on a blue background to indicate that it is mandatory to wear a hard-hat in a specific area)
- condensed versions of large amounts of information (e.g. a pie-chart showing a breakdown of the causes of accidents).

In many organisations graphs are often used to provide ongoing feedback about a work group's production and quality performance. Unfortunately, they often result in confusion simply because too much information is presented on a graph. For example, research has shown that any more than three pieces of information on a graph tend to be confusing, and that graphs tend to be preferred by professionals, while pictorial representations are the preference of tradespeople. Line graphs are also thought to be easier to understand than bargraphs, particularly if the scale values on the vertical axis are in multiples of two, five or ten. Many organisations also have a tendency to place many similar looking graphs next to each other on large noticeboards (*situation*). The difficulty of finding a particular graph causes many people not to bother (*attitude*) to read or look at them (*behaviour*). In practical terms this means that particular areas of a noticeboard should be labelled, and colour-coded by function (e.g. quality, productivity, safety). If the information is important, however, it is best to convey it by verbal face-to-face meetings and then post it on a noticeboard.

Behavioural Cues

Behavioural cues also determine how information is perceived and used. This is because face-to-face communication also involves the way speakers present themselves, and in many ways this is more important than the actual words used. Although an exploration of behavioural cues is beyond the scope of this book, the extent to which they are important can be discovered easily by watching people interact with each other on a television with the sound turned off. You will probably be quite surprised at how much information you can surmise about what is happening. A great amount of eye contact between two people who are talking, for example, indicates that they are listening to each other, whereas someone who is listening but continually looking around and not maintaining eye contact with the speaker gives the impression that they are disinterested in what is being said. Four main areas of non-verbal communication can affect people's interactions with each other. They are:

- physical appearance (e.g. dress)
- tone and speed of voice (approving or disapproving)
- physical movements (arm and hand gestures)
- posture and position (e.g. being too close could indicate over-familiarity or aggression).

Although the receipt of these types of signals and counter-signals is largely unconscious, they can determine whether or not a transmitted message is actually received. They are therefore just as important as oral, written and visual communications, particularly as people have a strong tendency to conform to other people's perceptions of them (e.g. people who are treated as responsible adults tend to behave as responsible adults).

In some areas of workplace activity behavioural cues are formalised and used to communicate the need for particular actions (e.g. banksmen signalling to crane operators); in other areas non-formal hand gestures are used (e.g. thumbs up), perhaps to indicate that it is all right to carry out an activity in a noisy area. In both cases, accidents commonly occur because the line of vision between people is not clear, or people misunderstand the signals. In the construction study examining 30 random accidents previously mentioned, three of them (10%) were due to misunderstandings of arm/hand signals. Thus if arm/hand signals are to be used, it is vital to ensure that people know what the signal means, that they can clearly see each other, and that only one person at a time uses hand signals to communicate with the other.

Complex Communication

The complexity of a communication transmission will also affect people's understanding of the information. Simple communications refer to those that convey a limited amount of easily understood information, and encompass such things as memos reminding someone to do something, telephoning to order new stocks, sending a fax to a customer or client, sending an e-mail to another part of the organisation, or writing letters. 'Complex communication' usually refers to the need to analyse and extract meaning from such things as reports, technical data sheets, production data and dials and displays in control rooms. Thus the amount of data processing and problem-solving increases with the complexity of the information presented by a particular communication format. However, because a person can only process so much information at any one time, people will only pay attention to those parts of the transmission thought to be important. Termed 'selective attention' this refers to people's propensity to listen and act upon only part of the information they receive, while ignoring the rest. This has obvious implications for health and safety as illustrated by the case of the KLM airline captain in the Tenerife runway crash which killed 580 people. Visibility was very poor and a Pan-Am aircraft was taxiing on the runway when the KLM captain decided to take off. A message from the Pan-Am flight was received by the KLM flight engineer which warned that they were still taxiing on the runway. This message was immediately passed onto the KLM captain who ignored it (apparently because he thought the content of the message conflicted with his interpretation of the situation). He continued taking off and crashed into the Pan-Am flight.

Communication Overload

Selective attention can also be brought about by the amount of information that someone is expected to process as they try to cope with communication overload (particularly when under extreme time pressures). Trying to cope with communication overload will almost certainly lead to a communication failure, simply because information thought to be less important will tend to be ignored. Unfortunately, this could lead to safety-critical (or other important) information being totally ignored, as it gets forgotten. Communication overload can be further compounded when people are presented with complex information which requires a great deal of processing capacity. In many day-to-day situations, it is supervisors or managers who tend to be overloaded with information as they also have to deal with requests from others. For example, a supervisor may be expected to deal with requests for permits to work while simultaneously dealing with the telephone and production-related problems. In these circumstances, the supervisor is likely to become

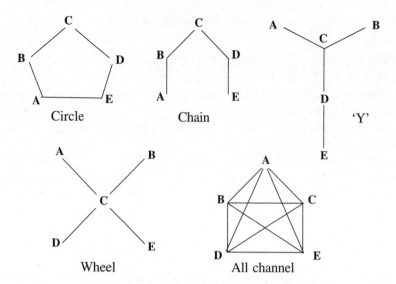

Figure 3.5   Communication Networks

so severely overloaded that he or she does not complete the work permits properly (which could put many people in jeopardy), or does not actually supervise day-to-day production. In these days of 'lean' organisations, communication overload is becoming much more of an everyday problem, and may explain why communication issues form a major part of the cause of many accidents.

Communication Networks

Although no simple formula can be applied to the design of a work group's communication network, optimising the information flow within the group may be one way of reducing the problems associated with communication overload. This can be done by assessing the complexity and amount of information that has to be transmitted in relation to the group's reporting structure. In the main there are two types of communication networks: those that are centralised and those that are de-centralised (see Figure 3.5: *Communication Networks*). De-centralised networks include the 'chain', and the 'circle', whereas centralised networks use the 'wheel' and the 'all-channel'.

De-centralised Networks

In work groups that operate in a hierarchical fashion, the communication flow nearly always follows a chain whereby information passes through several hands before reaching its destination, i.e. operator–chargehand–

foreman–supervisor–manager. At each stage, a decision is made about what and how much information to pass on and by what medium (e.g. verbal or written). This means that the information tends to be filtered or distorted by each person's interpretation of its meaning or importance. In addition, because the information flow tends to be one-way (i.e. either up or down) feedback tends to be non-existent (I have lost count of the number of times people have told me that they passed safety-critical information on up the line and have never heard about it since). As such, chain networks tend to lead to poor performance and poor co-ordination, which in turn leads the work group to become dissatisfied with the speed and flow of information, which in turn leads to poor morale (all of which can adversely affect the work group's safety performance). The circle tends to represent the communication flow found in leaderless groups and is analogous to a badly formed committee. Leaderless work groups tend not to be good at reaching decisions or in passing on information and ideas, simply because nobody knows who is responsible for what. They also tend to exhibit poor co-ordination and are very slow to arrive at solutions to problems, which could lead to poor safety performance. However, these problems might be overcome by ensuring that every group member has a clear job description, and that any group discussions start from a clear and explicit point of reference.

Centralised Networks

The wheel network is derived from the chain and is more typical of most work groups. The managerial or supervisory function is placed at the centre of the wheel and he or she acts as the central co-ordinator or facilitator who passes information to the people at the end of the 'spokes'. Because the opportunity for two-way communications is much greater, this type of network works well and leads to fewer errors, provided that the central person can receive, process and transmit information in an efficient manner. The wheel arrangement is also the quickest for solving problems as fewer messages need to be transmitted between everybody, and this facilitates good performance and co-ordination.

The all-channel network is participative, all-involving, and is good for quality decision-making, simply because it operates like a good committee and accepts that cross-communication is essential to prevent the distortion of information. Similarly, it provides good opportunities for feedback because two-way communications are the norm. However, like all well run committees it needs one person to act as an arbitrator, co-ordinator and controller. All-channel networks are better for solving complex problems, rather than simple problems, but they do not stand up well to time pressures or competition. When faced with pressure all-channel networks often revert to the wheel, or disintegrate.

Choosing the Appropriate Network for the Task

Given that each type of network has varying degrees of effectiveness, it is important to select the right one for the task, while simultaneously trying to make sure that one person does not become too overloaded with information. The chain tends to be quicker when simple information needs to be passed on, but it is prone to communication errors. To some extent this could be avoided by ensuring that two-way communications take place at each link in the chain (i.e. the recipient confirms his or her understanding of the message). It is also important to ensure that people receive feedback about the actions taken in response to safety-critical information (i.e. who is dealing with it and by when). Because the efficiency of the circle is so poor and ripe for rumour mongering or gossip, it should be converted into a wheel arrangement, so that one central person has responsibility for handling communications. This is because the wheel arrangement has been shown to be the most effective structure for communicating information and solving simple problems. Care must be taken, however, to ensure that the person at the centre of the wheel does not suffer communication overload because of large amounts of complex information. Wheel arrangements therefore depend on having a good manager at the centre. If a manager is weak and the information received tends to be complex and ambiguous, an all-channel network might be needed to supplement the wheel, i.e. holding regular team briefings to discuss the issues.

Communication Networks and Group Cohesiveness

The structure of the communication network operating in a work group will affect the group's cohesiveness and norms (i.e. standards and styles of behaviour), which in turn can exert an enormous influence on an individual group member's behaviour and attitudes. Because the essence of most safety improvement programmes is to help work groups positively to redefine their own safety related norms, the degree to which group norms exert an influence on safety performance cannot be underestimated. In general, the more cohesive a group is, the more a person will conform to the group's norms. However, the likelihood of a person conforming to a group's norms is dependent upon:

- the strength with which the whole group pressurises each individual to conform (e.g. the whole group insists upon everybody behaving safely)
- what sanctions are applied to non-conformance (e.g. teasing, sending somebody to Coventry, etc.)

- what rewards are applied for conforming (e.g. complete social acceptance, respect from established members of the group, and praise or
social approval for doing things right)
- the degree to which the group's values and beliefs coincide with each
individual member's values and beliefs.

Thus cohesiveness refers to the patterns of social interaction between the
group membership, which can be either task oriented or socially orientated.

Analysing a Group's Social Interactions

It is possible to identify situations in which potential communication failures
might arise within a group by using the Interaction Process Analyses System
(IPAS) developed by Robert Bales in 1950 (see Figure 3.6). The IPAS is
essentially a classification system consisting of 4 main categories and 12 sub
categories that assesses the content and patterns of a group's communications. The 12 sub categories fall into two main classes: those in the middle
form the task class (categories 4–9), while those on either end form the social
class (categories 1 to 3 and 10 to 12). These two major classes are further sub-
divided into two orientations: the task orientation categories 4 to 6 are concerned with giving information, opinions and suggestions, whereas categories
7 to 9 are concerned with asking for information, opinions and suggestions.
The social orientation categories 1 to 3 are concerned with positive reactions,
while categories 10 to 12 are concerned with negative reactions. Each of the
categories is also paired (as shown on the right hand side of Figure 3.6) to
identify possible problems in certain areas, as follows:

Table 3.1   Classification of a Group's Social Interactions

Sub category	Function
6 to 7	deal with communications related to setting out a problem and giving information
5 and 8	deal with evaluation of a problem (e.g. Have we done . . .?, or 'Should we do . . .?)
4 and 9	are concerned with control (e.g. We should do . . .? Or What ought we to do about . . .?)
3 and 10	concern decisions to accept or reject suggestions, opinions, etc.,
2 and 11	concern emotional responses related to the heightening or reduction of tension
1 and 12	are concerned about the degree of group integration or disintegration.

Conducting Assessments of a Group's Social Interactions

An assessment usually occurs when a group is given a problem to solve
within a certain time limit (usually 40 minutes). Because of time and cost

98

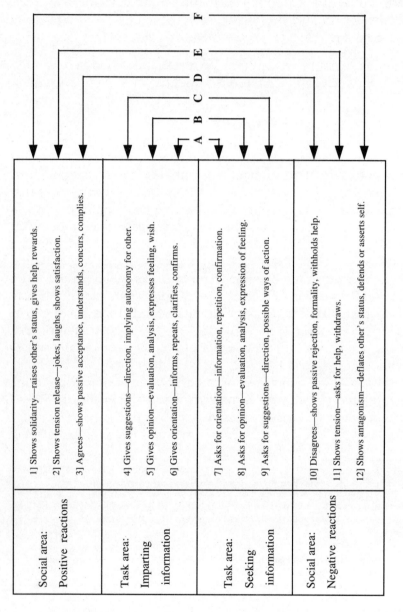

Social area: Positive reactions	1] Shows solidarity—raises other's status, gives help, rewards.	
	2] Shows tension release—jokes, laughs, shows satisfaction.	
	3] Agrees—shows passive acceptance, understands, concurs, complies.	
Task area: Imparting information	4] Gives suggestions—direction, implying autonomy for other.	
	5] Gives opinion—evaluation, analysis, expresses feeling, wish.	
	6] Gives orientation—informs, repeats, clarifies, confirms.	
Task area: Seeking information	7] Asks for orientation—information, repetition, confirmation.	
	8] Asks for opinion—evaluation, analysis, expression of feeling.	
	9] Asks for suggestions—direction, possible ways of action.	
Social area: Negative reactions	10] Disagrees—shows passive rejection, formality, withholds help.	
	11] Shows tension—asks for help, withdraws.	
	12] Shows antagonism—deflates other's status, defends or asserts self.	

Task area:

A Problems of orientation   (6 and 7)
B Problems of evaluation   (5 and 8)
C Problems of control   (4 and 9)

Social area:

D Problems of decision   (3 and 10)
E Problems of tension management (2 and 11)
F Problems of integration   (1 and 12)

Figure 3.6 Bales (1950) Interaction Process Analyses System – Adapted from Bales, R.F. (1950) Interaction Process Analysis: A Method for the Study of Small Groups. Reading, MA: Addison-Wesley. Reprinted by permission

constraints, however, it is usually better to observe and assess a work group when they are dealing with a real problem in the workplace. Each person in the group is arbitrarily given a number so that it is easier to record who speaks to whom. For example, the notation 1–5 would indicate that group member 1 spoke to group member 5. The analyst then assesses the type of communication between the two group members according to the IPAS categories. In this way, every communication act is assessed and classified according to its quality, who performed it, who it was directed at, and when. Typically, groups start by trying to solve the problem (categories 6 and 7), deciding upon the goals (categories 5 and 8), and addressing questions of how the goals can be achieved (4 and 9). The quality of the social interactions are rated according to categories 1, 2 and 3 (positive) and categories 10, 11 and 12 (negative). In relation to task orientation, problems can be identified when there is a mismatch between each of the paired sub categories. For example, if someone requests information (category 7) of another group member, and doesn't receive it (category 6), this would indicate communication problems. It is important for the assessor simultaneously to record the social aspects of the interaction according to the social orientation categories.

The quality of the interactions between people discovered with the IPAS during a problem-solving exercise can often be seen in the group's everyday communications. Thus the value of the exercise resides in discovering who interacts with whom, in what style. Typically, it is found that subordinates tend to be less open with their supervisors, and that supervisors seek less information from, or give less feedback to, their subordinates. In the main this appears to be related to the degree of trust between each of the parties. Low trust leads to less information flow, which in itself is also likely to lead to the information being distorted. Thus, groups operating in a low trust climate will tend to have weak group norms whereas high trust groups will tend to have stronger group norms. Members of high trust groups, therefore, are more likely to adhere to a group's safety norms than low trust groups. This can often be seen in organisations where breaches of standard operating procedures (SOPs) are not reported because of a lack of trust and a fear of sanctions. Conversely, breaches of SOPs tend to be reported in high trust groups because the group tends to examine the effectiveness of the SOPs themselves, rather than apportioning blame or disciplining an individual.

JOB ANALYSIS

So far this chapter has concentrated on analysing the organisation and the work group rather than individual tasks or jobs. Because individual jobs are the basic building blocks of work design, they also need to be examined so that a risk-reducing interaction between people, the production processes and the physical working environment can be achieved. Numerous examples of job/task analysis exist in the scientific and management literature, each varying according to the type of data required, the method of data collection, the information sources, and the methods of data analysis. For a fuller description of some of these the reader is referred to Barry Kirwan's and Les Ainsworth's excellent book on the subject published in 1992 by Taylor & Francis which includes many real life examples relating to safety.

In general, job/task analyses are used to break down a task into its constituent components, to identify such things as:

- the most cost-effective methods for achieving the task goals
- training needs
- staffing requirements
- the potential for error

or developing:

- maintenance schedules
- method statements
- safe systems of work
- permit to work procedures
- standard operating procedures.

Job analyses are carried out in a series of steps.

Step One—Define the Objectives

Job/task analyses can be used to help in the design, operation and maintenance of a work system, to address specific issues related to a task (such as hazard identification), or to conduct accident investigations. Because job analysis requires a systematic examination of many inter-related activities, the tools or methods used will often be determined by the purpose of the analysis. This means that the first step of any job/task analysis must be to *define the objectives* of the exercise (for example, identifying training needs, developing a standard operating procedure, etc.).

Step Two—Collect Job-Related Information

The next step requires the analyst to collect and gather job-related information. One of the best sources of job information is the job holder, as he or she will have the most detailed knowledge of the job requirements. However, exaggeration or distortion of information, forgetting, etc., remains a very real possibility. It is therefore wise to widen the information net by approaching superiors, subordinates, peers and others who come into contact with the job holder. Decisions also need to be made about the data collection method. Sometimes one method may be enough, but more often than not the use of several methods is more appropriate. The most common forms of data collection include:

- Self report methods — work diaries, written narratives, checklists, questionnaires, interviews, and group discussions
- Observations — direct observation, work study methods, video or close circuit television
- Existing records — procedures, job descriptions, quality/production records.

In relation to creating a positive safety culture, it may prove useful to set out to examine people's jobs in relation to the HSE's four 'Cs': Control, Co-operation, Communication and Competence. Although the HSE intended the four Cs to be examined from an organisational systems perspective, the author believes that they should also be examined for each person's job. In this way it is possible to review the efficiency and the effectiveness of arrangements from a top-down and bottom-up perspective so that a comprehensive integration of people's jobs with the organisational systems can be achieved.

Control

Because the notion of control is so wide and can be applied to many different aspects of a job, it becomes very important to fully examine the job holder's degree of control over:

- other people
- the work carried out
- the technology used
- resources (financial, time and material)
- documents and data
- planning
- decision-making
- training

- maintenance and servicing
- safety, health and environmental issues
- the working environment.

Having established *what* the job holder has control over, the analyst should proceed to establish *where* it is important for the job holder to exert his or her control, *when* it is important to exert or maintain control, and *how* the job holder actually maintains control. The end result of this exercise should be a detailed list identifying the person's responsibilities, the mechanisms by which the controls are exerted, how the person monitors his or her degree of control, feedback about the effectiveness of that control, and what *constraints* (if any) there are on the person exercising the control in any or all of the above areas. A systematic examination of these features for each job holder should make it possible to develop a work group's formal control systems, codify the appropriate rules and procedures, and establish people's responsibilities and accountabilities.

Co-operation

In line with the HSE's guidance on co-operation, it is useful to examine the extent to which job holders take part in health and safety by focusing upon the degree to which people are involved and participate in:

- developing and reviewing departmental health and safety policies
- health and safety committees
- setting performance standards
- devising operational systems
- developing rules and procedures for the control of risk
- conducting risk assessments
- monitoring and auditing safety systems
- investigating near misses and accidents.

However, the notion of co-operation is much wider than this as it also includes the degree to which people or work groups co-ordinate and co-operate with each other over the whole range of their activities. As such it is worth examining *who* the job holder has to co-operate with, *why* they need to co-operate, *when* they need to co-operate, *where* the need is for co-operation, *how* they actually co-operate and *what form* the co-operation should take. By analysing a person's job from this perspective, it is possible to identify areas of the job where potential failures in co-operation might occur, and the potential risks involved in such a failure.

Communications

In relation to communications, the analyst would examine the extent and quality of the job holder's communications by focusing on:

- the person's internal and external lines of communication (to whom)
- the purpose of the communication(s)
- ascertaining whether or not the communications are one way or two way
- the methods of communications used (oral, written, visual, electronic, etc.)
- the complexity and timing of the communications with which the person is required to deal
- the quality of the person's communication skill(s)
- the timing of the need to transmit or receive emergency communications
- the effectiveness of the person's communications during emergencies
- any additional communications the person requires
- whether or not the communications are affected by critical incidents
- areas of possible communication conflicts
- the consequences of a communication failure
- the degree to which he or she attends meetings, briefings, toolbox talks, etc.

In addition, it would be useful to examine the extent to which the job holder is aware of the company's health and safety policy, the extent to which the person is familiar with the company's mission and vision statements, the degree to which he or she is aware of the frequency of senior management safety tours, the person's ease of access to written risk assessments, standard operating procedures, etc. affecting the work area and the extent to which the person reads health and safety information posted on noticeboards, etc. In this way it is possible to build up a good picture of the organisation's effectiveness at communicating health and safety information and to identify areas where improvements might be needed.

Competence

An employee's competence exerts an enormous effect on an organisation's health and safety performance. Competence is defined as 'a person's *ability to perform* a task'. Because task performance is dependent upon people's levels of knowledge and skill, motivation and physical capabilities, it is important to examine each of these to determine if people are actually competent to undertake the task in hand. Assumptions that someone is competent to undertake a task can have catastrophic effects, as indicated by the case of a time served gas fitter who failed to fit a flue to a heater. Two people died from fumes because the fitter did not believe a flue was available or necessary for the type of heater fitted. Examinations of a person's competence should at the very least focus on their:

- levels of knowledge and skills as *demonstrated by the possession of appropriate qualifications for their job* (i.e. NVQs or SVQs, City & Guilds, Industrial Training Boards Certificates, designatory letters from a professional institution, etc.)
- levels of motivation (this can be determined by using the job design questionnaire presented in Figure 3.4)
- physical attributes to ensure that people are not handicapped in any way to do their job (e.g. good levels of hearing, good colour discrimination, appropriate and sufficient strength, height, etc.)

Assessing the levels of knowledge and skill for those employees who do not possess formal qualifications could be achieved by giving them work sample tests. This entails their demonstrating their proficiency and competence on a range of tasks that are representative of their jobs and the required performance standards. Local Skillcentres run by the Manpower Services Commission tend to have a range of work sample tests available. Alternatively, registered Chartered Occupational Psychologists can devise appropriate tests for any type of job (managerial, manual or clerical). They can also determine people's levels of motivation. Any discrepancies identified in a person's competence would indicate an immediate training need. Any discrepancies in people's levels of motivation may require their jobs to be restructured, and any discrepancies between the physical demands of the job and a person's physical attributes would demand either a restructuring of the job or the person being placed in a job that is more closely aligned with their physical attributes.

Step Three—Analyse the Information Collected

Once the necessary data has been collected, it needs to be analysed to ascertain the complete situation. In many instances it is likely that data collection and data analysis will coincide, as the methods for both may be mutually inclusive, with the data collection methods being determined by the data analytic techniques, and *vice versa*. It may be useful to use a combination of such techniques. Common data analytic techniques include:

- *Hierarchical Task Analysis (HTA)* which involves the systematic examination of a task in terms of nested hierarchies of operations. Initially the task is specified in fairly broad terms. Each element of the job or operation is then progressively re-described in more and more detail to produce the nested hierarchy.

- *Activity analysis* which examines the particular activities involved in a job and the psychological demands placed on the job holder (e.g. memory, perceptual and decision-making functions).
- *Skills analysis* which involves an examination of the job holder's relevant body movements for effective performance. The emphasis is placed on the informational cues presented by a task and the types and amounts of task feedback cues to enable the person to sequence, co-ordinate and control their activities.
- *Critical incidents analysis* which involves identifying the types and causes of human errors or mistakes. Based on their own experiences people are asked to identify critical incidents (e.g. unsafe behaviours, or other factors that contribute to a failure of some sort), so that particular behaviours associated with the incidents can be either eliminated or encouraged.
- *Role analysis* which involves the job holder, his or her superior, or possibly others in a work group to list their duties, individual responsibilities and expected behaviours.
- *Performance analysis* which involves assessing the appropriate basis for judging the job holder's performance by determining what productivity outcomes are appropriate (e.g. productivity output, quality levels, materials wastage, etc.), what job factors are important (e.g. accidents, absenteeism, lateness, etc.), and what standards and objectives must be achieved.

Step Four—Assemble the Information into an Appropriate Format

Having analysed the job-related information to provide an overall view of the person's job or task and the required performance outcomes, the next stage is one of assembling the information into an appropriate written form (e.g. a job description, a set of standard operating procedures, or a list of training needs). For any formal document it would probably be wise to divide the information into various categories or headings to make it more meaningful, such as that presented in Table 3.2 *Categorising Job-related Information*.

Step Five—Review the Outcomes

Having completed all the above steps, the analyst should review the final document *with the jobholder* so that its accuracy can be assessed and changed

Table 3.2   Categorising Job-related Information

Category of information	Type of information
General Information	Job identification data (i.e. job title, department, etc.)
	Organisational data (e.g. organisational position, reporting relationships, contacts with other people, work groups, etc.).
	Job summary (e.g. a basic summary of the job in terms of functions and purposes).
Job Content	All the data about specific tasks, operations, duties, responsibilities, accountabilities, etc., including the purpose of each task, the methods involved and the importance of each task.
Working Conditions	The physical environment, the physical demands placed on the jobholder, the ambient temperature, machinery used, noise levels, hazards, accident and health risks, etc.
Working Relationships	Membership of formal work groups, committees, working parties, etc.
Performance Evaluations	The required standards which are used to evaluate the jobholder's performance.
Physical Attributes	The physical or psychological attributes required of the jobholder.

if necessary. Because the final document is to be used for communication purposes, it will be subject to the normal problems of any written communication. Thus, it is essential that the document is written in the language of its intended user (i.e. jargon is avoided, the sentences are clear and concise and it is laid out in a logical sequence).

WORK SAFETY ANALYSIS

Work or job safety analysis is concerned with identifying the hazards or risks associated with each element or component of a job. Although it explicitly uses risk assessments to identify the most appropriate accident prevention measures, job safety analysis is basically an extension of task or job analysis. The intention of job safety analysis is to provide a basis for the development of written job safety instructions such as standard operating procedures so that a safe system of work can be developed and implemented by the organisation. Most job safety analyses:

- specify the job to be examined
- break down the job into its constituent components
- analyse and assess each job component to determine the hazards and risks
- develop appropriate control measures to eliminate or reduce the hazards/risks
- develop a safe system of work
- write the job safety instructions (standard operating procedures).

Subsequently, the analyst (or other significant person) ensures that the results and recommendations are:

- brought to management's attention
- implemented in a safe system of work
- reviewed at periodic intervals to take account of changing circumstances.

Because any job constitutes a reciprocal relationship between people, the production processes and the working environment, it is important for the job safety analysis to take these factors into account, separately and in combination. Although the following lists are certainly not exhaustive, they do indicate the types of factor that the analyst should examine in order to identify the hazards and risks associated with people's jobs. These include:

- people factors such as
  - the skills, knowledge and abilities required to do the job
  - potential areas for unsafe behaviour
  - potential stressors (e.g. work overload and work underload, role ambiguity, etc.)
  - hours of work
  - health or physical disabilities
  - the use of agency or contractor workers
  - factors affecting young workers (e.g. shiftwork)
  - pregnancy
  - responses to emergency or unusual situations
  - the quality of communications
- production-related factors such as
  - the tools, plant and machinery used
  - the methods of using tools, plant and machinery
  - the use of raw materials (e.g. chemicals or biological agents)
  - the sequencing of production operations
  - the timing and sequencing of maintenance activities
  - standards of supervision
  - provision of safety equipment
  - resource allocation (e.g. time, finance and materials)
  - bonus and incentive schemes
- factors associated with the working environment such as:
  - potential fire hazards (e.g. locked fire doors)
  - stressors (e.g. noise, heat, cold, ventilation, lighting, vibration, etc.)
  - access and egress
  - workplace design (e.g. layout)
  - the quality of floor surfaces
  - water
  - the types and placement of audible and visual alarms.

A thorough examination of these types of factor should lead to the codifying of rules and procedures, establishing accountabilities, elimination and control of hazards, etc. Such examinations can also result in improved productivity and quality as they tend to lead to plans that make the most efficient use of people, plant and materials within a safe working environment. However, no matter which type of analysis is undertaken it is important that the analyst:

- conducts a detailed examination of the workplace
- takes time to talk to people and does not rush things
- always questions why things are being done the way they are
- asks what the consequences might be of doing things in the wrong way.

4

Developing Risk Control Systems

INTRODUCTION

Achieving a balanced risk-reducing interaction between people, production processes and the working environment requires the assessment of risks involved in all of an organisation's activities (e.g. risks presented by a communications failure). Indeed, achieving this aim is one of the central features of the MHSWR 1992. Regulation 3 requires every employer to make a suitable and sufficient assessment of the risks to the health and safety of employees and others not employed by the organisation, to which they might be exposed whilst they are in the workplace. The purpose of this legislative requirement is to ensure that an organisation identifies, evaluates and decides what needs to be done about the risks it creates for people, whether employees or not. Organisations must therefore be able to demonstrate to interested parties (e.g. the HSE) the justification for their subsequent actions. Although there is no legal requirement to assess the risks associated with damage to plant, machinery, equipment or the working environment unless a person is involved, it makes good commercial sense to do so at the same time that a 'normal' risk assessment is undertaken. Thus, risk assessments are an integral component of the immediate level of effort from three perspectives: legislative, developing a positive safety culture and commercial. It is important, however, to stress at the outset that risk perceptions and risk assessments are *subjective* assessments of a situation, simply because estimates of risk tend to be socially constructed, regardless of the methodology used. This can be demonstrated by the fact that managers nearly always underestimate the risks involved in a task compared to those who actually do the tasks. This is because group characteristics exert important influences on perceptions of risk. For example, because managers are normally too far removed from daily operations, they tend not know the full details of a person's job, and therefore are unable to make meaningful assessments. In practical terms this means that any risk assessment must be conducted by a minimum of two people (i.e. the person doing the task and a manager or safety advisor), but preferably by all three so that a balanced, broad-based perspective is brought to bear in the analysis and evaluation of risk.

WHAT IS RISK ASSESSMENT?

Risk assessment is a process concerned with identifying the hazards presented by a task- or work-related undertaking (risk analysis), and estimating the extent to which any risks may result in harm or injury (risk evaluation), while taking into account any precautions that have already been operationalised. Common terms used in relation to risk assessments are:

- *Hazard*—something that has the potential to cause harm
- *Risk*—the likelihood of the potential hazard causing harm
- *Frequency or degree of exposure*—the number of times that people are, or could be, exposed to a hazard
- *Severity*—the degree of harm, or consequences if the hazard is realised
- *Risk assessment*—an evaluation of the likelihood that a potential hazard will actually cause harm, while also taking into account the frequency of exposure and severity of outcomes
- *Risk control*—measures taken to control or eliminate the hazard or risk on the basis of the risk assessment.

Types of Risk Assessment

In general there are four types of risk assessment:

1   those for large-scale complex hazard sites (e.g. chemical plants) that require quantitative risk assessments (QRA).
2   those specifically required by legislation, i.e.
    - Control of Lead at Work Regulations 1980
    - Ionising Radiations Regulations 1985
    - Control of Asbestos at Work Regulations 1987
    - COSHH Regulations 1994
    - Electricity at Work Regulations 1989
    - Pressure Systems and Transportable Gas Containers Regulations 1989
    - Noise at Work Regulations 1990
3   Assessments specifically required or implied by legislation for a wide range of activity, i.e.
    - The Management of Health and Safety at Work Regulations 1992
    - Manual Handling Operations Regulations 1992

- The Provision and Use of Work Equipment Regulations 1992
- The Personal Protective Equipment at Work Regulations 1992
- Health & Safety (Display Screen Equipment) Regulations 1992
- Workplace (Health, Safety and Welfare) Regulations 1992
- The Construction (Design & Management) Regulations 1994

4   Assessments of behavioural risk for each individual job, workplace or work process.

The first type of risk assessment, QRA, attempts to quantify the probability of 'things' going wrong by using expert judgement and quantified analysis to make predictions. In the main, QRA techniques are used to determine those situations where the consequences of a minor human error could be disastrous or the costs exhorbitant (e.g. nuclear power plants), although they have also been applied to such events as traffic accidents involving child pedestrians. The methods used involve collecting enough information about actual incidents to build statistical tables (from actual events or observation sampling techniques). On the basis of this information, judgements are made about any potential errors that can be made within a given sequence of tasks or events. Each potential error is then assigned a 'probability' value based on the ratio between the number of incidents and estimates of exposure. These are then multiplied by other factors (e.g. the numbers of people at risk). The resulting figures are then placed in descending order to provide an indication of the priority to be given to those 'events' requiring control measures. However, as pointed out by the ACSNI report and others, multiplying together such 'probabilities' (which may or may not be independent of each other) may hold true for physical engineering situations but is less likely for human errors. This aptly reinforces the point that all risk assessments are made on the basis of the risk assessor's underlying beliefs and values about the accident causation process and are, therefore, subjective.

The remainder of this chapter focuses on the practicalities of conducting risk assessments for the latter three types of risk assessment rather than that required for QRA, simply because a detailed explanation of QRA is beyond the scope of this book.

The Process of Risk Assessment

In essence, the identification, evaluation and control of risks involves a six stage process (see Figure 4.1: *The Risk Assessment Process*) that involves:

- identifying the hazard
- assessing the risks
- documenting the risks

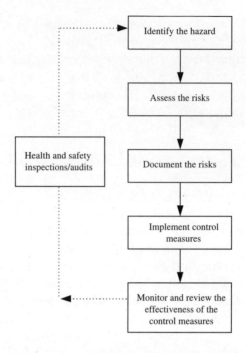

Figure 4.1   The Risk Assessment Process

- developing appropriate control measures
- implementing the control measures
- monitoring and reviewing the effectiveness of the control measures.

The complexity of the task, job or operation will determine what detailed actions are required at each stage of the process. However, the actual methodologies used to evaluate the potential risks and the procedures are broadly similar whatever the type of task, job or operation.

Identifying Hazards

The general principles involved in any risk assessment begin with identifying all the hazards associated with a task or activity by considering:

- the type of activity or work being carried out
- how it is carried out
- where it takes place (i.e. environmental considerations)
- what plant, equipment and materials are involved
- when a particular activity takes place
- who undertakes the work or activity
- how many people are involved

- whether the task activity is of a short or long duration
- the potential for safety management failures
- the potential for technical failures
- the potential for human error failures
- what the consequences would be of a failure in any area of the activity.

It becomes clear, therefore, that the first essential step of a risk assessment requires the assessors to possess a full and comprehensive understanding of the working environment, the production processes involved, the materials used and the numbers and types of people involved. The possession of relevant information is, therefore, essential. To ensure the assessors are fully conversant with all the requirements for each type of activity they need to have access to relevant legislative documents and approved codes of practice (ACOPs), HSE publications and other available guidance, product information, British and international standards, industry or trade publications, and near miss and accident reports and statistics.

Assessing the Risks

The main purpose of a risk assessment is to discover whether or not preventive measures are in place and whether or not they could and/or should be improved. Thus, it is important to ensure that *all* the hazards associated with an activity have been assessed. The only way that this can be achieved satisfactorily is for the assessors to actually observe the activity under consideration and critically ask themselves 'what if . . .' questions.

To determine whether or not a hazard presents an acceptable risk, values are assigned to various weighting factors to determine the priority of the necessary remedial actions (if any). It must be emphasised that the values assigned tend to be somewhat arbitrary, in that the scale of values and their associated category variables will tend to be organisation-specific. This does not normally present a problem provided that the organisation consistently uses the same values and scale variables when determining the risks involved in all its different tasks or operations. Notwithstanding the above, many safety professionals are now moving to simpler forms of risk assessment which do not involve the assignment of scale values to determine the priority of remedial actions. Instead, questions are asked on the basis of whether or not 'things' are satisfactory or unsatisfactory. If found to be satisfactory, no further action is taken. If found to be unsatisfactory, more detailed risk assessments of the type described here are triggered.

Risk assessment formulae. A widely accepted definition of risk in the safety literature states that risk is 'the likelihood that a specific hazard will result in a specific undesired event'. This definition is often expressed in risk assessment formulae used to determine the level of potential risk posed by a hazard, by estimating and assigning a value to both the likelihood and the severity factors. The assigned values are then multiplied to provide a risk rating, for example:

$$\text{Risk} = \text{likelihood of harm} \times \text{severity of harm}$$

However, definitions of this type tend to be limited as they ignore the frequency of exposure to a hazard on the basis that it is *implicitly* included in estimates of the likelihood of a hazard being realised. It is probably much better to *explicitly* include the frequency of exposure to specific hazards, simply because it helps to determine the priority of remedial actions with much greater precision. It is quite obvious, for example, that the risks of repetitive strain injury (RSI) increase with the frequency and amount of typing someone does. A manager who types one or two letters a week is much less likely to suffer RSI than a secretary who types 20 documents every day of the working week. However, risk assessment formulae that only take into account estimates of likelihood and severity could arrive at the same risk rating for both the secretary and the manager. Including the frequency estimate, therefore, would clearly distinguish who is at greater risk. Given the above, it makes sense to rate each identified hazard in terms of:

- the frequency of exposure (F)
- the likelihood of harm (L)
- the severity of harm (S).

Each of these components should be further broken down into a number of elements, each of which is assigned a value (e.g. 0–5), so that the degree of risk presented by a hazard can be discovered. Table 4.1 *Risk Assessment Formulae* provides an indicator of the type of scales assigned to each element of the risk formulae components:

The degree of risk presented by a hazard or combination of hazards would be derived from multiplying the three components together (e.g. potential risk = F × L × S). With the classification scheme presented in Table 4.1 each risk score could range from 0–80 (i.e. 4 × 4 × 5).

Determining objective risk formula weightings. It is possible to use a more objective basis for determining the scale values assigned to various risk assessment weighting factors by examining the organisation's existing accident and near miss databases (assuming they are large enough). This can also help to guide the organisation's initial risk assessment efforts, by

Table 4.1   Risk Assessment Formulae

Value	Frequency of exposure
0	Never
1	Hardly ever
2	Often
3	Very often
4	Continuously
	Likelihood of harm
0	Extremely unlikely
1	Unlikely
2	Likely
3	Extremely likely
4	Certain
	Severity of harm
0	No harm
1	Minor injury with no medical attention
2	Minor injury with medical attention
3	Injury resulting in one to three days off work
4	Injury resulting in three or more consecutive days off work
5	Major injury requiring hospitalisation or resulting in death

indicating which departments, work groups, tasks or operations are over-represented in the database. Because some or all of the risk factors associated with each of the accidents will already be known, the risk assessors will be able to focus their remedial efforts (if the causes have not been addressed) to good effect. At the very least it could provide focused training opportunities for those new to conducting risk assessments.

Most organisational accident databases tend to be divided into categories under such headings as:

- Nature of injury (e.g. part of body injured and severity)
- Cause of injury, such as
  - contact with:
    — moving parts or materials on a machine
    — electricity
    — a harmful substance
  - being struck by moving or falling objects
  - exposure to
    — a harmful substance
    — fire
    — explosion
  - striking against something not moving
  - handling, lifting or carrying a load
  - slipping, tripping or falling on the same level

- falling from a height
- being trapped by something which has collapsed or overturned
- drowning or asphyxiation
- Type of equipment involved
- Work location
- Victim's occupation
- Immediate causes (e.g. unsafe behaviour).

Overall, these types of categorisation enable useful analyses of the actual hazards associated with specific tasks, the frequency with which they are involved in accidents, and the severity of outcomes due to the risk being realised. Typically, however, because these types of categorisation tend to lead to the belief that an accident or near miss has a single cause, they also make it difficult to analyse the underlying contributory causes. Because accidents and near misses tend to have multiple causes (see Chapters 1 and 9), additional categories focusing upon organisational features could also prove extremely useful for examining the underlying causes. In accordance with the views of Dr Alan Waring in his book on Safety Management Systems, these could and should be divided into safety management failures, technical failures and human error failures that encompass:

- safety management failures
  - safety management systems non-existent or defective
  - inadequate safety strategies (organisational or departmental)
  - inadequate safety policies (organisational, departmental, or functional (e.g. pressure systems))
  - inadequate management control
  - inadequate procedural controls
  - inadequate contractor controls
  - inadequate communications
  - inadequate training
  - conflicting system goals
- technical failures
  - engineering or process design
  - engineering construction
  - process operations
  - inadequate maintenance
  - protective devices inclusive of PPE
  - inadequate workplace design
- human error failures
  - unsafe acts
  - errors in recognition (displays and controls, etc.)

- errors in judgement
- operational errors (e.g. non adherence to standard operating procedures, etc.).

In relation to developing a safety culture, one immediate advantage offered by this categorisation of organisational features is that attention can be focused on those underlying causation factors related to the immediate, intermediate and ultimate levels of effort. Another advantage is that it explicitly forces accident investigators to take these categories into consideration. In the context of risk assessment in particular, the categories can be used to determine the weightings for the frequency, likelihood and severity components of risk formulae for these underlying contributory factors.

The following example, based on a study in the chemical industry, shows how this can be achieved. The researchers divided the accidents and near misses into 'hard' errors (i.e. technical failures) and 'soft' errors (safety management or human error failures). They then calculated the ratio of hard to soft errors. This revealed that overall, safety management or human error failures (soft) occurred one and a half times more frequently than technical failures (hard). Thus the *frequency* of 'soft' errors was one and a half times greater than the 'hard' errors. Further examination of the 'soft' errors revealed that almost twice the number of 'actual' accidents were related to safety management failures, whereas almost twice the number of near misses were related to human error failures. Thus the *likelihood* of a hazard being realised was twice as great for safety management failures as for human error failures (presumably because of the ability of people to recover from an error of judgement, etc.). This was determined by dividing the percentage of types of actual accident by the percentage of their related near misses (i.e. same causal factors), and multiplying the result by 100 to provide an 'index of realisation', i.e.:

$$\frac{\% \text{ of type of actual accident}}{\% \text{ of related near misses}} \times 100 = \text{index of realisation}$$

From the resulting index it became apparent that two safety management factors, inadequate communication of operational information and inadequate standard operating procedures, were high realisation factors. The human error failure most likely to be realised was shown to be errors of judgement. In this study the errors of judgement were related to ergonomic design issues: the installation arrangements for a large number of valves were confusing, because they were all of the same type and size, but were for functionally different purposes. The same formulae applied to the technical failures revealed that the main realisation factor was related to poor maintenance, which is once again related to a management system failure (demonstrating the interactive nature between safety management, human error and technical failures). In summary, based on the above examination, a risk assessor in this chemical plant would assign a greater *frequency* weighting to the 'soft' rather than 'hard' failures, and a greater *likelihood* weighting to safety management failures than human error failures. The *severity* weightings associated with each type of accident would be derived from an examination of the actual consequences (i.e. types of injury, costs of damage, etc.)

An example risk assessment.   The following risk assessment uses the example of a scaffold team (who are generally only paid for the amount of work they do) to show how risk formulae are applied using the scales outlined above. When the team are dismantling a scaffold, the assessor assumes that they will throw materials to the ground, because they are only paid for what they do, and past experience has shown that people will take short-cuts when rewarded for doing so (e.g. time saving). The frequency of throwing down materials was rated as *continuously* (4); the likelihood of harm to the labourer on the ground if something hit him was rated as *certain* (4), while the severity of injury if something hit the labourer was rated as *major* (5). The potential risk to the labourer from materials being thrown down during dismantling is therefore very high, i.e.

$$\text{Risk} = 4 \text{ (F)} \times 4 \text{ (L)} \times 5 \text{ (S)} = 80 \text{ out of a possible 80}$$

The rater then conducted an assessment based on the scaffolders' lowering the materials to the ground by passing the materials down through each of the scaffold platforms. However, the potential hazard changed to one of unsafe stacking of scaffold materials on each of the scaffold platforms as the material is passed down. Based on past experience the frequency was rated as *often* (2), the likelihood of harm if any material fell off and hit the labourer was rated as *certain* (4), and the severity of injury resulting from the falling material was rated as *major* (5). This gave a potential risk score to the labourer of falling materials as:

$$\text{Risk} = 2 \text{ (F)} \times 4 \text{ (L)} \times 5 \text{ (S)} \times 1 = 40 \text{ out of a possible 80}$$

Thus, although the potential risks were thought to be halved by lowering the materials through each of the scaffold platforms, it was still recognised that this carried certain risks. The rater then evaluated the risks involved in doing the job right by lowering the scaffold materials to the ground with a 'ginney wheel'. Again, however, potential risks were posed by the fact that materials would be 'tied off', which might slip through and fall. Based on experience, the frequency with which materials slipped from the rope was rated as *hardly ever* (1), the likelihood of harm if any material did slip and hit the labourer was rated as *certain* (4), while the potential resulting injury was again rated as *major* (5). The resulting potential risk score to the labourer of falling materials was again halved:

$$\text{Risk} = 1 \text{ (F)} \times 4 \text{ (L)} \times 5 \text{ (S)} \times 1 = 20 \text{ out of a possible 80}$$

The above examples illustrate the point that even if a job method is changed, certain other risks may be introduced and it is important that these new risks are also identified and assessed. It also demonstrates the precision that can be derived from using the frequency component. Because the likelihood and severity components have remained constant, no distinctions in risk would be made for doing the job the wrong or right way, regardless of the actual risks involved, if the frequency component had not been assessed and utilised.

Risk categorisation.   A risk score has little meaning if it is not compared to other risk scores, or placed within a band of risk scores. With the above categories, for example, the maximum potential risk score possible is 80. This could be split into four threshold bands, each comprising of a multiple of 20 to enable any remedial actions to be prioritised. These might be as shown in Table 4.2.

Table 4.2   Categorisation of Risk

Band	Risk score	Result
Band 1	(0–20)	No action required (No real risk attached)
Band 2	(21–40)	Some action required (low risk attached)
Band 3	(41–60)	Some control measures warranted (Some risks attached)
Band 4	(61–80)	Control measures vital (High risks attached)

As this banding classification shows, the higher a risk assessment score, the more there is a need for control measures to be put in place. Thus, these types of classification lend themselves to the development of some form of guide to help prioritise the importance given to a particular risk (see Figure 4.2: *Risk Prioritisation Bands*). These types of risk classification schemes can be applied to all forms of risk (e.g. communications failures), to help determine the need for control measures.

Date:	Risk Rating Score – Prioritisation Bands			
Assessor(s)	Band 4 (61–80)	Band 3 (41–60)	Band 2 (21–40)	Band 1 (01–20)
Activities assessed	Controls vital	Controls warranted	Some action required	No action required
Throwing down materials when striking scaffold	80			
Lowering materials through scaffold			40	
Lowering materials with ginney wheel				20

Figure 4.2   Risk Prioritisation Bands

RISK CONTROL MEASURES

Choosing and *implementing* the most appropriate risk control measure will determine the success or failure of the risk reduction effort. Unfortunately, regardless of the size and nature of organisations it is all too common for risks to be identified without the appropriate remedial actions being taken. For example, seven months after a world renowned soft drinks manufacturer conducted a risk assessment and became aware that a lack of guards on a palletising machine could cause someone a disabling or fatal injury, the spine of one of their machine operators was crushed. This person was severely injured simply because the company had failed to implement the appropriate control measures. Disregarding the potential compensation costs to the injured person, subsequent court fines and costs in the region of £12,000 demonstrate that on cost/benefit grounds alone it would have been less expensive to have fitted the appropriate machine guards. (Since the incident, the company has spent £1.9 million on safety improvements.) Numerous other examples of failure to implement the appropriate control measures abound in monthly safety practitioner journals. Which control measure(s) to put in place, however, is dependent upon the type of activity that has been assessed, how thoroughly it has been assessed, and the relevant legislation (e.g. COSHH, PUWER, etc.). Although risk control measures must satisfy the production needs of the organisation, the quality needs of the job and the health and safety needs of employees, the control measures for any type of risk are basically the same. In essence, based on the two principles of risk avoidance or risk reduction, there is a hierarchy of control (ASIRP) that should be employed. This is shown by Figure 4.3.

In accordance with this hierarchy of control the first efforts should be to avoid the risk altogether. If this is not possible, efforts should be made to combat the risk at source by substitution, and so on. Where possible therefore, the steps to be taken are as follows:

1. Eliminate the hazard altogether to avoid the risk (e.g. stop using a dangerous substance if it is not necessary)
2. Change the activity or process to one that is less harmful
3. Separate people from the hazard or limit the number of people exposed by enclosing or physically guarding the hazard
4. Design a safe system of work that reduces the risk to an acceptable level
5. Provide written procedural controls (e.g. standard operating procedures)
6. Provide adequate supervision
7. Identify training needs and provide training
8. Provide instructions/information (e.g. warning signs, visual/audible alerting signals)
9. Protect people by providing the appropriate PPE (this should always be the absolute last resort, not the first option as appears to be the case in many organisations)
10. Always re-evaluate the chosen option to see if the hazard (or aspects of it) can be eliminated.

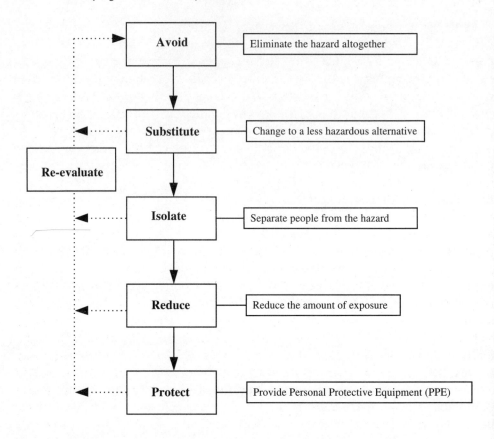

Figure 4.3   ASIRP Hierarchy of Control for Risks

In many instances, a combination of these control measures may need to be employed. Often, however, it is feasible that any number of alternative measures would reduce the risk. In these instances, the hierarchy of control should always be used as a guide to decide which measure to use, rather than pure economic cost/benefit considerations: i.e. eliminate the risk when-ever and wherever possible. Importantly, as pointed out by the Institution of Occupational Health and Safety (IOSH) the amount of managerial or supervisory effort needed to establish and maintain the above controls is in inverse rank order, i.e. the amount of effort needed to provide and ensure that people continuously wear the appropriate PPE (item 9), is infinitely greater than that required to eliminate the hazard altogether (item 1). Thus, the more an organisation provides PPE as a first rather than a last resort option, the more it is actually increasing its operational costs by minimising its manager's time for dealing with other organisational issues.

Control Measures Related to Organisational Policies and Practices

Given the importance assigned to the concept of risk management by many safety bodies (e.g. HSE, IOSH, British Safety Council, ROSPA, etc.), it is curious how silent these same bodies are about highlighting the need to develop control measures to minimise the risks caused by various organisational practices and policies. Incentive schemes that reward accident free periods are a case in point. Such schemes inevitably lead to the under-reporting of both minor and major accidents, and yet they abound in industry. Changing or adapting such policies and practices is an obvious organisational control measure. For example, providing incentives to report accidents would provide a much truer reflection of an organisation's safety problems, and enable the appropriate remedial actions to be taken. Such a change would also demonstrate the organisation's commitment to eliminating all its possible sources of risk. Similarly, other organisational control measures to reduce the likelihood of risk are related to the process of tendering for contracts. In the scaffold scenario, for example, the scaffold estimator could build the extra time required for safe dismantling into the tender price for the job. Although this might mean that the scaffold company is not awarded some contracts (because other scaffold contractors are not so concerned to ensure safe systems of work, and therefore offer a lower tender price), in the long run it could prove to be the most cost-effective option as it becomes known that the company is sufficiently concerned to provide a safe working environment for its employees and customers. In addition, the likelihood of increasing operational and insurance costs associated with accidents will be diminished. In essence, therefore, there appears to be a need to develop organisational risk control measures derived from an examination of the effects of all of an organisation's existing policies and practices. These examinations should be undertaken at the operational, tactical and strategic levels of an organisation (see Chapter 5). Moreover, it is important that the effects of these existing policies and practices be assessed both separately and in combination so that the interactions between various policies, at different organisational levels, can also be fully assessed.

Re-evaluating the Risks in Light of the Proposed Control Measures

Once a control measure has been proposed or put in place, a further risk assessment needs to be undertaken to ensure that:

- the original risks have indeed been reduced or eliminated
- no new risks have been introduced.

If the control measure satisfactorily addresses the situation, the next stage becomes one of documentation. If the control measure is found to be unsatisfactory, a further round of risk assessments to identify the appropriate control measure will be necessary. This makes the point that the risk assessment process is an iterative one. The exercise must be repeated until such time as it is impossible to reduce the risks any further.

Document the Risks

Although it is a legal requirement for organisations to record and document the significant findings of risk assessments if they employ five or more people, it makes good commercial sense to record them so that a check can be made that all of the organisation's activities have been assessed. It is not unknown, for example, for gaps in risk assessments to be discovered during the implementation of behavioural safety initiatives, i.e. assessments have been made of engineering tasks in workshops, but not for engineering tasks on a plant. However, discovery of these gaps can only be achieved if the records are kept. Again, for expediency, it is not unusual for daily permit to work procedures to be used as the only proof of compliance to the risk assessment requirements. Although the incorporation of on-the-spot risk assessments in permit to work procedures is laudable, these records tend to be discarded after about three months, resulting in the data being lost. Moreover, it is very difficult for such companies to know whether or not they have conducted risk assessments for all their activities. This often occurs in those companies which view the requirement for risk assessments as a bureaucratic burden. However, the advantages of keeping such records outweigh the perceived bureaucracy, as they can be used in many ways. For example, they can be used to:

- demonstrate to employees, board members, shareholders and statutory bodies (e.g. HSE) that the organisation is actually identifying, assessing and controlling risks
- identify or reinforce the need for capital expenditure to be allocated to control the risks
- reduce management's time during periodic reviews of risks
- identify safety training needs
- identify potential unsafe behaviours during the implementation of behavioural safety initiatives.

What Should be Documented?

A record of a risk assessment must include details of the measures chosen to eliminate or control the risks, and the reasons for choosing them. The record is focused primarily on the activities taking place, while taking into account any particular situational constraints, the risks posed and the solutions adopted to overcome them. IOSH recommend the documentation should specify:

- the activity, operation, location
- the hazards identified
- the adverse effects which the risks could have on people, plant and the environment
- the numbers of people at risk
- those groups of people especially at risk (e.g. pregnant women, young workers, etc.)
- serious and imminent risks
- the probability of harm and realistic worst case outcomes (e.g. major injury, death, etc.)
- any relevant health and safety information required by people (e.g. warning signs, visual and audible alerting signals, etc.)
- any additional training needs
- references to existing controls, and their quality
- remedial actions required in order of priority
- a firm time scale for action
- allocation of responsibility for completion of the remedial actions.

There is also a strong case for including the associated organisational policies or practices that have been identified as being associated with the creation of hazards, or reinforcement of risk-taking behaviour. In particular, the form should contain the assessors' names, their job titles and the date the assessment was undertaken. Figure 4.4 provides an example of a risk assessment pro forma.

Risk assessment documentation should always be readily accessible to those people who need to see it. Dedicated risk assessment 'software' now on the market makes access to risk assessment information very easy for numerous people in an organisation. It also eases the administrative burden. Even without such software, a good organisational safety management information system should overcome these types of problem (see Chapter 5).

Reviewing Existing Control Measures

Once risk control measures are put in place, they need to be periodically reviewed (e.g. every 24 months) and updated, so that any changes in circumstances can be accommodated (this requirement emphasises the need

Ref No:	Date:	Location:
Name(s) of assessor(s):		Job titles

Activity assessed (task, job or operation):

Hazard(s) identified:

Potential risks arising from identified hazard(s):

Frequency of exposure to risk(s):	Likelihood of harm if risk(s) realised:
0 Never 1 Hardly ever 2 Often 3 Very often 4 Continuously	0 Extremely unlikely 1 Unlikely 2 Likely 3 Extremely likely 4 Certain
Severity of consequences if risk(s) realised:	Numbers of people exposed to risk(s):
0 No Harm 1 Minor injury (no medical attention) 2 Minor injury (medical attention) 3 Injury (1–3 days off work) 4 Injury (3 days or more) 5 Major injury (hospitalisation or death)	Risk Rating = ____ •Band 1 (0–20) No action required Band 2 (21–40) Some action required Band 3 (41–60) Control measures warranted Band 4 (61–80) Control measures vital

Existing control measure(s):	Adequate: Yes No

Recommendations for remedial actions:

By whom:	By when: Completed: Y N	Review date:

Figure 4.4   Example of Risk Assessment Pro Forma

to record every risk assessment). The timing of these reviews may be dictated by a number of circumstances, including:

- the occurrence of accidents or near miss incidents
- addressing any recommendations arising from safety audits or inspections
- receiving safety suggestions or complaints from employees and others
- receiving updated safety information from suppliers
- the introduction of new equipment or materials
- planning and installing new plant and equipment
- planning and introducing new working methods
- the introduction of amendments to existing legislation
- the introduction of new legislation.

IOSH recommend that these reviews are best achieved by using a combination of methods, such as:

- preventive maintenance inspections
- safety committee/representative inspections
- statutory maintenance inspections, tests and examinations
- managerial/supervisory safety tours and inspections
- occupational health surveys
- safety audits (see Chapter 6).

Whatever remedial actions arise from these reviews, it is essential to ensure that they are put into effect. This is normally best achieved by allocating the responsibility to a named person, who must complete the task within a specified time scale. However, there is still a need for checks to be made that the named person has actually completed the remedial actions by the due date.

Section Two

The intermediate level of effort

5

Integrating Management Information Systems

INTRODUCTION

Having established a solid foundation on which to build a positive safety culture by analysing and restructuring people's jobs, production processes and the working environment, the next stage is to implement the *intermediate* level of effort. This is concerned with developing management information systems to provide reporting, monitoring, and feedback mechanisms to facilitate organisational learning, error correcting, problem-solving, decision-making and forward planning.

It is important to establish what is meant in this context by 'management' 'information' and 'system'. In essence, 'management' refers to the planning, organising, directing and controlling of people or 'things' to achieve a desired end state or goal. 'Information' refers to knowledge that is processed and understood, while 'system' refers to an 'organised whole'. A Management Information System (MIS), therefore, refers to *'knowledge that is organised into a structured whole which is used to control an organisation's ongoing activities'*. This has obvious implications for all areas of an organisation's functioning, including health and safety. For example, if information covering all aspects of the organisation's functioning is not readily available, the organisation's goals (e.g. creating a positive safety culture) will be very difficult to achieve, simply because the means for establishing and maintaining effective controls will either be non-existent or extremely limited. A MIS, therefore, can be viewed as the *nerve centre* of any type of business or organisation.

MANAGEMENT CONTROL MECHANISMS

Companies that successfully manage health and safety (and other operational areas) tend to be those that place a heavy emphasis on controlling their safety activities. However, effective managerial control (in any sphere of activity) is heavily dependent on:

- setting standards and goals
- evaluating ongoing performance against these standards and goals
- taking corrective action if performance is lower than the desired standards or goals
- rewarding people, business units, etc., for performance that exceeds the desired goals.

In essence, therefore, good management control is *the* essential ingredient of continuing success, the principles of which should be applied at all levels of a business, in every sphere of its activity. Because every employee has to perform well to contribute to the organisation's aims, management exerts control by setting performance targets or goals for individual employees, work groups, departments and business units. These performance targets form the basis for assessing ongoing performance, as they provide the benchmark for comparing actual performance in order to discover whether or not expectations are being met. In relation to safety culture, example performance targets may include:

- a specified reduction in accident rates for a department or business unit over a three year period
- all line managers to attend and pass a safety training course (e.g. National Examination Board in Occupational Safety and Health (NEBOSH) Certificate or Diploma within two years
- all employees to personally undertake and complete an annual safety project
- every member of the senior management team to conduct a safety tour once a month
- every safety representative to conduct a weekly toolbox talk with their respective work groups.

Setting Organisational Performance Targets

Whichever type of performance target is set, it must be clearly expressed, measurable in some way, with responsibility and accountability attached, realistic and achievable, with a deadline for completion. An easily remembered acronym for setting performance targets is SMART:

Specific	—	clearly and precisely defined
Measurable	—	so that levels of performance can be monitored and assessed

Agreed	—	with those responsible and accountable for achievement
Realistic	—	achievable but also difficult
Time bound	—	deadlines for achievement.

Specific

Because specific performance targets or goals (e.g. conduct a weekly safety tour) remove any doubt as to what is expected, they are much better than non-specific goals (e.g. improve safety) which allow people to interpret the effectiveness of their performance against a multitude of performance indicators. A goal, therefore, needs to be clearly and precisely defined.

Measurable

It follows that, to know how well people are achieving their target or goal, there has to be a corresponding means of measuring their performance so that feedback about the rate of progress can be provided. Although each has its own advantages and disadvantages, some of the most common safety performance measures include:

- accident statistics
- number of near miss incidents
- number of accident-free days
- accident costs
- safety audit scores
- number of safety inspections
- number of employees safety trained
- number of senior management safety tours
- levels of employees' safety behaviour
- safety attitude survey scores (safety climate)
- benchmarking.

Although some goals can be easily quantified and monitored (e.g. conduct chest x-rays for every employee within 12 months), other goals are less easy to quantify as they are a mixture of fact and opinion (e.g. creating an identifiable safety culture) and are, therefore, *subjective*. Nonetheless, subjective goals can be quantified by using rating systems. For example, a scale of 1 to 6 which ranges from 'alarming' to 'excellent' could be used to represent an organisation's current levels of safety climate, although great care is needed when devising these types of scale (see Chapter 8).

Agreed

If people are to become committed to a goal or target, it is important to gain the agreement of those responsible and accountable for actually achieving it. Research conducted by the author and colleagues in the construction industry, for example, has shown that imposing a safety-related goal or target on people serves as a de-motivator which may lead to them rejecting it. Agreeing a goal with those responsible for implementation also enables potential obstacles to goal achievement to be clarified, identifies the best strategy for overcoming any obstacles, and indicates the resources which may be needed to maximise the goal's achievement.

Realistic

The main aim of a target or goal is to place sufficient demands and challenges on people in order to motivate them to achieve higher levels of performance. The degree of challenge represented by the goals will determine the amount of effort that people are willing to exert to achieve that goal: i.e. the greater the challenge, the more people will exert effort (assuming they agree with the goal and are committed to achieving it). However, people will be reluctant to attempt to achieve a target or goal that they think is unrealistic or impossible to achieve, such as zero accidents in the workplace, or 100% safety perform-ance, and this is a further reason for agreeing a target or goal with those charged with implementation. Thus a goal needs to represent a challenge, while also remaining realistic and achievable.

Time Bound

Setting a deadline for the achievement of an organisation's targets or goals is in one sense a goal in itself. It focuses people's attention and actions, and mobilises their efforts so that the aims of the goals are achieved within the specified time. The time frame for goal achievement also has important implications for management control because some targets or goals (e.g. developing an identifiable safety culture) will only be achieved over the longer term. In essence, these longer term goals tend to be *strategic* simply because they are forward looking and directional (see Chapter 2). As such they imply that many resources (financial, human and time) will be directed at ensuring their achievement simply because the directional element tends to have significant implications for the organisation as a whole. *Tactical* goals are those set for the short to medium term (e.g. examining existing systems to identify structural problems; conducting job analyses and risk assess-ments, sending every line manager on a safety training course within two years). They tend to be co-ordinated and interdependent, and in combination

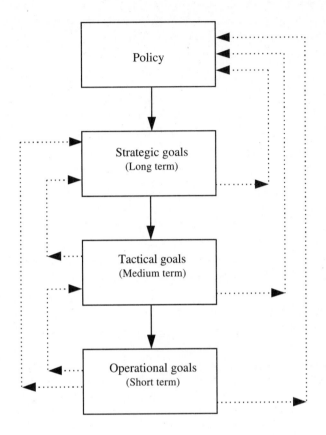

Figure 5.1   Hierarchy of Organisational Goals

will help to achieve the organisation's strategic goals. Similarly, although more concerned with the organisation's day-to-day activities (for example, safely achieving production goals, safety representatives conducting weekly toolbox talks, etc.), *operational* goals are specifically designed to support the achievement of the organisation's tactical and strategic goals. Thus, it is possible for combinations of different kinds of goal to be set, depending upon what needs to be improved and what is to be monitored.

These different types of goal, and the causal relationships between them, are illustrated in the hierarchy of organisational goals presented in Figure 5.1: *Hierarchy of Organisational Goals*. An important practical feature of this hierarchy is that the time frame for strategic goals will be longer than that for tactical goals, which in turn will be longer than that for operational goals. Accordingly, because organisations tend to be more successful at goal achievement if they give higher priority to those short-term goals that are linked to longer term goals, the emphasis for earlier goal achievement should first be placed on the operational goals, then the tactical goals, and then the strategic goals. In this way, the organisation is more likely to achieve its goals at all three levels without creating unnecessary conflicts between them as, for example, might be caused by them all falling 'due' at the same.

This also highlights the importance of ensuring that the actual goals set for each level in the hierarchy (i.e. strategic, tactical and operational) are aligned with and consistent with each other. Thus, checks should be made to ensure that the organisation's strategic goals (e.g. 'achieve a balanced risk-reducing interaction between people, our production processes and the working environment') are aligned with, and consistent with, the specific organisational policy (e.g. develop a positive safety culture). In turn the tactical goals (e.g. conducting job analyses and risk assessments, examining workgroup communications, etc.), should be consistent with the organisation's strategic goals *and* the specific organisational policy. Similarly, the operational goals (e.g. 'conduct safety audits and inspections') should be checked to ensure they are consistent with both the tactical and strategic goals and the organisational policy that the goals have been set to achieve.

Types of Monitoring Activity

Setting strategic, tactical and operational goals also has important implications for the development of information systems, simply because they determine the type of monitoring activity and the type of evaluative information that is generated at each level. As shown in Figure 5.2: *Goal-related Monitoring Activities and Types of Evaluative Information Generated.* Different types of monitoring activities are:

- Pre-monitoring   — feedforward control
- Live monitoring — concurrent control
- Post-monitoring — feedback control

Pre-monitoring or feedforward control is used to anticipate potential problems so as to avoid future problems (e.g. using forcefield analysis to identify problems before implementing a strategic plan). Although it is impossible to evaluate actual performance because it has not yet happened, *pre*-monitoring tends to focus on the resources and types of activity needed to achieve a goal, or to identify potential problems in the wider environment (e.g. forthcoming legislation). Live monitoring provides information about what is actually happening on a day-to-day basis in relation to goal-achievement, whereas *post*-monitoring provides information about what actually happened (i.e. whether or not the goal was reached). Thus, each type of monitoring activity provides different evaluative information.

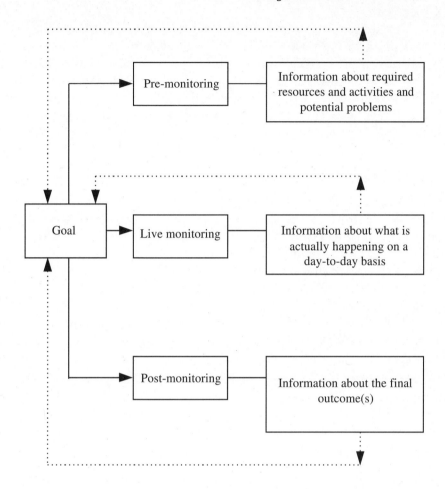

Figure 5.2   Goal-related Monitoring Activities and Types of Evaluative Information Generated

Strategic Goals and Example Monitoring Activities

In relation to strategic goals, an example of a pre-monitoring activity would be an organisation intending to build a new liquid petroleum gas plant, which identifies and invites tenders from only those contractor companies which already have excellent proven health and safety systems. During the construction phase, live monitoring of the wider environment (e.g. forthcoming EC legislation) might indicate that new safety regulations are to be applied to liquid petroleum storage vessels. This would enable the organisation to modify the construction of its storage vessels to meet the new safety requirements, thereby saving the considerable costs associated with post-construction modifications. Post-monitoring of the number of accidents or near misses during the construction project would show the efficacy of the employing organisation's policy of only contracting companies with proven health and safety systems. If the accident rate were minimal, the contractor would be considered for future projects; if the accident rate was very poor the contractor company would not be invited to tender again. This latter point illustrates the difficulties associated with post-monitoring at the strategic level: the success of the strategy is known only after the event because the strategic level is heavily dependent on long term objectives.

Tactical Goals and Example Monitoring Activities

Pre-monitoring activity in relation to tactical goals is similar to that for the strategic goals, with the aim being to minimise the possibility that the goals will not be met. For example, if every line manager were required to attend and pass a NEBOSH safety training course within two years, pre-monitoring activity would concern finding a suitable course provider who could tailor the course to suit the organisation's needs. Live monitoring would entail monitoring the performance of the course provider to ensure the course content satisfied the company's needs, that line managers are actually attending the course, that the administrative arrangements are satisfactory, etc. Post-monitoring on the other hand, might, for example, focus on the number of line managers who actually passed the course compared to the number who attended. If 20% or more failed to pass the course, the organisation would try to discover why.

Operational Goals and Example Monitoring Activities

Pre-monitoring in relation to operational goals would concern ensuring that the conditions were right for goal achievement. For example, if a behavioural safety initiative were required to address unsafe behaviour, the organisation would either look in the market place for a suitable expert, buy in an 'off the shelf' programme, or develop its own initiative. In any event it would need to be clear about which unsafe behaviours to focus on, how to develop appropriate monitoring instruments, how to select and train people in their use, and how to set appropriate safety improvement targets. Live monitoring would focus on how people were behaving on a daily basis, and identifying resident 'pathogens' in the working environment, while post-monitoring would focus on each work group's weekly performance so that feedback could be given at team briefings.

Pre-monitoring, therefore, is used to guide management's choices by seeking information with which to evaluate possible alternatives ahead of time. On the other hand, live monitoring is concerned with providing information that can be used to guide ongoing progress towards goal achievement so that it is possible to influence the final outcome, whereas post-monitoring provides information about the outcomes of goal-directed activity, which can be used to modify the next cycle of activity. It follows, therefore, that good management control is heavily dependent upon the supply of good information.

INFORMATION REQUIREMENTS

The information *output* produced by the monitoring activities outlined above is the essential ingredient for both evaluative and control purposes, as it provides the *input* to managerial decision-making (see Chapter 2). However, knowing what to monitor, and what to do with the resulting information is dependent upon *knowing what information is important for the decision-making process*. Which information is deemed to be important depends on its relevance to:

- the type of person who needs it
- the person's position or work group's role in the organisation
- the decisions or actions that might depend on it
- those who have the power and influence to change things.

Relevance To Those Who Need It

The relevance of information to the user is usually context dependent. This means that there is not much point in giving a bakery marketing manager information concerning the health and safety requirements of welding. Although the marketing manager may find it interesting, it does not count as information since it is not relevant to his or her job. Similarly, because large amounts of irrelevant information will hinder, rather than help, someone to make the appropriate decisions to achieve their goals, it makes sense to identify people's specific information needs as far as is possible.

Relevance to a Person's Position

A senior manager's information needs will differ to those of a line manager, whose information needs in turn will differ from the people under his or her control. Consequently, each organisational level needs to receive the right amount and types of information to enable them to do their job properly. Senior managers, for example, tend to require summary details of the company's ongoing accident rates to decide on the future allocation of resources to the safety function, whereas a line manager needs detailed information about the workflow processes causing accidents so that the work can be restructured, while operatives need information about how to overcome the immediate problems presented by the accident-causing process. Giving each of these people too little or too much information could result in its significance being lost, which means that it will not influence any decision-making processes and defeat its original purpose.

Relevance to the Decisions or Actions That Might Depend On It

As the above indicates, the quality of any information should be judged by how useful it is in helping people to arrive at a decision. This means that information has to be communicated in a user friendly format. The way that information is structured and presented will determine its overall significance and meaning to the end user. This can be illustrated by accident reports which contain columns and rows for entering victims' names, their works number, where the accident took place, what the person was doing, and the type of injury sustained. Any entries on the form (such as the name and number, the workplace area and the type of injury) will probably be different for each person. Were this raw data to be presented to senior managers 'as is' it would not help their decision-making as they would have to try and make sense of it all. Although the data may be helpful to the safety manager, he or she would need to extract trends from it (for example, the number of accident victims associated with particular work areas, and the associated types of injury) if the information were to help senior management realise the importance of taking remedial actions to improve the work areas concerned.

The Data, Information and Knowledge Relationship

The accident reports, for example, also illustrate the difference between data and information. While data consists of detailed facts and figures, information is more about knowledge extracted from the facts. In a sense, therefore, any management information system can be viewed as a type of 'processing factory' that takes raw data and transforms it into a product called information which is subsequently used to communicate 'knowledge' between various organisational functions and hierarchical levels. It follows from this that knowledge is also a means of clarification to reduce uncertainty and increase control. For example, knowing the specific outcomes of a pilot safety improvement activity (for example, implementing a behavioural safety initiative) will enable a manager to evaluate its effectiveness, thus clarifying his or her future goals (i.e. whether to continue, to adapt, or to discontinue the behavioural safety initiative) and the means to achieve them. Accordingly, the ability to instantly extract knowledge from an information system and communicate it widely will, in many cases, determine the overall effectiveness of the organisation's efforts to achieve its goals. Information, however, does not just suddenly become available out of 'thin air'. Its availability is generally dependent upon a formally organised means of obtaining, storing, extracting and communicating information or knowledge. Such systems may be computerised, manual or partially both. Nonetheless, the effectiveness and efficiency of any management information system is usually judged by its *ability to assemble data in a format required by the user, so that the right information can be extracted at the right time.*

The HSE's four Cs of control, co-operation, communication and competence could also be used to assess the efficiency and effectiveness of a management information system. Control, for example, comes into play because any information system is a sub system of a control system, which is a sub system of a management system (See Figure 5.3: *Hierarchy of Management, Control and Information Systems.*) Similarly, co-ordination is required between the information, control and management systems to ensure that the right information is communicated to the right people at the right time, all of which is dependent upon the competence and integrity of mechanisms such as computerised information databases, filing archives and libraries used to store and interrogate data to provide useful information.

Relevance to Those Who Have the Power and Influence to Change Things

Because managers tend to be the people who need the information, it becomes very important for them to be deeply involved in the design, development and operation of such information systems. Again, good information management requires a recognition of the role that management policy and values play in determining the relationship between *how* an information system is implemented and *what* it can produce or achieve, i.e. the organisation's goals will define the role of the information system. Similarly, one of the major functions of management is to determine an organisation's structure to meet its business goals. Given that the organisation's structure influences the structure of information systems, management need to be involved to ensure that any organisational changes are reflected in the corresponding information systems. The more complex the organisation's design, the more complex the information system(s) will need to be (the failure of many organisational culture improvement initiatives result from a failure to change the corresponding information systems). Since the goal of a management information system is to deliver useable information

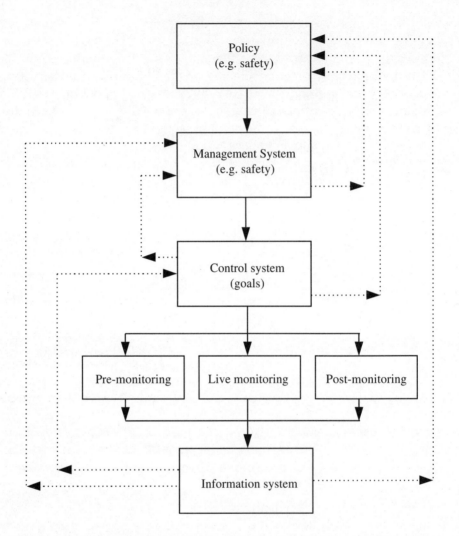

Figure 5.3   Hierarchy of Management, Control and Information Systems – Adapted from Harry, M.
(1995) 'Information Management', in T. Hannagan (1995) Management: Concepts & Practices. Pitmar
Publishing, pp. 447–480. Reprinted by permission

or knowledge to enable an organisation to achieve its operational goals, i
follows that such a system is only as good as the information it provides
Thus developing such a system is dependent upon asking the right questions
within the context of the organisation's specific requirements, such as:

- What kind of information is *needed* by whom and when?
- What kind of information is *wanted* by whom and when?
- What type of decision-making will the information support?
- How quickly is the information needed?

- How quickly will the information be out of date?
- Are there better ways of obtaining information?
- How will the data be stored and processed?
- What information systems are already in use?
- Can existing information systems be better used or adapted?

What Kind of Information is Needed?

Questions concerned with *what* kind of information is needed by whom and when force system designers to define the system's scope and boundaries by identifying which work groups, departments and functions will be involved in various decision-making processes at various organisational levels. It also forces them to consider how the information should be tailored, packaged and delivered to each type of user, where the appropriate sources of data and information reside, and how they might be obtained.

What Kind of Information is Wanted?

Questions revolving around what sort of information is *wanted* by whom and when allows the designers to discover what the ideal information system might look like. These information 'wants' can then be compared to people's information needs, to assess the feasibility of delivering them within existing budgetary and system constraints. Nonetheless, to keep the development and operational costs of the information system under control, it is important to help people to clarify the 'wants' in terms of asking what information they *must* have, what would be *useful* to have and what would be *nice* to have. In all cases, the criteria for assessing the 'wants' should be the impact the information will exert on aiding people's decision-making, not the person's status or position in the organisation.

What Type of Decision-making Will the Information Support?

Questions aimed at discovering the types of decision which the information will support should reflect strategic, tactical and operational decision-making concerns. For example, strategic decision-making will require information from external sources (such as HSE or EC) as well as summary information, such as production trends and accident rates, about the organisation's ongoing performance from internal sources. Information requirements for tactical decisions have implications for the speed with which information is delivered to the user, the level of detail required, and the interrelationships between various pieces of data that might be required by all the organisation's departments or functions. Similarly, consideration needs to be given to the types of information that will assist in everyday operational decisions, and how these can be delivered to the end user at the time that it is needed.

How Quickly is the Information Needed?

Questions aimed at discovering the speed with which information is required has resourcing and cost implications. For example, because operational decisions nearly always have to be made immediately, how is the information to be provided? Alternatives might include the use of personal computers (perhaps linked to a network) or a dedicated telephone 'helpline' to enable specific information to be requested from company libraries or company archives. If the information is to be accessed via personal computers consideration will also need to be given to the numbers required, their specification, the provision of peripherals such as modems, printers, etc., and the total costs involved. If information is requested from libraries or archives, consideration has to be given to the costs of information supply, storage, staffing, telephone systems, etc.

How Quickly Will the Information be Out of Date?

Questions concerning how quickly information will be out of date should again revolve around the organisation's strategic, tactical and operational goals. Because of the storage implications, consideration should be given to the speed with which information is needed, and the most efficient means of accessing it. Again, these considerations are useful because they force the system's designers to prioritise and provide structure to the information flow.

Are There Better Ways of Obtaining Information?

In some organisations, it is common to find the same or similar information being presented on different forms within the same department. Some information may also come from verbal reports, or paper and pencil recordings derived from physical inspections (for example, reading a gauge). Consideration therefore needs to be given to the possibility that there might be better ways of obtaining and presenting this information.

How Will the Data be Stored and Processed?

A number of practical questions also need to be asked about how the information will be entered into the system, stored, processed, extracted from the system and moved around the organisation. The main issues in relation to entering data into a system will concern the technology to be used, the number of access points, the numbers of people that might be required to enter data at the same time, and the associated staffing requirements. Extracting information from a system might include considering the use of computer monitors, printers and the associated peripherals such as ink ribbons or cartridges and paper, or manual searches through filing systems by experienced staff, each of which has cost implications. Storage can include filing cabinets, manuals on shelves, company archives or libraries, or using modern technology such as databases, CD-Roms, floppy disks, tapestreamers, etc. Each of these should be able to cope with the addition of further information and with the maximum amount of data which might be required in the future, so decisions will need to be made about what needs to be stored, and for how long. Information processing issues will be concerned with the system's integrity when a number of people wish to use it at the same time, and in terms of what happens when the system is actually accessed by large numbers of people who all extract information at the same time. In terms of moving data around to ensure that the right information is given to the right person at the right time, consideration needs to be given to the feasibility of telecommunication links, computerised networks and staffing.

What Information Systems are Already in Use and Can They be Better Used or Adapted?

Given that good management control is heavily dependent upon good information, it is possible for an organisation to compare its existing information system with the above requirements as an integrity check. Many organisations experience communication problems simply because they have not given sufficient thought to their information requirements. At the very least, an examination of these issues will pinpoint where the organisation might adapt or improve its existing system. Although there will always be tensions between what is required and what is wanted, if the organisation's existing system is found to be less than adequate the appropriate remedial actions can be taken. The senior management team's commitment to this process is vital simply because of the time and cost implications.

SYSTEM CHARACTERISTICS

A system can be viewed in many ways depending upon the context in which it is used. Although there is no single definition of the word 'system', it is often taken to mean an 'organised whole' containing a number of *inter-connected* components (such as people, plant, factory) each of which *interacts* in an organised way to *transform* something (such as raw materials) into an identifiable *property* (product). The basic characteristics of a system can be summarised as follows:

- It is an assembly of objective (i.e. physical) and subjective (e.g. informational) components that are organised into a coherent whole.
- The components are structured to achieve an identifiable purpose.
- The system produces or affects something.
- Each component is affected by changes in other components, or changes in the system's functioning.
- The system has a boundary: internal components are within the system's control, but the system cannot control anything beyond its external boundaries even though it is influenced by these external forces.

System Structures

It is important to recognise that a hierarchical structure is found in some form or other in *every* system. Systems may, therefore, be viewed as structured, nested hierarchies. This is because they have sub systems that share the same basic characteristics as the system as a whole. For example, as illustrated in Figure 5.3 which showed the relationships between information, control and management systems, the purpose of each sub system is to help the next higher system reach its goal, and so on. As such, the whole will always be more than the sum of its parts. In practical terms, thinking of systems as nested hierarchies can help to unravel their complexity. This is achieved by identifying the boundaries of each system component and its associated sub systems. When it is no longer possible to break a system down into any more meaningful components, the limits or boundaries of the system and its sub systems will have been identified. In turn, this helps to generate questions about how effectively the system is functioning. The answers to these can be used to design an information system that accurately mirrors the organisation's activities. The safety management system illustrated in Figure 5.4, for example, could be used to generate questions about:

- whether or not the organisation has a health and safety policy
- how health and safety is currently organised
- how effective people, departments or business units are at planning for health and safety
- whether or not any problems (such as allocation of resources) surround implementation of these plans
- whether or not the means used to measure safety performance are adequate

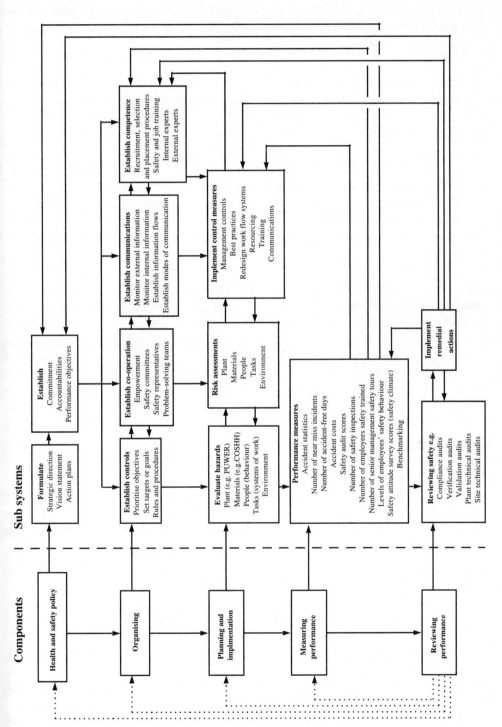

Figure 5.4 An Example Safety Management System

- how the information generated by the performance measures is used
- the methods used to review the functioning of the system.

Vertical and Horizontal Relationships

Figure 5.4 shows that there are likely to be *vertical* and *horizontal* relationships between the various sub systems of the overall system (which is why the HSE recommends both vertical and horizontal auditing of safety management systems). Vertical relationships refer to the hierarchical nature of systems and their associated sub systems. The vertical relationship is established by focusing upon the 'nodes' where each system or sub system joins another in the hierarchy. For example, a node exists where the organisation's health and safety policy is used to develop the organising system (i.e. establish controls, co-operation, communications and competence), which is then used as the basis for developing the planning and implementation system, and so on. Horizontal relationships refer to those where there may be a linear relationship between different systems and sub systems at the same level within the same overall system. These horizontal relationships reveal themselves at the 'node' where one system joins another. In most cases, horizontal relationships occur because the output of one system (such as risk assessment) provides the input for another system or sub system (such as developing a safe working method).

Depth Relationships

Where a system or sub system shares a resource (person, process, computer, vehicle, etc.) with another system, there is a *depth* relationship. In practice, this often means that systems or sub systems that share depth relationships have to compete with each other for the use of the very same resources. In turn this may lead to potential conflicts that may only be resolved by giving priority to one system over the other. This is illustrated in Figure 5.5: *System's Analyses for Issuing a Hot Permit to Work*. The actual conflicts identified are a result of the safety and productivity systems sharing two resources: the supervisor himself and the supervisor's time.

Emergent properties. A conflict emanating from a shared system resource can be described as an *emergent* property, which may or may not be predictable or desirable. Every system has its own emergent properties. In the main these properties are expected to result in gain(s) (for example, the hot permit to work illustrated in Figure 5.5), but it is often difficult to know what might result from a system's design until some time after it has been set up. Many accidents, for example, can be traced to people using their own initiative when attempting to cope with something that has gone wrong within a particular workflow system. Similarly, negative emergent properties could arise from the optimisation of a single sub system without giving due regard to its effect on other parts of the system. Many companies issue corporate health and safety policies stressing the utmost importance of safety (optimisation) without increasing the safety budget while, at the same time, stressing the importance of increasing shareholder return on investment. This often leads to the situation where line managers no longer take the policy at its word, and shut down an unsafe production plant simply because they fear dismissal or other sanctions (although they also tend to be the scapegoat when things go wrong). On the other hand, operatives tend to apply severe upwards pressure to get health and safety problems rectified in accordance with the espoused policy. Being squeezed from both the senior levels and the bottom of the organisation places the line managers under extreme stress on a daily basis, which can have negative knock-on effects on their performance. In other words, many companies optimise their health and safety policy without considering its knock-on effects on other systems (e.g. production) or people (e.g. line managers). In practical terms, this means that efforts must be taken to assess the likely impact (i.e. the effects of emergent properties) of optimising a single sub system on other systems or sub systems, *prior* to actual optimisation (forcefield analyses discussed in Chapter 3 may be appropriate here).

Environmental Disturbances

In a sense, the impact that one system has on another system can be viewed as an environmental disturbance which can create uncertainty and/or instability. This is again illustrated in Figure 5.5. The supervisor's absence is causing both uncertainty and instability in the production system because he or she cannot complete the shift handover until such time as the hot permit to work has been issued. Given that the stability of a system is dependent upon its ability to control these environmental disturbances, a system must also have the ability to monitor and respond to any changes which might affect it (such as re-assign the timing of permit issuing until such time as the shift handover is complete). However, the system's ability to monitor and respond to changes is dependent upon the frequency with which the environment is monitored and feedback is obtained. Behavioural safety systems, for example, would not work without frequent observations (monitoring) of actual safety behaviour, as it would be impossible to provide work groups with information about their ongoing levels of safety performance (feedback), so they can assess their ongoing progress and adapt to the changing circumstances (control).

150

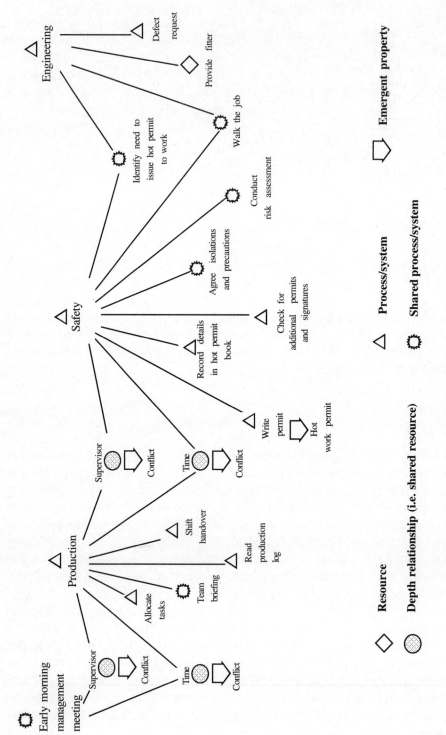

Figure 5.5 System's Analyses for Issuing a Hot Permit to Work

Monitoring Frequency

The optimal levels of monitoring frequency are usually determined by balancing the costs of monitoring against the costs of any errors emanating from a failure to monitor. The costs of monitoring are normally associated with implementing the control system itself (for example, the amount of time taken and the resources used to issue a hot permit to work). The costs of errors are made up of the costs (human and financial) associated with a system's failure to achieve its goals (a failure to issue a hot permit to work could cause a serious incident). The more frequently a system is monitored, the higher the costs of monitoring will be. Conversely, less frequent monitoring could lead to greater costs of errors. Thus, depending upon the importance of the system or sub system in relation to the whole, the optimum balance tends to reside somewhere between these two extremes.

Real time or batch processing?   Since the purpose of an information system is to monitor the organisation's activities and the external environment (such as pre-monitoring of market trends, forthcoming legislation, etc.) each information system and associated sub systems will inevitably have their own in-built monitoring costs and costs of errors. These can often be determined by assessing whether or not the information system is dependent on 'real time' or 'batch' processing. Real time processing refers to situations where any changes in the state of a system are immediately reflected in the information stored about the state of the system (for example, behavioural safety observation data is converted into a safety percentage score and knowledge of the results given to the work groups each time an observation is carried out). Batch processing, on the other hand, refers to the monitoring, recording and storing of information for a period of time, before information is provided (for example, behavioural safety observation data is collected each day, but allowed to accumulate over a week before being converted into a safety percentage score). Because real time processing requires a greater frequency of monitoring, it will incur higher monitoring costs than batch processing information systems. Conversely, batch processing could incur greater costs of errors because of the time-lag between the information collection (input) and the dissemination of the results (output).

Although much of the above may seem removed from the real world, the issues discussed provide a useful framework to help build up an overall picture of the structure of an organisation's existing information systems. By breaking these systems down into smaller manageable parts to clarify the relationships and interrelationships between them, and identifying each system's emergent properties, it becomes possible to map out an ideal information system.

DEVELOPING AN INTEGRATED MANAGEMENT INFORMATION SYSTEM

As any information system is a sub system of a control system, which in and of itself is a sub system of a management system, the only way a business can develop its goal-related control mechanisms (such as a safety management system) and monitor its ongoing goal-related performance (such as safety performance), is to structure the appropriate information systems (for example, safety management information system) to connect the control and monitoring mechanisms together to provide an organised whole. Initially this requires an analysis of the organisation's existing information, control and management systems by:

- identifying the components of each system
- identifying the boundaries of each system
- examining the purpose of each component
- comparing the system's output with the system's purpose
- mapping out an ideal information system.

Identifying System Components

Unravelling all these systems to develop the ideal information system begins with the pinpointing and defining of all its individual components. As stated earlier, a component can be objective or subjective. 'Objective components' refers to physical entities such as factories, office blocks, functional departments (such as accounts, personnel, safety), physical work equipment (such as computers, bulldozers), raw product materials, etc. 'Subjective components' includes data, information, organisational goals, interrelationships between departments, people, etc. It is the way that these components are organised into a whole that determines the effectiveness of a system. Historically, for example, the safety department was a separate function with full responsibility for an organisation's safety performance. In many instances, partly because of a lack of status and authority, and partly because of an over-reliance on safety training, the safety function tended to have little effect on an organisation's safety performance. Legislation in 1992 that *explicitly* required the integration of safety into the line management function has forced many companies to reorganise their safety management systems. The impact that this system change has had on annual accident rates in recent years testifies to its effectiveness.

Identifying System Boundaries

Since each system has a boundary within which it can control its various components, it is advisable to identify the limits of these boundaries so that each system and associated sub system can be clearly differentiated. For example, production and maintenance systems are clearly linked, but they are separate systems in their own right. Often this differentiation between systems will identify misplaced boundaries that are causing co-ordination, communication and scheduling problems which in turn can lead to role ambiguity (i.e. people not being clear about what their job entails or about how much authority they have), unsafe working systems, poor quality services or products, and/or low levels of productivity.

Examining the Purpose of Each Component

Once each component has been identified, its reasons for existing and its purposes should also be examined and recorded from all its users' perspectives (e.g. engineers, technicians, managers, safety personnel, etc.). Safety management systems, for example, are supposed to be designed to achieve and maintain high standards of safety performance. Depending upon the perspective taken, however, the purpose of a safety management system may be seen in different ways. If, for example, it is thought to be a system that is designed to merely deliver safety training and personal protective equipment, the system components will be geared up to meet these perceived demands. Alternatively, if it is believed that such a system should deliver an organisation-wide integrated strategy to improve safety by, for example, following the HSE's guidance on organising, planning, implementing and reviewing safety performance, the system will comprise many components and sub systems. Thus, people's beliefs about the purpose of a system and its reasons for being will differ depending upon their views on the importance of the system, their particular specialism, and how frequently the system impacts on their daily lives. Examining and recording all of these beliefs will help information system designers to provide the right information to the right people at the right time.

Comparing the System's Output with the System's Purpose

The next stage becomes one of comparing the quality of what the system normally produces (such as risk assessments) with the expressed aims of its purpose (for example, creating a safe working environment), to establish whether or not the system is actually delivering what it is supposed to deliver (safe working methods). Because each individual component is affected by changes in other components or in the purpose of the system's functioning, the likely effects of any changes also need to be evaluated. For example, if a company tries to reduce its labour costs and overheads by contracting out some of its services, the company will need to evaluate its methods for selecting contractors and contractor control, *and* assess the effects this has on their purchasing, production, finance, quality, engineering, safety and information systems.

Mapping Out an Ideal Information System

Once each system has been clearly defined it should be possible to map a communications or information system onto the structure of each system and sub system. This can also help to identify the formal and informal interrelationships between each of the different systems operating in an organisation, so that the impact that each system exerts on other systems can be identified. Similarly, although a system cannot control anything beyond its external boundaries, it is still influenced by external forces. For example, a safety management system could be profoundly influenced by public policy and legislation, case law emanating from the courts, suppliers of goods or services, insurers, etc. The potential influence each of these types of external force has also needs to be recognised and provision made for assessing any potential risks to the system's functioning.

A Strategy for Analysing Management Information Systems

Mapping out an ideal information system that corresponds with an organisation's structure of systems is dependent on the analyst asking the right questions and using an appropriate strategy.

The most appropriate strategy is *difference reduction* which involves simultaneously adopting two approaches for modelling the systems involved. The first focuses on the way that the information necessary for managing and controlling each of the organisation's systems is *currently* produced; the second focuses on the way the organisation *ought* to collect information. The resulting *differences* between the two approaches identify the strengths and weaknesses of the existing information systems. As such, this approach highlights areas where changes might best be made to existing organisational practices or structures so that the organisation's goals can be more efficiently achieved. If the analysis shows that current practices or systems arrangements are ineffective, it is advisable to make any changes to organisational practices or structures *prior to installing* a modified information system, otherwise the purpose of the whole exercise could be defeated. In principle, the analysis of an organisation's systems can begin anywhere. However, due to the complexity of most organisations it is much better to use a bottom-up, rather than a top-down approach when attempting to analyse the existing information systems. The main reason for doing so is that a bottom-up approach is much more likely to identify the actual systems that exist and the way they behave, as opposed to a top-down approach that is likely to merely identify the systems that are supposed to exist and the way they are supposed to behave.

An Overview of a Five Stage Analysis

The analysis should proceed in five stages:

1. Identify just one particular system (such as accident reporting), which is deemed to be of importance, identify its sub systems (such as accident administration, processing, analyses, etc.) and the various components that reside within each sub system.
2. Identify the particular system's location within the organisation's larger hierarchy of systems (e.g. safety management system), to evaluate the system's horizontal relationships with other systems at the same level (e.g. risk assessments) of the hierarchy, and the system's vertical relationships within the overall hierarchy of systems.
3. Identify the system's relationships with other systems (e.g. accident reporting and contractor control) in terms of its:
    *   shared resources (e.g. personnel, administration, etc.),
    *   emergent properties (e.g. organisational learning, conflicts, etc.).
4. Compare the effectiveness of the current system with the way the system ought to function in terms of satisfying the organisation's information needs.
5. The analyst turns his or her attentions to other systems that have been identified by the examination conducted, and repeats the first four stages of the analysis, until all the organisation's systems and sub systems have been identified and mapped.

At each stage different questions will need to be asked that revolve around system characteristics, information needs and management control mechanisms. This will require the analysts to possess good communication and interviewing skills (see Chapter 6 for an overview of interviewing techniques). Moreover, given the scale of the task (which could take many months in a large organisation) the analyst should be assigned to the task until it is complete. In large organisations it may prove wise to set up a small project team under the leadership of the information technology manager who, in all probability, will already be experienced in the analysis of complex information systems. Indeed, he or she may have already been engaged in this type of exercise for other purposes, and so may have useful information to hand. Similarly, if an organisation has conducted a workflow analysis as advocated in Chapter 3, much of the groundwork for an information system's analysis may already have been completed.

The remainder of this chapter looks at each of the five stages in detail.

Stage One—Identifying Existing Systems

The first set of questions will centre around what systems or sub systems exist and the way they are organised with a view to discovering how a system collects the data it needs, and how it delivers information in the required format to the end user. Closely allied questions will revolve around the identifiable purpose of the system and the best ways of delivering the required information. Assuming, for example, that an analyst had started with an organisation's accident investigation system. Because the goal of an accident investigation is to provide adequate information to ensure that:

- preventative and remedial actions can be promptly taken
- the organisation is complying with legislative requirements
- the implementation of the organisation's safety policy is being adhered to
- information is available to assist in decision-making, planning and resource allocation,

the analyst's questions would centre around what sub systems exist and the presence and quality of their components to help achieve these goals. Ideally, as illustrated in Figure 5.6: *The Components, Sub Systems and Sub Components of an Accident Investigation System* the analyst would find that the accident investigation system would comprise various sub systems that include an accident investigation policy, an accident reporting system, an accident investigative system, an accident analyses system, a verification system and a transformational system.

If all these sub systems were found to exist, the analyst would probe further to identify the various components of each sub system. If any of the sub systems were missing they would be recorded as such, and efforts would then be made to assess the potential impact of their subsequent inclusion within the existing system.

Identify the sub components of each sub system.   The analyst would probe further to identify the sub components that comprise each of these sub

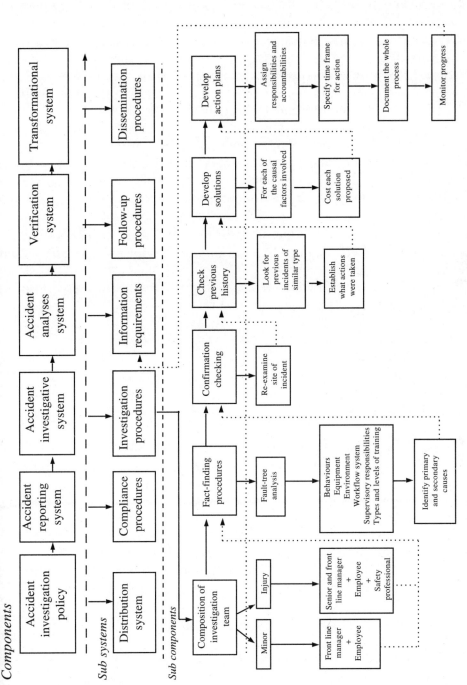

Figure 5.6   The Components, Sub Systems and Sub Components of an Accident Investigation System

systems. Taking each sub system in turn, it would be expected, for example, that the sub components of the accident investigation policy would include:

- a written document that fully describes the requirements for investigating accidents
- descriptions of the nature of the types of accidents that need to be reported (i.e. first-aid injuries, occupational illness, near misses, third party injuries, property damage, chemical spills, gas leaks, fires, etc.)
- details of who should be involved in accident investigations (i.e. safety professionals, line managers, safety representatives, etc.)
- standardised reporting forms for injury investigations, near misses, fire incidents, chemical spillages, etc.
- details of the investigation follow-up procedures.

A system for distributing the document to all line managers and supervisory staff (inclusive of contractor/sub contractor supervisory staff) should also be in place and documented.

It would also be expected for the sub components that comprise an accident reporting system to include compliance procedures to inform:

- statutory bodies (e.g. HSE)
- senior management
- safety committees
- contractor management
- line management.

As illustrated in Figure 5.6, the sub components of the accident investigative system would include specified procedures for deciding upon the composition of the investigative team, the fact-finding procedures to be employed by them, a requirement to check the incident against the organisation's previous accident history to discover what recommendations and remedial actions were taken (if any), a requirement to develop and cost solutions to each of the causal factors involved in the incident, and a requirement to develop action plans. Similarly, the components comprising the accident analysis sub system would include information requirements for:

- the location or department where incidents took place
- the workflow processes involved in incidents
- the supervisory arrangements and responsibilities at the time of an incident
- the levels and types of training previously undertaken by victims
- the primary and secondary causes of incidents

- types of injury and position on body
- frequency of particular types of accident
- a breakdown of the severity of the injuries sustained from the accidents
- the costs involved in accident investigations
- the costs of any property damage
- the costs of production downtime
- the compensation costs paid out to victims
- the legal costs associated with compensation claims
- the costs recovered from insurance
- the effects of incidents and associated claims on insurance premiums.

The components of an accident verification system would include follow-up procedures to assess:

- the adequacy of existing risk assessments
- the adequacy of existing procedures, systems and work methods to comply with legislation and company policy,

while the components of an accident transformational system might include procedures to disseminate completed investigation information to other organisational systems such as:

- senior management
- safety committees
- finance
- legal
- insurance
- purchasing
- engineering
- production
- human resources
- training.

Identifying the purpose of each sub component.   Having identified the presence (or absence) of the sub system's components the analyst would then try to ascertain whether or not the system, its sub systems and components clearly produced something or at least had an effect on the system's purpose or goal. In this way it is possible to identify specific information products derived from each specific system or sub system. For example, Figure 5.6 illustrates that each sub component either has a clear purpose (for example, deciding upon the composition of the investigative team) or produces

something (such as a fault tree analysis of the incident). If a specific information product cannot be identified, it may be that the structure of the
system or sub system and its activity is associated with more than one
information product and hence is too general. In these instances it might be
wise to consider:

- the system or sub system's purpose
- how it achieves this purpose
- the data needed for the system to achieve its purpose
- what information product is supposed to be derived from the data
- what resources the system needs to fulfil its purpose.

Focusing on the purpose of a system or sub system, and the way in which
its purpose is achieved, also helps the analyst to identify its boundary, and
this then makes it possible to establish its relationship(s) with adjoining
systems or sub systems. For example, in Figure 5.6 the boundary of the team
composition sub component is reached when the compositions of all the
types of investigative teams have been specified for different types of
incident. Having identified the boundaries of each sub component, the
relationships between them can be established (as indicated by the arrows
and/or dotted lines in Figure 5.6). Only when these boundaries and relationships have been established is it possible to examine the effects that any
environmental disturbances may have on the performance of the system or
sub system.

Identifying potential system disturbances.   Only the data that is relevant for an
information system to achieve its purpose can be considered to be the
system's environment. Other factors impinging upon the system can be
considered as disturbances, i.e. if a resource from one system is continually
shared with another system the free availability of the resource could be
constrained by competition from the other system. This was illustrated in
Figure 5.5 in the analysis of the hot permit to work system. At the beginning
of a shift, a supervisor was required to simultaneously process a hot permit to
work request from a maintenance engineer, attend an early morning
management meeting and deal with the shift handover. Such disturbances
could signal potential problems with the overall system that might become
(or actually be) a serious management issue. Other environmental disturbances may emanate from the information flow, changes in company policies,
changes in personnel, management styles, or the introduction of new
technologies. In practical terms, the inability of a system to cope with these
disturbances would signal that some restructuring of the existing information, control and/or management systems or sub systems is required.

Stage Two—Identifying the System's Location Within a Hierarchy of Systems

The second stage is to identify the system's location within the organisation's larger hierarchy of systems. This helps to increase the analyst's understanding of the factors that determine the system's overall performance by evaluating the system's horizontal interactions with adjacent systems at the same level of the hierarchy. In other words, the analyst needs to examine the linear sequencing of information outputs (e.g. accident investigation results) that provide the inputs to another associated system (e.g. risk assessments), which in turn processes this and transforms it into the output for another associated system (e.g. standard operating procedures), and so on (see Figure 5.7: *Linear Sequence of System Inputs and Outputs*). The aim is to examine the influence each adjacent system has on other systems. This can best be achieved by examining the effectiveness of the sequence in coping with the required information flow in terms of the time lag between information supply and demand. (This might also reveal where duplication of effort is occurring.)

The longer the interaction chain, the greater is the potential for instability in the linear system. Similarly, the more two systems are separated along a sequence, the greater the potential destabilising effects of this method of transmitting information. In many instances, these could be avoided by providing access to a common database (for example, a dedicated safety management information database that explicitly encompasses all aspects of the safety management system). However, it is unlikely that every time lag can ever be totally eliminated. Therefore, as well as reducing the potential for time lags, consideration should be given to explicitly designing the system to cope with potential time lag effects.

Assessing time lags in a linear sequence. Assessing the time lags associated with a linear sequence of inputs and outputs can be achieved by using either a forecasting or buffer approach. 'Forecasting' means anticipating what future outputs might be needed, so that the current inputs can be set in an appropriate form to produce the desired output at the end of the lag time. The forecasting approach is dependent on the analysis of past trends of information flow and lag times, on the assumption that the same is likely to hold true in the future. Referring to Figure 5.7, for example, it may be the case that due to other pressing issues the time lag between comparing the findings of an accident investigation against the adequacy of current risk assessments has always taken a week, followed by a further week to review the appropriate SOPs. Although there is much scope for improvement, the information system designer may build this two week time lag into the system's capacity for processing the necessary information.

162

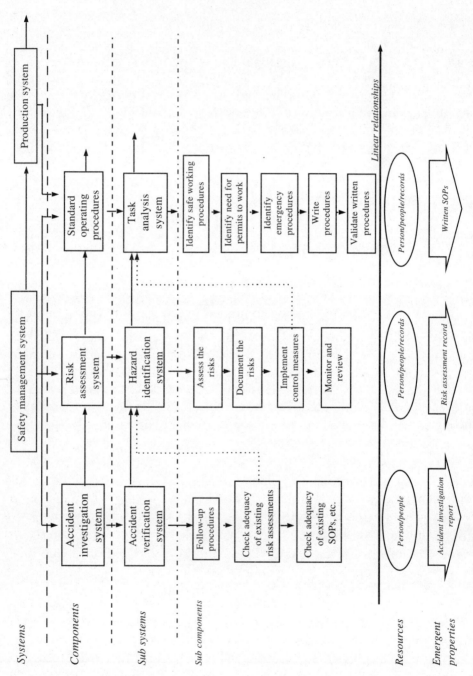

Figure 5.7   Linear Sequencing of System Inputs and Outputs

Alternatively, the designer may adopt a 'buffer' approach. This refers to the holding of information when it is difficult to satisfy demand due to poor system co-ordination. Since demand for information is an environmental disturbance that cannot always be predicted and therefore cannot always be controlled, it may be possible to develop a means of holding the information 'in stock' for a certain time, which is then released as demand on the system diminishes. In other words, the designer may take the view that no accident investigation information is to be entered into the system until such time as the whole sequence of tasks has been completed (i.e. comparisons have been made against the risk assessments, and the appropriate SOPs reviewed and changed). However, this requires the analyst to ask the appropriate questions, which might include:

- What is the linear sequence of information supply?
- What is the time lag between information demand and supply between each of the adjacent systems?
- Does the length of the sequence increase the time lag and add exponentially to the instability of the overall system?
- Are the linear relationships between the systems ideal?
- Should any of the systems be combined to reduce duplication of effort?
- Does information supply ever exceed demand?
- Does information demand ever exceed supply?
- Does the linear sequence allow information to reach the end of the supply chain before it is actually required?
- Does unwanted information feed into the linear sequence of systems?

Examining the vertical relationships between the systems in the sequence. The vertical relationships between the system under scrutiny and other organisational systems are examined in relation to the same factors as the horizontal relationships i.e. what is being provided to whom and by when. Moreover, the interactions between the associated control mechanisms for each system and the interactions between the associated management systems should also be examined. These latter relationships should be explored to identify what tactical or strategic information is required and how it is delivered, for example, by focusing on whether:

- the system currently provides the required information
- the control systems are operating as intended
- the control systems interact with each other in a co-ordinated way
- the management systems are clearly associated with their intended control systems
- the management systems interact with each other as intended

- the same information outputs are found in any other system (i.e. is the same information emanating from two different sources).

This combined examination of the vertical and horizontal relationships between systems and sub systems makes it explicit where each system or sub system resides within the whole system. An examination of the vertical relationships should reveal which particular systems are serving and being dominated by the purpose of other systems, whereas an examination of the horizontal relationships should reveal which adjacent systems are exerting a direct or indirect influence on each other.

Stage Three—Identifying Depth Relationships

Having identified the horizontal and vertical relationships between the different systems the third stage is to examine the depth relationships between them. The very notion of a depth relationship implies that there will be an element of competition for resources between different systems. The analyst therefore needs to focus on:

- the resources shared by systems (such as documents, personnel and equipment)
- the properties emerging from these depth relationships (such as documents, information and conflicts).

As illustrated in Figure 5.7 some of these may have been identified at stage two. However, stage three explicitly focuses the analyst's attention on these factors, which otherwise might be ignored or at least not be fully considered.

Resource implications. Focusing on the resources used by an information system and how they might be shared with other systems is important because it has implications for the effectiveness or efficiency of the system's functioning and for the organisation as a whole. In essence, the main concerns centre around issues such as:

- How is data entered into the system?
- How is data stored in the system?
- How is the data processed?
- How is data moved from one system to another?
- How is information extracted from the system?
- How is information communicated around the different systems?

An examination of each issue will reveal the current use of resources, and (perhaps) the resources that are actually required. An information system that is very slow to deliver, for example, could indicate a lack of available manpower (human resources) to manage and maintain the system. Whenever a number of people have the capacity to access an information system, the analyst should ascertain what actually happens to the performance of the system when everyone who can access it actually does so. It may also be wise to know what happens to the system's performance when additional access is made available, what happens when significant amounts of additional data are entered into the system, and at what point a system becomes overloaded. Importantly, when consideration is given to the way information ought to be collected, the analyst should consider the resourcing implications that the introduction of a new information system will have both in the short term and in the longer term.

Emergent properties. When two or more systems share depth relationships, it is not always clear what properties might emerge, and therefore this issue needs to be explicitly explored. Both the beneficial and negative properties need to be considered. Obviously, the most beneficial property to emerge would be the required information at the right time, in the format specified. It is often the case, however, that negative properties emerge: for example, competition for resources that ends in system conflicts which may or may not previously have been recognised as such. The analyst should, therefore, pay particular attention to pedantically examining both these issues, and the influence that the negative properties may be exerting on the corresponding control and management systems.

Stage Four—Difference Reduction

By the fourth stage the analyst should have completed a thorough review of a particular information system, identified its sub systems and its associated components and established their purpose. The vertical, horizontal and depth relationships between the system and other adjacent systems should also have been examined, providing a clear view or understanding of how data is collected, processed into appropriate information and delivered to the end users. Similarly, the relationships between the system's associated control mechanisms and management systems should have been identified and explored. As a result, the analyst should be in a position to compare the effectiveness of the existing system with the way the system ought to logically function if it is to satisfy the organisation's information needs.

Modelling and comparing the existing system with the proposed system.   At this point both the existing system with all its relationships and the new proposed system should be drawn out as models (if this has not yet been done) in diagrammatic form. The analyst should highlight the differences between the two models in a preliminary report that makes the case for implementing any changes to the system. Because a new information system could exert a profound influence on the way the organisation is structured to meet its goals, it is very important that the analyst fully considers and justifies each proposed change. Particular attention should be paid to a need to introduce:

- new data collection methods to be used for management control purposes
- additional information requirements for management
- new types of information that could help the organisation to meet its goals
- new resources or reconfiguring the use of existing ones
- changes to management control systems
- changes to management systems
- changes to organisational structures.

It may also prove wise to estimate the financial costs involved.

Stage Five—Repeat the First Four Stages

Having completed a preliminary report, the analyst then repeats the first four stages of analysis with all of the organisation's remaining systems until such time as all the organisation's information systems and sub systems have been identified and mapped. At the end of this process the preliminary report that recommends change can be modified to reflect all the necessary changes to each individual information system. This can then be presented to senior management in the normal way.

6

Safety Management System Auditing

INTRODUCTION

Having developed or checked the capacity of the organisation's management information system to absorb and deliver the appropriate information at the right time to the right people, the next stage of the intermediate level of effort is to examine and test the adequacy of the existing safety management system. The mechanism by which this is achieved is normally termed 'auditing', which is an essential element of any management system. Audits are usually carried out to discover to what extent the organisation's policies and procedures are being adhered to and how they may be improved. As such, any management system audit should be able to identify, assess and evaluate the organisation's problems so that recommendations for improvements can be made. The results of these audits also enable the management system to be kept under continuous review. It should be recognised that although an audit may be able to identify the most serious problems, it cannot possibly identify every existing problem no matter what type of audit is conducted or whatever the audit's focus (e.g. quality, safety or the environment) might be.

DEVELOPING A SAFETY AUDIT SYSTEM

Since one of the main requirements of the intermediate level of effort is to develop and establish feedback and monitoring systems which help to facilitate organisational learning, it becomes evident that potentially disastrous consequences could flow from a poorly developed safety audit system, as it might fail to identify significant safety issues. Accordingly, a high quality safety audit system is essential. Figure 6.1 presents an overview of the auditing process so that a system designer can give due consideration to the required audit standards of each part of the process when developing a safety audit system.

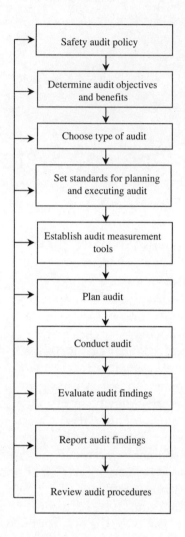

Figure 6.1   An Overview of the Auditing Process

These standards should provide clear guidance on all aspects of the audit, including audit policy guidelines that cover the philosophy and principles of audits, the training and selection of audit teams, good audit practices, the audit programme and the audit report. The setting of such standards is an important part of the auditing process that forces the designers of an audit system to consider:

- why audits need to be undertaken, and their objectives
- what types of audits need to be undertaken
- the frequency of audits

- the standards required for the planning and execution of the audit programme
- the audit's elements
- auditing practice
- the standards required of the audit report
- the arrangements for responding to the audit findings
- arrangements for reviewing the audit system.

It is important for each of these standards to have the strong support of the senior management team, including a commitment to provide the necessary financial and time resources, to allow the audit team to go about its activities without hindrance from anybody, to instruct all levels of the organisation to co-operate with the audit team, and to act upon the findings within a particular timeframe. Obtaining this support is crucial but sometimes fraught with difficulties, as not every senior manager fully appreciates the need for safety systems to be audited. In these instances it may be appropriate to emphasise that safety auditing provides the means for senior management to demonstrate that they are meeting their health and safety responsibilities, that safety auditing is a way of improving the organisation's overall safety performance, that the results of the safety audit can be used to further refine the company's safety strategy, and that it is a cost-effective way of identifying potential losses that could damage bottom line profits.

ESTABLISHING THE NEED FOR SAFETY AUDITS

Although safety audits may be undertaken for a number of reasons, the main purpose is to enable management to measure the effectiveness of its safety efforts, and to present the findings in such a way that it is able to undertake the appropriate remedial actions. Nonetheless, because of the time, money and effort involved it is wise to ensure that an audit can be justified at any particular point in time. Since the element being assessed and evaluated needs to be justified against some reference standard, it is the wise auditor who focuses upon the objectives of an audit, and the benefits that can accrue. The objectives of the audit might include assessing:

- senior management's commitment to safety
- the effectiveness of safety policies, safety strategies or safety management systems
- a site's safety performance at a particular point in time
- one site's safety performance against other sites
- high hazard or risk areas
- the need to set future safety targets

- people's training needs
- people's safety awareness.

The benefits of conducting safety management system audits could include one or more of the following:

- improving actual safety performance at all levels of the organisation
- establishing the need for the provision and management of resources
- establishing a prioritised list of health and safety issues that require attention
- establishing the importance of health and safety in the minds of the organisation's personnel at all levels (i.e. senior directors, line managers, operational personnel, sub-contractors, etc.)
- establishing the people's health and safety responsibilities and accountability
- increasing the degree of control that line managers can exert within their sphere of influence
- clarifying the organisation's health and safety objectives which then provide a basis for strategic decision-making
- identifying the potential for losses (e.g. property damage, compensation claims)
- reducing the costs of insurance premiums
- limiting the amount of exposure to public liability claims
- meeting statutory requirements.

These expected benefits could also be used to help determine the audit's objectives and focus. For example, an audit could be used to examine specifically an organisation's exposure to public liability claims arising from its current activities. In the chemical industry this might mean examining particular activities to assess the potential for toxic releases into the atmosphere. Within the construction industry it might mean examining current arrangements for traffic management when undertaking activities on or near the public highway. Whatever objectives are decided upon, it is important that the audit should be tailored so that it meets the organisation's needs for improvement, is matched to the size of the organisation, and is relevant to the industrial or commercial sector that the organisation operates within.

TYPES OF SAFETY AUDIT

Many people believe that identifying problems by looking for hazards in the workplace constitutes an audit, but this is not the case. Hazard-spotting exercises constitute a safety inspection, not an audit. This is because safety inspections are usually confined to a particular area of a business, and are concerned with the regular (e.g. weekly, monthly, quarterly) identification of actual workplace hazards during half hour workplace tours, which often results in a list of remedial actions to be undertaken within a short time scale (e.g. week, month, etc.). Safety auditing on the other hand is much broader than this as it usually refers to an independent examination of the whole safety management system itself that takes between two to five (or more) days depending on the size of the organisation and the scope of the audit.

At least four types of safety audit exist which, when used in combination, will provide a full and comprehensive examination of an organisation's safety management system. Given that an organisation will set strategic, tactical and operational goals to develop its safety culture, a corresponding three-level framework is offered for the four different types of audit that encompasses the strategic, tactical and operational levels of an organisation. These are:

- Strategic
    Compliance or verification audits
- Tactical
    Validation audits
- Operational
    Plant technical audits
    Site technical audits.

Compliance and Verification Audits

At the strategic level, compliance audits assess whether or not particular legal requirements have been met by the organisation, and whether or not the organisation's own policies, procedures and standards are being adhered to. The purpose is to examine the effectiveness of the existing safety management system in relation to both internal and external standards i.e. to verify that the safety management system is doing what it is intended to do, and functioning as well as it should be.

Validation Audits

Validation auditing is mainly concerned with the scope and design of the safety management system at the tactical level. Validation audits are used to check whether or not the appropriate safety management sub systems are in place (for example, a near miss reporting system) and their constituent components (such as availability of reporting forms, procedures for entering the data into the system, on-site investigations, drawing up action plans, etc.) are being adopted and followed, and whether regular monitoring of the systems and sub systems is actually being undertaken.

Plant and Site Technical Audits

Conducted at the operational level, plant technical audits are concerned with an in-depth review of the design and integrity of the plant and equipment being used, the efficiency of the associated technical systems, and the interface between people and the equipment. Whereas plant technical audits involve assessments of the operation of complex technological facilities (such as chemical plants), site technical audits cover specific technological work activities (for example, offshore drilling) where the equipment used is relatively standard and the main focus is on organisational control. Site technical audits are usually carried out at pre-determined intervals by both site staff and specialist experts from another part of the organisation or from outside the organisation.

Strategies for Using the Three-level Audit Framework

As shown in Figure 6.2: *Three Level Audit Framework* the main advantage of using the three level framework outlined above is that it can be mapped onto the equivalent levels of an organisation to help guide the audit strategy and its scope. The head office of many organisations, for example, is in a different geographical location from its business units and would be categorised as the strategic level of the organisation where compliance or verification audits would be carried out. Each subsidiary business unit would be categorised as the tactical level, where the safety management systems in place would be subjected to validation audits. Similarly the actual production elements of the business would be deemed to be the operational levels and subjected to plant or site technical audits. Thus, the most appropriate audit could be applied to the most appropriate level (this is not to exclude the possibility of conducting compliance or verification audits at the tactical or operational levels). This three level framework also helps organisations to conduct both vertical and horizontal auditing as recommended by the HSE. For example, if the focus of the audit were upon the effectiveness of safety communications, the vertical communication flow up and down the organisation could be tracked between the strategic, tactical and operational levels of the organisation to identify where a communication breakdown might occur. Similarly, the horizontal communication flow between different departments

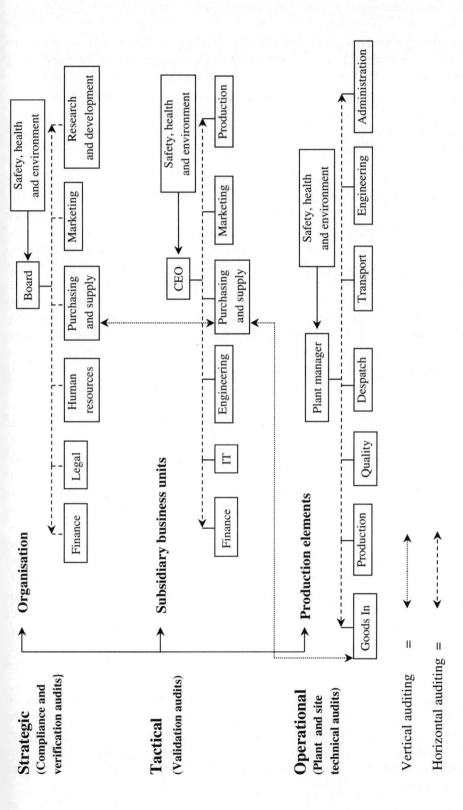

Figure 6.2 Three Level Audit Framework

or functions at each organisational level could be tracked. As different types of audit can be carried out at each of these organisational levels, they could all provide useful information centred around a common theme, but from a variety of perspectives. This information could then be integrated into a whole by the audit team or the safety department, etc.

The three level framework could also be used within a particular area of operations to identify and target various people and groups within the organisation to assist the audit team during the audit process. Figure 6.3, for example, shows that a strategic level compliance or verification audit could be directed at the management level of transport and warehouse operations, while a tactical level validation audit could be undertaken at the supervisory level. Similarly, plant and site technical audits could be carried out at the operational level of this work area. Were this three level framework to be applied across the whole organisation, it would soon become evident which people would be suitable to assist in the various types of audit.

A further strength of this three level framework is that it can be used to guide the focus of the audit itself by developing a three by three matrix so that the relationship between people, their jobs and the organisation is explicitly recognised and taken into account during an audit within the three major dimensions of a management system i.e. policy, execution of policy and assessment. This is illustrated in Figure 6.4, whereby, at the organisational level, audit questions could focus on people's awareness of the company's policies, how these are implemented in the organisation, and whether people know of and are involved in reviewing company safety policies. Similarly, at the job level the auditors could focus on a location's knowledge of safety policies that affect or govern their particular workflow activities, how the safety management system is executed in practice, and how the review procedures are executed. At the individual level, the auditor could examine people's awareness of the safety policies affecting their tasks, how well people adhere to procedures, and the extent of people's involvement in reviewing these procedures. The purpose of this type of matrix, therefore, is to assist auditors to fully develop an audit plan by defining the scope of the audit, selecting priority areas for auditing and allocating the appropriate resources to the audit team.

AUDIT FREQUENCY

The frequency of auditing depends on the size of the organisation, the scale of operations, the specific goals of the audit programme and the costs involved. Another major consideration is whether or not an organisation has been audited before. First time audits should be very comprehensive and carried out from the top to the bottom of the organisation. Follow-on audits

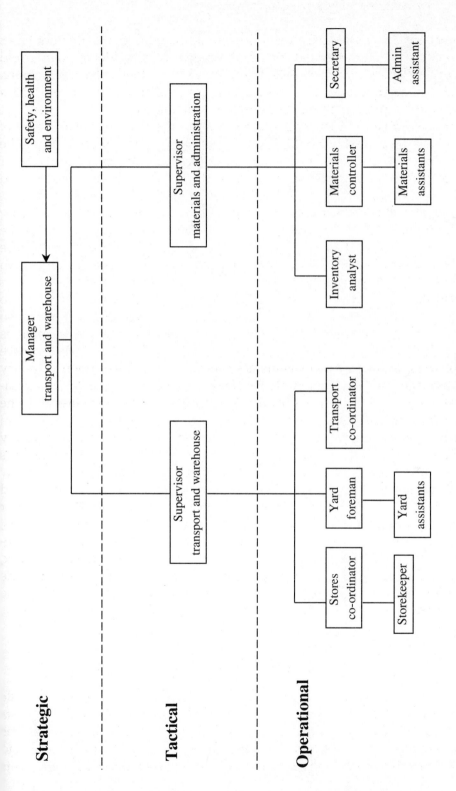

Figure 6.3   Three Level Framework Applied to Transport and Warehouse Operations

176

	Policy	Policy execution	Policy assessment
Strategic Organisation	Awareness of company safety policy	Understand safety policy implementation	Understand procedures for reviewing safety policies
Tactical Job	Awareness of company safety policies governing particular workflow activities	Examine execution of safety management systems (e.g emergency preparation)	Examine procedures for reviewing safety management systems
Operational Individual	Awareness of safety policies affecting the person's tasks	Examine adherence to task-related safety policies (e.g Permit to Work)	Examine extent of person's involvement in reviewing safety procedures

Figure 6.4   Example Three by Three Matrix Being Used to Guide the Focus of an Audit

could focus on those elements identified for remedial actions during the first comprehensive audit. As a rule of thumb, compliance (strategic) audits that focus on documentation are normally carried out every two to three years, whereas validation (tactical) audits are normally held on an annual basis. At the operational level, full scale plant technical audits are usually held about every five years, whereas site technical audits tend to be carried out on a six monthly basis. More frequent safety inspections of the workplace could also carried out by line managers on a weekly, monthly or quarterly basis to further enhance the organisation's ongoing safety performance. Any significant changes in an organisation's structure, policies, procedures and practices, or numbers of personnel could also signal the need for further in-depth audits. Many large organisations also have a policy of transferring or promoting managers around every three years. Accordingly it may well prove useful to conduct full in-depth audits about three to six months after these wholesale changes to ensure that the new role occupants are familiar with their new safety management responsibilities.

STANDARDS REQUIRED FOR PLANNING AND EXECUTING THE AUDIT PROGRAMME

Comprehensive audits of safety management systems can be accomplished in many ways. In every case, it is important to establish written guidelines or standards so that all the necessary planning can be undertaken properly to ensure that the auditing programme proceeds smoothly.

Terms of Reference

One of the first standards to consider is the audit system's terms of reference to provide the auditors with the necessary authority to carry out their remit. The scope of these terms of reference should be as wide as possible, so that the audit process is seen to be independent and not constrained by organisational politics. For most safety audit systems these are usually concerned with reviewing:

- management systems to rate their effectiveness in controlling activity
- the effectiveness of boundary interfaces (e.g. the degree to which information flows between the strategic, tactical and operational levels of an organisation)
- current working practices and supervisory arrangements
- the organisation's safety policies and procedures

- the design, construction and/or modification of equipment
- workflow processes, and any other activity that the organisation may be undertaking
- contractor control.

In addition, it should be the auditor's role to identify the boundaries of the operational systems to be reviewed, rather than the scope of the audit being dictated by senior managers.

Audit Scheduling

Once the terms of reference have been established, consideration needs to be given to the time scheduling of the various types of audit. The frequency with which audits should be undertaken has already been outlined above. However, it is also important to specify the expected schedule of each of the audit elements to be undertaken by an audit team. In essence, the audit schedule for each type of audit should acknowledge and encompass pre-audit, audit and post-audit activity as follows:

- Pre-audit activity
  - Select audit team leader/manager
  - Select plant or business unit to be audited
  - Select appropriate type of audit
  - Select audit team and confirm availability
  - Plan audit
    — define its scope
    — identify the priority areas
    — allocate resources
  - Review background information
    — prepare on-site agenda
    — prepare audit questions
    — conduct an advance visit
    — train audit team
- Audit activity
  - Develop audit team's understanding of the systems to be audited
    — interview selected personnel
    — review documents and/or standards
  - Assess strengths and weaknesses in relation to
    — internal controls
    — potential hazards/risks

- Gather audit data
  — select
  — test
  — verify
- Evaluate audit data
  — document audit findings, deviations and observations
- Compile audit findings
  — present draft findings to management of the audited facility.
- Post-audit activity
  - Prepare draft report
  - Issue final report
  - Present final report to management
  - Develop action plans
    — propose remedial actions
    — resolve conflicts
    — establish responsibility and accountability
    — set timeframe
  - Review and monitor
    — implement action plans
    — audit system

It is obvious from this list of audit activities that a first time comprehensive audit could take up to six months to complete, particularly if the audit team members are inexperienced. In his book on safety management systems, Dr Alan Waring makes the point that it might take experienced auditors up to ten weeks to carry out a large scale audit. Even for the most limited scope of audit, the minimum duration is six working days: one day for assigning tasks and developing an interview schedule (structured question set), two days for site interviewing and three days for drafting, discussing, editing and presenting the report.

Audit Personnel

The auditing schedule outlined above also emphasises that safety auditing needs should be conducted on a project team basis. Decisions therefore also need to be made about who should be appointed to oversee the audit effort. In principle, the team leader or manager should:

- not have direct responsibility for the site to be audited
- have been trained in auditing techniques
- have previously taken part in at least two audits led by an experienced auditor.

The responsibilities of the team leader are many and varied. He or she will, for example:

- ensure that all the administrative systems are in place before the audit programme commences
- ensure that those who form part of the team receive the necessary guidance and training in auditing techniques
- organise the audit team activities to ensure that the audit team's schedule is adhered to
- conduct team meetings at the end of each audit day to obtain feedback from each team member
- reassign or redirect each team member's responsibilities depending upon the progress and findings
- at the audit location, lead the opening meeting with the relevant managers
- liaise between the audit team and the audit location's management
- organise the preparation of the final report in conjunction with the whole audit team, to ensure that the required quality of the audit report is met
- give feedback about the findings to the audited location's management team
- review the progress of the audited location's remedial actions.

The team leader should be given full authority to select and train the audit team, select the plant or site to be audited, determine the type of audit to be conducted, plan the audit and the associated timetable, and be held fully responsible for ensuring that the audit is completed on schedule and within budget. Often, the audit team leader is a full time member of the organisation's safety department, and would normally report directly to the company's safety manager. The remainder of the audit team will vary depending on the site or activities being audited and the type of audit being conducted.

Audit Team Composition

Audits conducted by the organisation's own staff are internal audits. Internal audit teams normally comprise three or four people with extensive experience of the industry and auditing experience. If trainee auditors are attached to the team, the number of experienced auditors may need to be increased so that there is a one to one ratio. Similarly, if independent external auditors are used, it is a good idea to keep to a one to one ratio of internal to external auditors as this facilitates communications and understanding of the organisation's policies and practices. If plant or site technical audits are to be conducted it is very useful to include one or two specialist technical experts n the audit team. It is often said that the team members should be people who have held a responsible position in the organisation (e.g. managers, technicians, safety advisors, etc.). In the author's view, at least one of the audit team members should be a 'shopfloor' type person as this gives the audit team a balance that is often lacking. Of overriding importance, however, is the need for the audit team members to be independent. Wherever possible, they should be drawn from other parts of the organisation, not from the site or business being audited.

In the main the team member's responsibilities include taking part in opening meetings, conducting interviews or observations, helping the team leader to summarise the audit findings at the end of each day, and taking an active part in preparing the final report. A competent typist should be available to the audit team at all times, as a considerable amount of typing will be undertaken before, during and after the audit. It is usually best if the typist is assigned full time to the audit team from beginning to end so that he or she is intimately familiar with all its aspects.

Audit Training

An audit team should undergo a mixture of refresher training and briefings to ensure that all the members are consistent in the way they approach the audit and in the way they interpret and score the responses. Typically the audit briefings and training would encompass:

- the reason why the audit is being undertaken
- an overview of audit policy
- the aims and objectives of the audit
- the processes and strategy to be adopted
- an outline of the scope of the audit and the team member's individual responsibilities
- the diagnostic tools and questionnaires to be used
- refresher training in interviewing techniques
- the presentation of the audit findings
- an overview of logistics (e.g. travel and accommodation arrangements).

These briefings and refresher training will often take two days, and so need to be built into the audit schedule. Given that the team members will probably be drawn from different backgrounds and locations, the benefits of such guidance and instruction flow from the audit team learning to function as a single unit.

Budgetary Requirements

Auditing is an expensive business and therefore needs to be fully costed. Typical costs include travel and subsistence for the audit team, salaries or costs of consultancy for outside experts/auditors, materials (e.g. questionnaires, specialist equipment, etc.), training requirements and overheads (e.g. office space, telephones, computer equipment, etc.). Other costs include the 'downtime' of those selected to answer the audit team's questions.

If possible, a budget should be drawn up when the audit is proposed. However, if an organisation has not previously conducted a safety audit the proposed budget should be treated as a guesstimate, and the actual costs tracked during the audit. Alternatively, it may be possible to use the costs of any financial audits conducted by an organisation as a guide. Importantly, the costs of any remedial actions should also be recorded as these can be used to help determine the financial benefits that may flow from them. In this way, as an organisation gains experience in auditing, the costs and benefits will more easily be identified, and can be used to budget and control the costs of future audits.

AUDIT ELEMENTS

The information to be gathered and evaluated during an audit will obviously vary considerably from plant to plant or location to location and process to process. In essence there are four sources of information: documentation, workplace observations, technical or ergonomic data, and interviewing data. It is important to recognise that information sometimes resides in more than one location or may not even exist. Members of the audit team, therefore, need to be very clear as to what they wish to audit and where the information might be found.

Documentation

Typical sources of documented information that might be examined at the three levels include:

- Strategic level
  - Company safety policies
  - Minutes of Health and Safety Committees
  - Safety plans and objectives
  - Safety audit reports
  - Safety cases

- Occupational health plans
- Purchasing controls
- Environmental controls
- HAZOP & design reviews
- Tactical level
  - Standard operating procedures
  - Permits to work procedures
  - Maintenance procedures
  - Emergency procedures
  - Safety training programmes
  - Fire fighting training programmes
  - Engineering controls
- Operational level
  - Safety meetings
  - Risk assessments
  - Manual handling assessments
  - Near miss reports
  - Accident and investigation reports
  - Statutory inspection reports (e.g. seven day scaffolding inspections)

Workplace Observations

Observation in the workplace provides information about how safety is actually operationalised on a day-to-day basis. In the main the auditors will be focusing on unsafe or hazardous conditions or monitoring people's activity (for instance, are people following the correct procedures?). Typical features that auditors might examine include:

- Tools and equipment
  - Availability of the right tools for a job
  - The condition of the tools and equipment
  - Storage locations
  - Lifting equipment
  - Machine guards in place
  - Operational alarms
  - Isolation procedures
  - Personal protective equipment
- Working areas and plant
  - Housekeeping standards
  - Separation of people and traffic
  - Lighting standards
  - Noise levels

- The control of fumes, dust, smoke, etc.
- Access controls to restricted or prohibited areas
- Materials handling
- Labelling of chemicals
- Adherence to policies and procedures
- Fire and safety equipment
  - Availability and adequacy
  - Training in the use of the equipment
  - Inspection schedules

The choice of what will be examined is largely dependent upon the audit team's experience, the workplace factors implicated in the large majority of the organisation's accidents, previous audit findings, etc. The audit team will need to record their findings in note form. It is also important to record where and when the observations were done, what activity was being monitored, and people's comments. It may also be necessary to use checklists, photographic evidence or video recordings to support the audit findings.

Technical and Ergonomic Data

In high hazard industries it may also be prudent to examine technical and ergonomic data, although the necessary experienced technical or ergonomic expertise needs to be available within the audit team. The types of factor that might be examined include:

- Technical processes
- Design and layout of control rooms
- Design and layout of plant
- Emergency alarm systems
- Storage of hazardous materials
- Transportation of hazardous materials
- Occupational exposure limits
- Environmental issues.

Interviewing Data

When auditing an organisation's safety management system it is often necessary to conduct a series of interviews to examine how well the organisation is implementing its safety policies. Elements that could be addressed during the interviews include the extent to which personnel are familiar and knowledgeable about the issues surrounding:

- the existence and quality of health and safety policies
- senior management's leadership, commitment and accountability
- policy and strategy development (e.g. planning, standards, monitoring, co-operation and controls)
- resource allocation
- the organisation's safety-related rules, regulations and procedures
- skills, safety and management training
- safety communications
- risk assessments
- purchasing and engineering controls
- protective equipment
- incident/accident reporting
- emergency preparedness
- occupational health
- safety plans and objectives
- selection, recruitment and placement procedures
- the impact of the required workpace on health and safety
- involvement in safety-related decision-making
- safety committees and safety representatives.

Although this is not an exhaustive list, it does provide an indication of the range and scope of activities that auditing might entail.

Audit Tools

When a decision has been made to conduct an audit, a choice needs to be made about whether to purchase an industry-specific 'proprietary' audit or to develop an audit tool specific to the organisation. It cannot be emphasised enough that the audit must suit the organisation's needs, not the needs of the supplier. Proprietary audits abound in the marketplace, some being better than others. Some appear to be generic to all industrial sectors, while others are specific to an industry (e.g. construction, chemicals, etc.). However, they all focus on the issues outlined above. The differences between them are usually associated with the way the questions are scored and weighted. In the main the issues covered by these proprietary audits are covered by the HSE's document *Human Factors in Industrial Safety* (HS(G) 48), which includes an item bank of appropriate questions and which costs approximately £5, compared to proprietary systems that can cost thousands of pounds. The drawbacks are that a scoring system is not included, neither is the auditing expertise that forms part of the service for some proprietary brand audits. Similarly, HS(G) 48 assumes some level of prior knowledge about safety (in fact most organisations have resident safety advisors with the appropriate knowledge). However, the author has found it to be an extremely useful audit tool, albeit that he has further broken down each question into various elements based on scientific evidence to provide a 'frame of reference' (i.e. the ideal answers) for the responses. The author (with others from the organisation concerned) tested this version in the offshore industry by conducting 333 interviews at the strategic, tactical and operational levels of the organisation. Interestingly, when people were asked about safety issues, they tended to focus on their personal safety or the immediate working environment (e.g. whether or not they had had safety training, the presence and quality of emergency equipment, etc.). When asked about the impact their job function had on the safety of others in the organisation (see the section on task significance in Chapter 3) the large majority had absolutely no idea. If an in-house audit is to be developed, the HS(G) 48 document is a good place to start simply because of the audit question bank, which ranges from management practices to ergonomic considerations. It provides a pick and mix menu that can be used to tailor an audit to an organisation's specific needs. This can also save a considerable amount of time, because the development of an audit question bank can take many months.

Developing an 'In-house' Audit Tool

If starting from scratch, the development of the audit question bank will normally be achieved through a number of stages. The first stage is to derive the initial questions from a review of the appropriate legislation, scientific literature or other sources such as standard operating procedures or risk assessments. Other means include asking the organisation's personnel to describe critical incidents that have affected their personal safety by using the critical incident technique (see Chapter 8). Whichever method is used, the second stage involves testing this initial question set on a sample of personnel to ensure they are both logical and relevant. In light of this testing, a draft audit manual is written that reflects any changes made to the initial question set, and provides the necessary instructions and guidelines for the audit's use. The third stage involves subjecting this revised manual to further testing (in as many diverse settings as possible) to ensure that people understand the questions, instructions and guidelines. This manual is then further refined to reflect everybody's comments, and so on. As the latter makes clear, developing a question set is a process that is repeated over and over again until the developers are satisfied that it fully covers the topics under consideration.

Developing a scoring system.   One of the most difficult aspects of devising an in-house audit is the development of an appropriate scoring scheme. This can take months of painstaking work trying to establish the weighting factors for each of the various elements (i.e. determining the overall importance of a particular element in relation to all the other elements that comprise the whole audit tool). In fact, a simple *'yes' 'no' 'don't know'* format will suffice in most instances. This not only keeps the scoring system simple, but it can also be used to calculate an average percentage score for each audit element, for the audit as a whole, and for each individual respondent. Suppose, for example, that an audit team had devised ten questions to determine the degree of senior management's commitment to safety, and each of these questions was put to respondents, each of whom answered in different ways. The audit team would calculate each respondent's percentage score by adding up the number of *Yes* responses, the number of *No* responses, and the number of *Don't know* responses. In the first instance, the total number of *Don't know* responses is ignored. The percentage safe score would then be calculated by using the following formula:

$$\% \text{ safe} = \frac{\text{Total Number of 'YESses'}}{\text{Total Number of YESses} + \text{Total Number of NOs}} \times 100$$

i.e.

$$\% \text{ safe} = \frac{5 \text{ YESses}}{5 \text{ YESses} + 5 \text{ NOs}} = \frac{5}{10} = 0.5 \times 100 = 50\%$$

In this example, a score of 50% would indicate that senior management still have some considerable way to go to demonstrate their commitment to safety to the person who answered the audit questions. Obviously, if all the respondents' views on management commitment were around the same level in a particular business unit, the overall score would have much greater validity. To calculate an overall audit score for a particular audit element, the same formula would be used, except that you would add the number of *YESses* and *NOs* together for *all* the respondents, and then apply the formula. By extension, this means that it is possible to calculate a percentage score for a work group, department, business unit or the audit location as a whole simply by adding together the total number of *YESses* and *NOs* for all the respondents for each element audited. It is important to calculate the percentage scores by using the number of *YESses* and *NOs*, not by adding together a number of averaged percentage scores (i.e. averaging a series of averages), otherwise the total percentage score will be distorted.

Prioritising scale.   Before beginning the audit, it is also important to divide the actual percentage scores into various bands so that the priority of any remedial actions can be easily determined. The following bands provide a simple but effective prioritising method for the percentage safe score:

0–20%   Alarming
21–40%   Poor
41–60%   Average
61–80%   Good
81–100%   Excellent

Calculating the degree of certainty of safety knowledge. The number of 'Don't knows' could be used to calculate the degree of certainty of safety knowledge. i.e. the higher the percentage certainty response, the higher the degree of respondents' knowledge about safety in the organisation. In essence, the certainty score indicates the difference between the percentage of 'Don't know' responses and a perfect 100% score. For example, if a respondent were able to answer only eight of the ten management commitment questions, the percentage certainty score would be 80% (2 divided by 10 = 0.2 multiplied by 100 = 20% minus 100 = 80%). This means the respondent was only 80% certain about his or her knowledge of management commitment. The certainty score can provide a useful indication of the organisation's levels of knowledge about its safety management system. A score of less than 75% could signal a need for further improvements to the quality of safety communications, safety training or other such remedial actions.

AUDITING PRACTICE

A number of basic activities are common to all auditing programmes, some taking place before arriving on site, some during the audit itself, and others after the audit has been completed. Practically all audits involve gathering and analysing information, evaluating safety management systems against certain criteria, and reporting the results to management. Pre-audit activities involve the selection of the locations to be audited, scheduling the audit, selecting the members of the audit team, and developing an audit plan to help define the scope of the audit. Pre-audit activities also tend to include an advance visit to the plant or site to be audited to gather background information or to administer safety climate questionnaires (see Chapter 8). Determining an appropriate audit schedule frequently depends on the goals of the specific audit programme, as well as the number of facilities and functional areas to be included within the scope of the programme. These plants or locations can be selected by a number of methods. For example whether a site is potentially hazardous, how important in business terms the site is to the organisation, the frequency of accidents, the frequency of environmental releases, etc. As every organisation's safety management systems should be fully audited as a matter of course, a major consideration in choosing a site for audit is whether or not it has been audited before.

Pre-audit Visits

Once a location has been chosen for audit, a further consideration is to make sure that all key personnel will be available and that the facility will be in its normal operating mode at the time of the audit. Once this has been established an audit team leader will normally identify all the types of information that the team will need or require in advance of the actual audit. Advance visits prior to the audit early on in the development of the audit programme tend to increase the effectiveness of the subsequent audit. The objective of such a visit is to inform the plant management and staff about the audit's goals, objectives and procedures, obtain in-depth information about the facility and gain a good feel for the way the site is run. The advantage offered by this preparation is that it allows the audit team to develop a more comprehensive audit plan. Irrespective of whether or not there is a pre-audit visit all the information known about a particular plant ought to be reviewed by the team leader and the team members as appropriate at the time, as it helps to guide the issues to be developed in the audit plan. These types of pre-audit review often minimise the risk of omitting anything important during the planning stages of the audit.

Developing an Audit Plan

An audit plan is an outline of the steps that will need to be taken by the audit team in terms of who will do what, and in what sequence. These points are normally included in a written guide. Prior to an audit, the audit team leader should also have identified the priority topics for review so that, if necessary, the written guides can be modified. This also helps the team leader to make an initial assessment of the required audit team resources. Before the audit, and certainly within one month before the actual audit commences, each audit member should receive guidance and training in auditing techniques, and a briefing on the audit policy. The audit policy training should give the team members an overview of the audit process to be used and the strategy to be adopted. In this way everyone shares a common understanding of the way in which the audit will proceed. The training should also familiarise the audit team with the actual audit schedule and make clear to each team member the scope of their work and their individual responsibilities for the preparation, implementation and follow up of the audit. The audit practice training is used both to familiarise the audit team with the specific diagnostic tools that are being used and to familiarise or refresh their knowledge of interviewing techniques.

Selecting the Appropriate Number of People

Developing an audit plan also involves selecting the appropriate sampling method, and of course the amount of people who are going to be audited and reviewed. Selecting the appropriate sampling method will obviously be dependent on the objectives of the sampling (e.g. technical audit or a review of particular factors associated with the safety management system). The team leader often selects particular groups of people for interview across the organisation by referring to organisational charts (i.e. organograms) that show the names of departments and people and job titles. The number of people that are going to be interviewed must be adequate to be representative of the whole plant so that the audit team can make an accurate defensible judgement. A suggested scheme for determining the appropriate percentage sample size is as follows:

Table 6.1   Scheme for determining a sample size

Size of sample (people)	A	B	C
2–10	100%	100%	100%
11–25	100%	39%	17%
26–50	53%	21%	16%
51–100	26%	13%	9%
101–250	17%	12%	6%
251–500	13%	5%	3%
501–1000	6%	3%	2%
Over 1000	2–3%	2%	1–2%

A = suggested minimum for compliance audits
B = suggested minimum for validation audits
C = suggested minimum for plant/site technical audits

Interviewees should be chosen by the audit team leader and not by the location's management as this helps to minimise the potential for any biases to be introduced into the audit's findings. Similarly, all interviewees should be given at least one month's notice that they will be involved in the audit. This is often done with a standard letter that emphasises that the audit is a routine part of the company's safety improvement activities and that, while safety is the primary concern, other operational problems or concerns can also be raised. Everybody should also be asked to give their full support and co-operation to the audit team. Prospective interviewees could also be asked to provide a list of their current safety concerns so that these can be explored or discussed during the audit (this could also help to determine some of the audit's objectives).

Setting the Ground Rules for Evaluating the Audit Findings

The audit plan should include the ground rules for the evaluation of the audit team findings. For example, it might be that individual team members must formally communicate potential problems or deficiencies to the audit team leader as and when they are found. The team leader can then raise these issues during informal discussions with the audited site's management. This not only helps to reduce the possibility of any surprises at the close-out meeting, but also allows any misunderstandings to be rapidly cleared up. At the end of each interview, it is also a good idea to get each team member to check the information obtained to ensure that it has been thoroughly and completely evaluated, for example by asking questions such as:

- Did I adequately record the information I was given?
- Did I identify and ask the appropriate questions?
- Did I use the correct techniques?

The team members should also be expected to summarise their findings, draw a conclusion and record it immediately after an interview. Moreover, at the end of each day, before retiring for dinner, the audit team could also hold a debriefing meeting to review and constructively challenge the conclusions that each team member has reached during the day. The findings as a whole are then reviewed and agreed upon by the whole team, as this helps to identify any trends or pattern of deficiencies that might be caused by the same type of problems. The team's attention should also be drawn to the possibility of identifying deficiencies that in themselves are quite minor but which, when grouped together, point to much greater problems.

On-Site Audit Activities

The first thing that normally occurs when an audit team arrives on site is an introductory opening meeting lasting for about an hour. This meeting is intended to provide an opportunity for the audit team and key members of the plant staff to meet, so that the audit team can explain their objectives, their approach and the overall audit process. These meetings also allow the site management team to provide an overview of the location's activities, while also informing the audit team about the local rules and procedures. In addition, this meeting provides an opportunity for any politically sensitive issues to be identified and discussed. After the meeting the audit team is typically given a tour of the site.

The actual 'on-site' audit typically involves the following five basic steps:

- Understanding management systems
- Assessing strengths and weaknesses
- Gathering audit data
- Evaluating the audit data
- Reporting the audit findings.

Understanding the Site's Management Systems

Most of the audit team's on-site activities are dependent upon developing a working understanding of the site's integral safety management systems. Very often auditors are tempted to rush in and review a series of documents to verify that certain procedures are in place. Ideally, however, the audit should start with a thorough understanding of the management system itself. For example, when informal management systems are in place with little or no written documentation or procedures, the auditors must assess whether this form of management can be effective if the work or staff changes. Understanding the management systems also includes developing an understanding of the workflow processes and internal controls such as staff responsibilities, engineering documentation, emergency procedures, etc. This up to date knowledge helps to build on the information provided prior to the on-site audit, and is usually obtained from management interviews and verified later on in discussions with other staff as the audit proceeds. The auditor should record his or her understanding on a flow chart or narrative description or some combination of the two in order to have a written description against which to audit.

Assessing Strengths and Weaknesses

In order to clearly understand how safety is meant to be managed, the auditors need to evaluate the soundness of the safety management systems. This requires the audit team to check that the management systems actually perform as intended. The appropriate questions to ask might include:

- Are people doing everything the way they say they are?
- Are current methods and safety practices acceptable?
- Is the site complying with applicable requirements?

Assessing the strengths and weaknesses of management systems is usually achieved by looking at performance indicators such as written policies safety management programmes, standard operating procedures, safety plans, management responsibilities, systems of authorisation, the competency of personnel, administrative controls, documentation of actions taken and internal safety audits. It must be recognised that it is much easier to identify weaknesses in the site's internal controls than it is to determine their adequacy. As there are no widely accepted standards to guide auditors as to what is an acceptable internal control, each of the indicators usually requires the auditor to make judgements about their adequacy. The auditors should be guided by the objectives of the performance indicators in conjunction with the organisation's basic safety philosophy or safety management policy to decide its adequacy.

The advantage of establishing an understanding of the strengths and weaknesses of various systems early in the audit is that it allows the audit team to determine where best to focus its ongoing efforts. For example, where internal control is said to be really good, the auditor could spend time ensuring the existence of that particular control system and testing whether or not it functions effectively on a consistent basis. On the other hand, if the design of an internal system is thought to be inadequate, it would be more fully examined and tested. If the system is found wanting, it will obviously be recorded as a negative finding. Every negative finding should specify in detail what the inherent weaknesses are, along with specific recommendations for action.

Gathering Audit Data

Whichever type of audit is conducted, it will involve information gathering via observation and/or interviewing. No matter which method is used, information gathering involves three basic features. These are:

- Determine the objectives
- Devise a series of questions that will enable assessment of the area under scrutiny
- Compare answers to the questions, against the objectives.

For example, the purpose of observations might be to establish senior management's commitment to safety. To determine this, a series of questions might be asked such as 'Has the organisation appointed a director for health and safety?' 'Do senior management conduct regular safety tours of the workplace?'; 'Does a member of senior management always investigate accidents?'; 'Is health and safety the first item on the agenda at all management meetings?' An auditor would then observe and monitor senior management's activities in the workplace and record events. Analysis of the recorded events would provide answers to the questions posed. The answers would then be analysed as a whole and compared to the original objective of determining senior management's commitment in terms of their behaviour. However, there are certain procedures that should be followed, and some that should be avoided. The next few pages outline both observational and interviewing procedures so that the effectiveness of the chosen method can be enhanced.

Observational procedures.   Unlike information gained from interviews which are based on self-report assessments of what people think, observations focus on what people actually do, or what physical attributes exist in the workplace. However, like most things involving people, for many reasons differences will exist between observers in what they report, etc. The sources of differences in observations are likely to reside in the fact that some people:

- are more skilful or conscientious than others
- differ in their interpretation of what is observed
- may be attending to different things even though they are observing the same scene
- may unconsciously be biased.

Being aware of these sources of differences will help to overcome any difficulties that might arise. To a large extent this can be achieved with a little forethought and preparation. The first thing to establish is the objective of the observations. What is being observed? Why are we undertaking observations? Are we looking at people's behaviour or are we only concerned with the physical aspects of the workplace? If we are observing people's behaviour a different strategy is used than when we observe or monitor the physical aspects of the working environment.

Observing people's behaviour.   When decisions are made to observe people's behaviour in the workplace, it is important to ensure that those being observed are going about their normal daily activities, as there is little point in observing contrived situations, unless of course emergency procedures are being assessed under practice conditions.

The very act of observing itself may affect the people who are being observed. This is termed the 'Hawthorne effect' after a study which showed that the performance of factory workers improved simply as a result of being observed. Therefore, as far as is possible, the observers should be unobtrusive, although not invisible, and not interfere in the situation being observed. The main precaution against Hawthorne effects is to conduct multiple observations. For example, if a location is to be audited for a week, it is possible to observe people for a specific period of time every day, during that week. If multiple observations are to be conducted over a period of time (e.g. a week or more), it is better to observe at different times of the day, on different days, as the information collected is more likely to be representative of normal activity, since those being observed tend to accept and then ignore the observer.

If, however, a limited amount of time is available (which is more likely to be the case during an audit), it is possible to undertake 5 to 10 minute observations at predetermined times throughout the day. Once again the usefulness of this strategy is that the auditors do not have to rely on a single observation to form their opinions or conclusions. *Thus a rule of thumb is always try to get multiple data points, rather than relying on only one or two observations.* Reducing discrepancies between observers is fundamental to effective observational information gathering. The most obvious step to take to reduce discrepancies is to make sure that all the observers are in agreement as to what event is being observed (e.g. management commitment), the specifics of what behaviours are being observed (e.g. safety tours, encouragement of safe behaviours, criticism of unsafe working, etc.) and how each aspect of behaviour will be scored (e.g. yes/no/sometimes, etc.). This will entail devising an observational checklist of some sort which should also include a section for notes and comments to enable associated information to be recorded if necessary (e.g. a manager may have had to attend rapidly to two different situations, which may affect any actions taken). The checklist items should also specify what to ignore in specific situations. Thus, the purpose of the checklist is to narrow down the areas of interest, allowing closer agreement between observers. Sometimes legitimate differences of opinion will arise. If this happens, the observers can record their comments and the reasons why the difference has arisen. Inferences or judgements can be made later when all the observations have been completed, which illustrates the point that whenever possible the recording of events should be separated from making judgements. Further steps which can be taken to reduce discrepancies between observers include selecting observers with similar levels of experience and training; randomly assigning areas of interest to different observers; video recording of situations or events; and scheduling review meetings to discuss the findings and resolve any discrepancies.

Observing physical attributes.   The physical attributes of the working environment are checked by establishing the objective of the observation, devising a checklist of particular items with established standards next to each item to provide a frame of reference, and comparing the findings against the frames of reference. In this way the findings should be the same for any observer. Some differences may become apparent, however, depending upon the perspective and experience of the observer, but these can be addressed at review meetings.

One method of enhancing the quality of physical attribute observations is to look for signs of wear. The wear and tear on various parts of the floor or equipment can indicate the extent to which various system components are used. Similarly, dial settings which are left on a machine, particularly at night, may indicate the way the machine has been used as may the positions in which moveable machines and components are left after use. It is likely that when undertaking assessments of the physical working environment, the auditors will be talking to the operators involved. This is a type of interviewing, and all the rules for interviewing will apply. However, by talking to operatives you are likely to gain a deeper understanding of the process involved and any problems that the operator might consistently come across in his or her daily activities.

Interviewing

Within the context of conducting an audit, interviewing is defined as 'any oral communication conducted throughout the audit process'. Thus any verbal communication, whether in a formal and informal setting, is defined as an interview. The aim of an audit interview is to try and establish whether or not an effective safety management system is in place, is understood, and is functioning correctly. This will involve evaluating existing safety management systems against certain criteria by gathering and analysing information gained from both interviews and observations in the workplace. Regardless of the setting, duration and degree of formality, all audit interviews follow a common pattern: planning, opening, closing and documenting.

Planning the interview   Preparation is essential before conducting the interview to ensure that the interviewer is ready to meet the interviewee. This involves:

- identifying the personnel to be interviewed
- knowing what is to be accomplished in terms of what you wish to find out.

Similarly, to maximise the effectiveness of the interview, the auditor should try to ensure that:

- there will be no interruptions
- all the appropriate documentation is available
- the timing of the interview is convenient for all parties concerned

- he or she has some understanding of the interviewee's current job title, responsibilities, and reporting relationships
- the physical environment will lend itself to conducting interviews (e.g. an office rather than in the middle of the production process, etc.)
- he or she can keep track of the time, without having to look at a watch.

The atmosphere will probably be more informal and more conducive to information gathering if the auditor (where possible):

- does not sit behind a desk
- arranges the seating so that all parties will feel comfortable (e.g. in a semi-circle)
- ensures that office doors are closed to create an atmosphere of privacy
- avoids one interviewee being interviewed by several auditors, which may intimidate the person.

Opening the interview. Perhaps the most crucial part of the interview is to make the interviewee feel comfortable and co-operative. Interviewees are understandably often nervous and defensive as they normally expect to be asked a lot of questions, to which they hope they have the right answers. They should not be made to feel nervous or defensive.

The following basic guidelines should help to establish a good working relationship.

- *Introductions*—the auditor should introduce himself or herself, explain why the audit is being undertaken, ensure the timing of the interview is convenient, and inform the person of the amount of time that the interview is expected to take.
- *Inform the person about the topics to be covered*—people are entitled to know what to expect during the interview. Similarly, the auditor is entitled to decide what the interview will cover and include, and what the objectives are. Nonetheless, agreement about the topics to be covered forms the basis for establishing a good working relationship and will help to keep the interview moving forwards. It is also worth the auditor establishing, in a considerate way, that notes will be taken throughout the interview.
- *Reassure the person*—when the purpose of the interview is discussed it is worth stressing the point that, when the findings of the audit are reported, any specific comments made by the individual will be kept confidential. The auditor should also explain how the information

obtained will be used; that is, that the primary purpose of the information obtained is to help the audit team develop a complete understanding of how safety activities are managed in the interviewee's workplace, and that the auditor is not there to test or find fault with the interviewee.

Conducting the interview.   After opening the interview, the auditor should shift the emphasis to the main business in hand: obtaining, exploring and understanding specific information. The easiest way to maintain control and obtain the information required is to structure the interview.

- *Confirm the interviewee's position and responsibilities*—the auditor could (and should) ask for a brief overview of the interviewee's job, to confirm how that person fits into the overall organisation in their workplace, and what their primary responsibilities are. The auditor then follows on and probes for answers to specific questions, prepared prior to the interview. One of the best ways of changing from one topic to another is to summarise. This is done by simply covering the points raised since the last summary, and then changing to the next question if everything is agreed upon from the last topic.
- *Use open-ended questions*—during the interview the auditor will want to encourage the interviewee to give the fullest answers possible. However, the way in which questions are asked will affect the responses given. Open-ended questions, such as those that start with 'What', 'How', 'When' and 'Why' are the better type to use, simply because they help the interviewee to answer the questions in concrete terms, rather than in vague or abstract terms. The best types of question are those that start with 'What'. Most of the questions that might be asked can be prefixed with 'What'. For example, *'What evidence is there to demonstrate that a "responsible competent person" is assigned to each work group, with specific authority to verify adherence to procedures?'* The response to this should cover the 'how' and 'when'. If not, the auditor can use these to probe further.
- *Constructive probing*—when responses to questions are inconsistent or in conflict with other evidence, phrases such as 'Tell me about . . .', or 'Tell me more about . . .' should be used as they are neutral: i.e. they give no indication of approval or disapproval, but invite more than a yes/no response. If such phrases are used the auditor should ensure that the interviewee is given time to gather his/her thoughts and decide how the answer will be presented. An inexperienced interviewer often finds silence intolerable, and when waiting for a response from a good open-ended question, will often pose another question. Pauses are often a very useful device to elicit further information, but should not be used to put

the interviewee under stress, as this will result in defensiveness. Well managed silences build up a sort of tension, which interviewees often feel it necessary to fill with more information, but it requires good judgement to decide when a silence has gone on long enough. When the auditor asks 'Tell me about . . .?' questions, he or she may find that the interviewee drifts from the main point, and the auditor may be tempted to interrupt to try and correct this. Often, however, it is useful to let interviewees continue, as something important may be learnt, and they can always be encouraged back to the main point later on.

- *Avoid closed questions*—closed questions are those that invite a yes/no response, and as such tend to be of little value and tend to make interviewing more difficult (unless the scoring format of the interview schedule has been explicitly designed to elicit yes/no responses). Any question that can be answered with a simple 'yes' or 'no' are closed questions. Examples include questions that start with 'Do', 'Can', 'Will', 'Is', 'Did'. Sometimes these types of question will suffice, depending on what it is that you are trying to find out, particularly if the question is highly focused. However, in the main they should be avoided. The interview is quite a robust procedure, and often the interviewee is on the auditor's side, allowing him or her to get away with asking a closed question by giving a lengthy response. But this is not always so; therefore, although it is natural to start with closed questions, the auditor should try and start with open-ended questions, as the interview will tend to be much easier.

- *Avoid leading questions*—leading questions are a dangerous form of closed question, and make it clear to the interviewee what answer you expect to hear. This type of questioning not only invites agreement, but also makes the questioner appear naive and foolish. Similarly, gimmicky questions (those with a catch in them), which sound searching and deep must be avoided, as they do not yield information that can be sensibly interpreted. The most likely effect of this type of question is to bemuse, or even humiliate the interviewee. Moreover, if the auditor wants to keep receiving information he or she should never criticise the interviewee, although this should not occur if the auditor is focused upon the information being received.

- *Listen to the responses*—listening and being attentive is the single most useful and essential interviewing technique. Auditors may get away with slack questioning, social clumsiness etc., but they cannot get away with listening badly or inaccurately. Accurate listening implies attention, care, alertness and a keen awareness of the obstacles to accuracy. Establishing real communication requires that the receiver (the auditor) is every bit as accurate as the transmitter (interviewee). Attentive listening not only implies respect, but also reinforces the interviewee and conditions him/her to continue talking. The auditor should therefore never allow his or her attention to lapse or wander.

Closing the interview.   It is particularly important to close each interview in a concise, timely and positive manner, as this will reflect on the audit team as a whole. There are at least three components to closing the interview.

- *Ensure all the topics have been covered*—the auditor needs to make sure that there are no major gaps in the information acquired. In other words has the auditor obtained all the information wanted? There is no reason that the auditor cannot consult his or her list of points made before the interview. This should be done openly by explaining to the interviewee what the auditor is doing. Similarly, the auditor should invite the interviewee to ask about anything that they feel is important. However, the interviewee must be given time to think, and the auditor should even suggest that the person takes time to do so. The auditor would also be wise to invite the interviewee to expand on anything that has been said, to ensure that there have been no misunderstandings.
- *Summarise*—the auditor should summarise the information obtained. This may be as simple or elaborate as the auditor wishes, but it allows any misunderstandings to be clarified.
- *Close-out*—the auditor should thank the person for their time and candour, and state what is to happen next, i.e. the information will be written up as a report, and communicated to local staff at the end of the audit at the close-out meeting.

Evaluating Audit Data

Once the data gathering phase is deemed to be complete, all the data needs to be evaluated to identify and record the audit findings as either positive or negative conclusions. If the audit team makes an initial evaluation of the data throughout the audit itself by comparing notes at the end of each day and jointly discusses, evaluates and formulates tentative audit findings, the final evaluation tends to be somewhat easier and quicker. Importantly, the final conclusions should be arrived at by consensus, based on all the data collected and analysed during the audit. The auditors should be particularly careful not to base their conclusions on a single interview or single document. Rather, they should strive to confirm them from other data sources. During an audit, it is not uncommon for an audit team and the site's management to continuously discuss the important findings and the conclusions they are arriving at so that surprises at the final close-out meeting can be avoided. During this meeting, the audit team communicate all the findings noted during the audit. Any ambiguities about the findings can then be clarified prior to the audit team making any final recommendations. The criteria for evaluating the data obtained during an audit is usually based on assessing whether the data that has been obtained is sufficient and adequate.

- *Sufficiency of data*—audit teams frequently wonder whether they have collected enough information to confirm their understanding of the site's safety management systems and programmes. This begs the question of 'How much is enough?' In essence, the audit team have probably gained enough information if they:
  - understand both the design of the management system and how its is implemented.
  - have interviewed all key personnel involved in the system's operation
  - can adequately summarise all the safety initiatives in progress
  - understand the causes of any difference in the viewpoints of management and employees.
- *Adequacy of data*—determining the adequacy of any information obtained is usually achieved by assessing it against four properties. These are the information's:
  - relevance
  - freedom from bias
  - objectivity
  - persuasiveness.

Relevance refers to the information's usefulness in helping the audit team reach conclusions in relation to the audit's objectives (for example, the presence of, use and co-ordination of permit to work procedures would constitute relevant information about the control of critical situations). Freedom from bias means that the information received is free from any attempts to influence the audit report, and can be supported by an alternative information source. Similarly, data is deemed to be objective if it leads two separate auditors to reach the same conclusion. If the same piece of information leads to two different conclusions, then the information lacks objectivity and should not be used as a basis for decision-making. Alternatively the auditors may be biased, and it may be necessary for the team to discuss the potential findings before a decision is reached as a conclusion. Persuasiveness refers to the inevitability of the information leading to a single conclusion by two or more people, and may arise from the sheer volume of data or the type of data (e.g. accident records). If these properties are not satisfactory, additional information gathering will probably be necessary.

Reporting the Audit Findings

After the on-site audit is complete the audit team must complete its report within a reasonable time frame (e.g. two to four weeks). In all cases the site audit team must have the opportunity to review the findings at the reports draft stage. Sometimes these reviews will include a pre-defined group of other experienced auditors, technical experts, legal personnel or those who commissioned the audit. The purpose of the review is to ensure that the report is clear, concise and accurate rather than an attempt to modify the audit team's findings.

The final audit report should document the results of the audit indicating: where and when the audit was done, who performed the audit, the audit's overall scope, and the audit findings. The specific content of the report will vary. For example, a report that is focused solely on identifying deficiencies might remain silent on all other matters. Another report might merely offer comments on the subject areas reviewed. The content of the audit report itself should be defined as part of the audit programme and should be consistent with the objectives of the audit.

As there is no single correct way to determine the content of an audit report, it is important that, once the format and content has been decided, the audit team produces reports that are consistent with it. It is also important when writing audit reports to ensure that great care is taken to use the appropriate wording. The audit report must clearly and concisely communicate the findings and observations of the audit team. Accordingly it should be worded in such a way that it does not imply findings or observations that go beyond those actually intended. Where possible, facts should be reported very clearly and concisely and every statement should be capable of being supported by evidence, not conjecture or speculation. For example, writing 'The team were unable to verify . . .' instead of 'The plant does not have . . .' is much more accurate and therefore defensible. This makes the point that the language used in writing the report is very important.

AUDIT FOLLOW-UP

After issuing the report it will often be necessary for the audit team to develop a follow-up and corrective action stage during which an action plan is developed that reflects the areas in which improvements are required. The action plan should indicate what is to be done, who is responsible for doing it and when it is to be completed. The action plan itself is an important step in ensuring and demonstrating that the audit findings are being addressed. I should be developed in conjunction with the site manager responsible for the audited site, and should contain mechanisms for other senior managers to monitor progress. Copies should be distributed to everyone who has a responsibility under the plan, to all the members of the audit team, to the organisation's director of safety, health and environment, and to the company safety manager. The action plan should be subsequently reviewed and updated on a regular basis (e.g. quarterly) so as to track the status of the remedial actions. Sometimes the audit team are also required to monitor the completion of any action plan that results from the audit.

One of the last steps in the overall process is the verification of these corrective actions. This is generally a role performed by the audit team, simply because it is important to have an independent verification that corrective actions have been undertaken and that these factors directly address the audit's recommendations. In some auditing programmes, the verification of corrective actions is performed as part of the next scheduled audit. In other programmes, verification is performed sooner at a special separate review. In any event the same audit techniques used for verification in the programme implementation should be used periodically to verify the reported stages of the action plan.

REVIEWING THE AUDIT SYSTEM

The final step consists of examining ways in which the overall audit procedure could be improved. In the main, such reviews are conducted with a view to examining the effectiveness of the overall audit system, or may be conducted to ensure a particular audit was carried out correctly. There are several options for conducting an audit system review. These include both internal and external reviews.

Internal Reviews

Internal reviews should be conducted by senior members of the organisation who were not involved in the audit. The main purpose of an internal review is to confirm that an audit was carried out correctly according to the predetermined audit standards, that all the topics of interest were covered, and that all the logistical arrangements were satisfactory. In addition, the reviewers should seek information from the audited site that the audit team acted professionally. In other words, the audit team's actions during the audit should also be subjected to scrutiny.

External Reviews

Usually carried out by someone from another part of the organisation or from an outside organisation, external reviews are more concerned in ensuring that the audit standards and procedures themselves are satisfactory. The external reviewer should be someone with extensive auditing experience (the choice of an experienced financial auditor should not be discounted as they operate to very high standards and can bring an enormous amount of expertise to bear). Alternatively, it may be possible to set up an audit review panel comprising a number of experienced auditors. The advantages offered by independent reviews unconnected with the detail of an audit are immense. They could, for example, reveal that:

- the audit's guidelines were not followed
- there are gaps in the audit's standards and procedures
- technical matters of general interest need greater investigation
- the audit team tried to do too much within the allotted time scale
- there were deficiencies in the quality of the audit team or their training.

Section Three

The ultimate level of effort

7

Safety Propaganda and Safety Training

INTRODUCTION

Having addressed the organisational and managerial aspects of developing a safety culture during the immediate and intermediate levels of effort, attention is now specifically focused on the ultimate level of effort. However, the approaches used to address the most difficult aspect of developing a proactive safety culture, namely that of winning people's hearts and minds, can either enhance or undermine everything the organisation has already done at the immediate or intermediate levels of effort. In general, there are two types of approach: passive and active. The former tends to rely on general exhortations for people to think and behave safely, in combination with safety training being used to support the message, whereas the latter is dependent upon empowering those employees with real responsibility for the day-to-day safety effort. In other words, people are either treated as passive recipients of safety information, or as active participants in the safety effort. Not surprisingly, the outcomes of these two approaches will differ. The success of propaganda approaches (inclusive of safety training) in winning people's hearts and minds tends to be very limited, whereas empowerment approaches tend to be extremely successful. Accordingly, this chapter concentrates on passive approaches traditionally used to win people's hearts and minds. Proactive approaches for winning people's hearts and minds are considered in Chapters 8 and 9.

SAFETY INFORMATION CAMPAIGNS

Perhaps because of their high profile nature, informational safety campaigns have been widely used in many industrial sectors to educate employees to work safely. They are known to appeal to senior management and are believed to be cost-effective, simply because they reach large numbers of workers. Although the medium varies (e.g. posters, in-house publications, videos, films, gifts, etc.) these types of campaign are usually developed for the express purpose of educating employees and raising the profile of safety. As such, they usually contain elements which attempt to alter beliefs and knowledge as well as attempting to motivate and encourage particular safety-related actions. Unfortunately, there is a tendency for them to fail miserably on both these counts, as demonstrated by the fact that they rarely exert any significant downwards pressure on accident rates. This has been clearly shown in a recent two year safety propaganda campaign conducted by researchers in a Finnish shipbuilding yard with 3,400 employees. Based on previous evidence the campaign incorporated best practice that included:

- developing the campaign materials with the assistance of the workforce
- using specific instructional messages
- posting different messages at the relevant workplaces
- changing the posters periodically
- providing performance feedback.

Despite the campaign being well received by employees, no notable change occurred in either the number or severity of accidents. Similarly during the nation-wide 'Site Safe 83' campaign in the UK construction industry, which involved the use of slogans printed on posters, mugs, etc. there were a further 18 fatalities and 226 major accidents compared to the previous year.

Frightening Messages

One of the most common propaganda campaign methods involves trying to frighten people into being safe by using fear-arousing messages on posters in the workplace. One example is

'On one end of this CABLE is a 240 volt mains supply, on the other is a DEAD MAN'

supported by a photograph of a broken electricity cable with smoke curling upwards. These types of message are thought to induce high levels of fear which lead to people positively changing their attitude(s) towards the subject matter of the campaign. It is assumed that this change in attitude(s) will the cause people to change their behaviour so that they act in a way that avoid any involvement in a subject matter-related accident. Although this may sound logical, the available research evidence suggests that this assumption is only partly true. For example, despite some of these campaigns success-fully inducing fear and changing attitudes in the short term, they were not so successful in changing the associated behaviour. A number of such fear-arousing campaigns were also shown to be counter-productive as they led to defensive reactions that caused people to completely reject the message. Indeed, this latter reaction tends to be the most common, as people have a tendency to reject or ignore threatening messages, as they deny the possibility that anything bad can happen to them.

Induce Fear or Provide Factual Information?

Some campaigns that have deliberately manipulated fear levels have shown that moderate, rather than extreme, levels may alter some people's attitudes, although it does not always follow that the required behaviour will also change. A number of explanations are available, including the way the message is presented, the person's degree of control over what is advocated by the message, and the relationship between the message and the influence of the prevailing working environment.

Presentation effects.   The way a fear message is presented will exert a sig-nificant influence on the message's success in changing people's attitudes or behaviour. While some campaigns use only fear-arousing communications (such as the 240 volt scenario described above) or specific recommendations for action (for example, 'Wear eye protection'), others adopt a policy of only imparting factual information (for example, 'Know your fire extinguisher colour code').

In order to examine the success with which each of the first two types of message have induced fear and/or influenced people's attitudes and behav-iour, researchers have tested various combinations by presenting the fear element with specific recommended actions in four different formats:

1. specific recommendations first
2. specific recommendations and threatening material intermingled
3. specific recommendations last
4. no recommendations.

In terms of inducing fear, the 'no recommendations' (4) were most effec-tive, followed in order by 'recommendations first' (1), 'both intermingled' (2), and 'recommendations last' (3).

In terms of changing attitudes and behaviour, this research has shown that people more readily accept and act upon a message in which specific recommendations are available and presented all in one go, as a solid block.

This shows that specific information exerts a greater influence than fear *per se*. Therefore, posters and other forms of safety communication (such as safety training films) should broadcast specific recommendations for action rather than try to induce fear. Similarly, if fear arousal is to be used, specific information should be presented in one chunk either before or after the fear-arousing message as this aids understanding and facilitates acceptance. This and other research also shows that specific *new* information is far more effective for changing attitudes than general exhortations. This is because new information builds on existing knowledge and also targets specific behaviours.

The danger of vague general messages is that they allow employees to draw their own conclusions as to what is required or, as is more often the case, people tend to think the message applies only to others, not themselves. This may explain why personnel are more likely to remember specific rather than general safety messages.

Degree of control.   The interactive relationship between people's attitudes and their perceptions of the situation is also important. Their beliefs concerning their degree of control over the environment, the layout of the physical environment or the two in combination also affect the degree of attitude change. Although it is self-evident that messages aimed at changing something beyond people's control are not likely to exert any positive effects, they can too often be found in the workplace. One example is a poster sold through a national safety organisation that urges workers to 'replace worn parts'. This message is unlikely to have any effect on attitudes or behaviour simply because most employees tend to be reliant upon the maintenance department for repairs of this nature, and therefore are not in a position to change worn parts. A more fruitful message might be to urge people to report worn or defective parts, and stop using the equipment until the 'part' has been replaced. Although this may appear to be a costly route in terms of production, at least the message urges a behaviour that is within people's control. Moreover, urging people to stop using machinery until it is fit for purpose is consistent with the idea of a positive safety culture, as well as reducing costly accidents.

The influence of the prevailing working environment.   The important influence of the immediate physical environment (situation) is illustrated in a study that introduced a poster campaign to get employees to replace chain slings on crane hooks after a lifting task has been completed. Although the campaign had a small overall effect on behaviour, it was far more successful with those who worked in low-roofed premises, where the hanging chain slings presented a much larger danger, than in high-roofed premises. In other words, the degree of immediate danger present in the environment (situation) determined the importance (attitude) employees placed on the campaign's message, which influenced the number of times the slings were replaced on crane hooks (behaviour). Such campaigns might, therefore, be more successful if they are aimed at specific dangers thought to be important to the workers themselves, as this offers the advantage of taking into account the dangers presented by the immediate working environment. Indeed, this idea could be extended to include some form of competition among employees whereby they design their own posters to address problems related to their own operational areas. Safety advisors and line managers could assist in this process by providing information about the following 'golden rules of thumb' to enhance the effectiveness of the posters. For design and content purposes these include ensuring that the posters:

- are concerned with specific behaviours that are within the control of employees
- are specific to a particular task or situation
- provide clear instructions rather than threaten
- are positive rather than negative in tone
- are designed to grab attention
- reflect topics which the target group feel are important.

In addition, line management should ensure that the posters are:

- placed in relevant areas of the workplace
- changed on a regular basis, so that they do not blend into the background and become a part of the furniture.

Although the rules of thumb outlined above apply to both commercially available and self-developed posters, it is essential that the assistance of the target audience is sought if ownership is to result. Although such an approach will increase the likelihood of personnel heeding the campaign's message, without supporting systems such as on-going training and direct positive reinforcement from management or co-workers, poster campaigns exert little long-term influence on people's attitudes or behaviours.

SAFETY TRAINING

Attempting to change people's safety behaviour and attitudes via safety training is one of the most widely used methods for improving safety in the workplace. Largely based on the implicit assumption that trained people will automatically work safely on the job over extended periods of time regardless of the prevailing circumstances, most safety manuals have tended to recommend training as *the* means of accident prevention. Indeed, the importance attached to safety training is underlined by legislative requirements for employers to provide the appropriate safety training to personnel (e.g. MHSWR 1992, regulations 11(2) and 11(3)). Nonetheless, although some evidence shows that a variety of *high quality* integrated job and safety training programmes are one of the main features that distinguishes high from low accident companies, other research has shown that safety training *per se* does not bring about lasting changes in people's safety-related behaviours or attitudes.

Why Safety Training can be Ineffective

One of the major reasons why safety training does not work is that all too often there is a mismatch between the requirements of effective training and the training given. In other words, safety training programmes are often not tailored specifically to the needs of the trainees. Familiar examples include:

- the inappropriate use of teaching methods (e.g. lectures rather than practical hands-on simulations to manual workers)
- irrelevant training content caused by the trainers lacking an understanding of the trainees' jobs (e.g. giving construction site toolbox talks on the dangers of excavations to bricklayers, scaffolders and roofers)
- insufficient training time to ensure real understanding of the issues involved (e.g. merely showing a half-hour training film without further exploring the issues involved)
- the use of inexperienced trainers
- a lack of feedback to individual trainees about their learning progress through trainers assuming that the mere presentation of the training material is a sufficient condition for learning.

Even when an ideal training programme has been designed and delivered the credibility and importance of the training received is often undermined through day-to-day operational causes (e.g. line managers ignoring or actively encouraging unsafe behaviour for the sake of productivity). In other words, the training received is not continually reinforced by line management or followed up with constant coaching and refresher training. A notable exception to this is the UK offshore industries' survival training. All personnel must attend an intensive five day training course involving fire and evacuation procedures that leads to a survival certificate. Thereafter every helicopter journey to and from offshore platforms undertaken by personnel is accompanied by refresher training on evacuation procedures prior to boarding.

Designing Ideal Training Programmes

One method of training known to influence both behaviours and attitudes is Computer Based Training (CBT). In essence, CBT provides interactive, personalised training programmes that allow trainees to work at their own pace while receiving ongoing feedback about their performance. Despite heavy initial development costs, CBT also tends to be more cost-effective as more people can be trained in less time than by conventional methods. The flexibility of CBT also means that employees can be trained at their place of work (e.g. on PCs in operational areas) which facilitates the transfer of learning without the need for supervisors or training personnel to be present. In addition, CBT systems can be easily updated to reflect changes in operational or legislative requirements. Nonetheless, it is always a good idea for operational personnel to be involved in the development of a CBT package, as this helps to effect 'ownership' and ensures that the training material is directly relevant to trainees. Given that the majority of safety training tends to be via conventional methods, it makes sense to consider how an optimal training course can be designed, delivered and evaluated. As shown in Figure 7.1: *An Overview of the Training Process*, this consists of systematically proceeding through discrete stages that include the identification of training needs and learning objectives, creating a learning plan, deciding upon the most appropriate training methods, planning the administration of the overall training programme, conducting the training and evaluating the effectiveness of the training.

Identifying Training Needs

One of the most important but often neglected aspects of a training programme is the establishment of training needs to ensure that the course content is directly relevant to the trainees. These needs can often be identified by examining an organisation's safety information systems (see Chapter 5) such as standard operating procedures (SOPs), method statements (documented safe systems of work), risk assessments, permits to work, accident investigation records and near miss reporting systems. The advantages of using existing safety information systems is that they allow for the interactions between safety behaviours, attitudes and operational situations to be fully identified and explored. The general aim is to reveal discrepancies between existing knowledge and what personnel are required to do. Any such discrepancies will almost inevitably mean a training

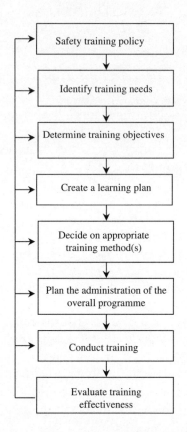

Figure 7.1   An Overview of the Training Process

requirement. The human resource department can assist in this process as they tend to record the training that personnel have previously undertaken. Moreover, they tend to possess in-depth knowledge of job analysis methods (see Chapter 3) if training needs are to be identified by examination of actual jobs or workflow systems.

Identifying Learning Objectives

Once training needs have been identified, the overall aims and objectives of the training programme should be established. The overall aims of the course are usually written as general statements of intent (for example, develop awareness, knowledge, and grasp of safety management procedures) whereas objectives are specific, precise statements of intent that focus on the outcomes of the programme, rather than what occurs during the training. When specifying the objectives, it is important to ensure that they are realistic and achievable.

In general, any training objective should encompass three distinct aspects:

- What the trainees should be able to do after the training
- The conditions (situation) under which the learnt behaviours should be exhibited
- The required performance standards.

Systematically focusing on each of these helps to clarify what is actually required of the training programme and ensures that the course content is directly relevant to the trainees' needs. In practice, training objectives could be concerned with knowledge, skills or attitudes, or a combination of all three.

Knowledge.   Knowledge *per se* refers to the retention, recall and understanding of facts or other items of information. Three types of knowledge are important: information about 'What'; information about 'How'; and information about 'Which, When and Why'.

   Information related to 'What' reflects the rules and concepts about the subject area in which a particular skill, or set of skills, is to be developed. Because subject matter information has to be retrieved from a person's long term memory and actively held in their working memory, this type of knowledge should be overlearnt through repeated practice, feedback and reflection. This is particularly important for safety-related information because people soon forget subject matter rules and their associated concepts if the training is superficial. This may lead to events unfolding which dictate people's unthinking courses of action, rather than them applying the correct rules or concepts for a given situation.

   Information about 'How' is more concerned with the way in which the topic's rules and concepts are put to good use. Good safety training programmes focus upon sequences of context-specific rules of behaviour that apply to both normal operations and emergencies. In other words, the particular behavioural sequences to be enacted in a given situation (i.e. If . . . Then . . .?) need to be taught. The outcomes that can be expected from enacting or deviating from the correct sequence should also be highlighted. Accordingly, it is vital that the correct sequences of events are taught the first time around, and further reinforced throughout the duration of the programme, as it is extremely difficult for people to unlearn, or relearn, a given sequence of behaviour.

   Even though information about *when* to apply *which* knowledge and *why* generally develops through ongoing experience, training programmes should provide information, guidance and/or opportunities for practice, to enable trainees to apply the most appropriate knowledge in particular situations. For example, when and under what conditions it is appropriate to use different types of fire extinguisher (i.e. foam, water or powder) with different types of fire (e.g. petrochemical or electrical), and why the distinctions are important.

Skills. Although skill-based training may be concerned with problem-solving, decision-making, communication or other 'intellectual skills' involving rules and analysis to guide behaviour, the objectives of skill-based training will usually refer to specific behavioural 'motor' skills involved in practical applications of the subject matter. For example, when working in confined spaces employees will need to know how to check their breathing apparatus, how to correctly don the equipment, how to monitor their air supply, and how to overcome any difficulties that might arise. As such skill-based training usually requires a mixture of classroom-based training (*instructive* phase) and 'hands-on' practical training in realistic conditions (*practice* phase). The classroom-based training would normally focus on the sets of rules and concepts associated with the subject matter, whereas the practical hands-on training would implement these rules and concepts. The distinction between these two phases of skill acquisition forces the trainer to consider how the training materials should be sequenced and structured, and what the functions are of particular training devices (e.g. simulators). Similarly, the trainer is forced to decide between teaching trainees the whole task at the same time or breaking it down into smaller manageable components. More often than not, breaking tasks or skills into their constituent components is the better course of action, as each component can be thoroughly learnt before being integrated into a whole task or skill. Careful consideration of these types of issue can considerably ease the burden on the trainer, and ease the stresses on the trainees arising from trying to teach them too much, too quickly. A critical feature of the practice phase is the provision of *constructive* feedback to assist the trainee to get it right every time. Constructive feedback means giving feedback about specific behaviours or actions so that people know what to correct, and why they are going wrong. The feedback needs to be objective, accurate and easily understood, all of which is best achieved by judging a person's performance against a set of pre-determined observable behaviours. When giving feedback, the trainer should begin by focusing on the positives (i.e. what the trainee has done well), then focus on the negatives (i.e. what the trainee is not so good at), and then finish on a positive note (i.e. although the trainee was not so good at something, they were good at other aspects, and if they can address the negatives they will improve considerably). Presenting feedback in this way is known to help to motivate the trainee to want to learn.

Attitudes. Safety training literature often gives the impression that it is the easiest thing in the world to change people's attitudes via training. However, it is not as easy as it sounds, simply because strong links between attitudes and behaviours are only likely to occur in certain situations. Given that situational influences (i.e. social and/or environmental) may exert a greater impact upon people's behaviour than their attitudes, the link between attitude(s) and behaviour(s) becomes even more tenuous. Notwithstanding this, attempts by many safety professionals to change people's attitudes are often predicated on the notion that, because they have tried everything within *their* power to improve safety, it must be people's poor safety-related attitudes that are at fault if things go wrong (see Chapter 8). Indeed, it is often written on accident reports that 'if this person had taken more care, and had a better attitude towards safety, this accident would not have happened'. It is notoriously difficult to describe what an 'attitude' is, given that it is an elusive phenomenon that means different things to different people. Accordingly, when people talk about attitudes they commonly discuss them in terms of people's behaviour (e.g. a predisposition to respond in a given way to particular situations). It seems appropriate, therefore, to ask what exactly is meant by the term 'attitude'. The term is actually a psychological construct or label which is used by people when they attempt to make sense of, or describe, how people *consistently* think, feel and behave towards a particular subject. After many decades of research, psychologists have broken down the concept of 'attitude' into four constituent components. These are:

Cognitive — What a person thinks about a topic
Affective — How a person feels about a topic
Evaluative — Whether or not the person's views about a topic are negative or positive
Conative — Whether or not the person actually behaves in ways that are consistent with their views.

If we consider that these four components relate to one single attitude, and that people generally hold a set of related attitudes about a specific topic, it becomes apparent that each separate component of each separate attitude that comprises one person's complete set of attitudes must be targeted if they are to be changed. To do this for one person would be extremely difficult, even if their attitudes towards a particular topic were known. To do it for a number of people attending a training course would be impossible. Thus, evaluating a one-day or even a one-week safety training course on the basis that it has or has not changed people's safety-related attitudes is clearly a nonsense. In addition, even if a trainer successfully managed to change people's attitudes, could he or she be certain that the trainees will actually behave in accordance with these new attitudes?

Again the answer has to be no. People's behaviour is not only determined by their attitudes, but also by their evaluation of the immediate situation and the likely outcome of their behaviour in that situation. In other words it is not possible to predict how someone will behave simply by knowing (or guessing) what their attitudes towards a topic are. Research has also clearly demonstrated that the best way to change people's attitudes is to change their *behaviour* (see Chapter 9), simply because people tend to re-adjust their values and beliefs to fit with the new behaviour. As such the objectives of a safety training course should be much more concerned with imparting safety-related knowledge and skills than with attempts to change people's attitudes.

Creating a Learning Plan

Once the training objectives have been established and written, it is important to create an optimal learning plan that will fulfil the training objectives. Since people need to know where the training is taking them and how they are going to get there, it is a good idea to specify the desired sequence of training events and make these available to the trainees before they attend the course. This also offers the advantage of the training provider being sure that he or she will have sufficient time available to cover each part of the training topic. On the day it is also a good idea to present '*induction organisers*' to enhance the trainees' motivation, interest and attention, and to set the context for what follows, for example, by showing a brief video of what happens to those who ignore safety issues. This should then be followed by an '*advance organiser*' to establish the learning context and provide a framework for the main content. 'Advance organisers' are overviews of what is to follow, and may include learning objectives, introductory information, etc. (see Figure 7.2: *Advance Organiser for Hot Work Permit Training*). These should be organised hierarchically in descending order of inclusiveness. Each organiser should precede a unit of detailed, differentiated training content. Ideally a graphical representation of the end process/product should be made available (e.g. a flow chart that shows how each element of the training content relates to all the other elements). The learning plan should also identify what trainees should be able to *do* at successive stages throughout the learning process, with the level of difficulty increasing progressively from stage to stage. Each stage should specify exactly what knowledge or skills the trainees should know by the end of it, and how to apply this knowledge or skill to emergency or other unusual situations.

Whole or part learning. It is when the learning plan is created that the training provider makes decisions about whether the training content should

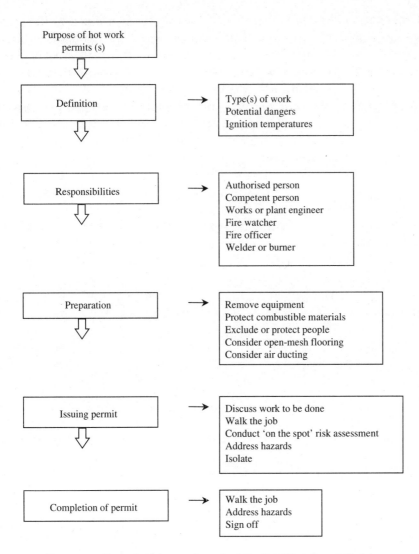

Figure 7.2   Example 'Advance Organiser' for Hot Work Permit Training

be taught as a whole or broken down into discrete steps. In general, whole learning is better for more complex tasks or those with a high degree of organisation, structure and inter-relatedness between task components (i.e. where there is a great deal of cross-flow of information between independent parts). For example, whole learning is probably better for training control room operators in their plant shutdown procedures, simply because each element of the shutdown procedure is inextricably linked and it is therefore less likely that crucial steps will be left out in a behavioural sequence during a real emergency. Conversely, if an operator learns each element separately from the other elements, he or she will have to re-learn the procedure while linking each element together into a whole shutdown sequence, and this could lead to important elements being missed out during a critical event. Another vital aspect of a learning plan for *complex* activities is to provide opportunities for the trainees to receive sufficient information for them to be able to completely understand how a system and each of its interrelated parts are linked together with other parts of the system. Too many infamous disaster investigations have revealed that key operators did not appreciate how the system they were in charge of worked, particularly when the system deviated from its normal operational limits.

Part learning, on the other hand, is better where the parts are sequentially organised, and where poor performance at the initial stages will disrupt the trainees' task performance during the later stages. Welders, for example, are taught how to identify and select the appropriate gas cylinders, hoses, fittings, flashback arresters, regulators and torches before being taught actual welding techniques. Only if they choose the right equipment for the job will the quality of their welding be adequate. In principle, a good learning plan also ensures that there is sufficient time built into the training course to allow in-depth practice of each behavioural sequence so that trainees 'over-learn' (over-learning simply means that the trainee rehearses a skill or procedure until it becomes so automatic that he or she cannot get it wrong). Similarly, for material that imparts new information or concepts, sufficient time must be allowed for reflection and discussion so that people can fit them in with their previous knowledge and experience, and apply them to various situations.

Choosing Appropriate Training Methods

Only after creating a learning plan is it possible to decide on the appropriate training methods to use. It is important to recognise that the choice of training methods will influence the trainees' motivation to learn, and how much they actually learn. There are two types of learning: active and passive. Active learning is more concerned with trainees *doing* something with the knowledge they have been taught (through performing a task or discussing the training material), whereas passive learning merely requires the trainee to receive and digest information (through listening or watching). Researchers have shown that active learning results in between 70% and 90% of the training material being remembered, compared to between 10% and 50% for passive learning. It is therefore generally better for trainees to become actively involved in the learning process as they tend to remember much more, and many safety training courses actually use a mixture of passive and active training methods. The advantages and disadvantages associated with some of the more common instructional methods used for safety training are discussed next.

Lectures and presentations.   Passive learning methods include the traditional lecture and presentations which generally involve one-way communication to a group by someone who is knowledgeable about the subject. The advantages of lectures and presentations are that large chunks of information can be imparted in a relatively short time period to a large number of people at the trainer's own pace. Conversely, because there is little opportunity for two-way dialogue, the audience's attention can easily wander, and people may only remember approximately 20% of the material. However, this type of training method could be made more active by the trainer asking questions of the audience, or getting the audience to ask questions to stimulate discussion. One proven method for stimulating learning and discussion is the use of 'buzz groups'. At the end of the lecture or presentation, people are asked to form small groups, discuss the topic that has just been presented among themselves for 10 to 15 minutes, and formulate a number of questions about the lecture. The questions are then asked of the trainer, who responds as the questions dictate. The advantage of this method is that people are able to ask questions in an enabling atmosphere, while the trainer can reinforce his or her message, and also receive feedback about what people have been unable to understand.

Demonstrations.   A complementary alternative to the lecture or presentation is the use of demonstrations. These are primarily used to demonstrate how to use a particular piece of equipment (e.g. a fire extinguisher, breathing apparatus, etc.) or how to conduct a particular task in a safe manner (e.g. how to safely turn upright an overturned liferaft). The trainees are then invited to 'have a go' themselves. The advantages of demonstrations reside in the interest and attentiveness they can generate among trainees. Most people are able to remember about 50% of what they have seen, and this rises to 90% for those who 'had a go'. If the training group is not too large it may prove useful for everyone to have a go at the task. The disadvantages of demonstrations are mainly related to the amount of time that they can take (particularly if everyone has a go), and that the demonstrator may go too fast for some people to fully absorb the information. If the task involves a number of discrete steps it may be best to go through each of these slowly and explain what is happening at each step, before proceeding through the whole procedure in one go.

Role modelling.   Behavioural role modelling is a very proactive approach to training and refers to a trainee watching and emulating an experienced person conducting a task 'on the job'. In a training environment it is possible to use videotapes of the modelled behaviours followed by rehearsal and role playing. Research has demonstrated that role modelling is most effective when one or two observers are present during the trainees' rehearsal, which in turn is videotaped and played back to the trainee, with constructive feedback provided by the trainer. The advantages of this approach reside in the one to one tuition, the provision of immediate feedback, and the retention rate of about 90%. The drawbacks are related to the costs of providing video equipment and, as it is very time-consuming, the small numbers of people who can be trained at any one time. Nonetheless, it is an ideal aid for crisis management training in jobs where many people's lives are dependent upon a significant person doing the right thing at the right time (e.g. offshore installation managers).

Role playing.   Role playing requires people to act out parts of a situation in as realistic a setting as possible. In other words not only should the physical environment be reproduced as accurately as possible, but the roles should be acted out within the normal everyday limits of managerial authority and within the constraints of the organisation's systems, procedures and policies. There is not much point in acting out a role just for the sake of acting, even if some people enjoy being amateur actors. The role play needs to be conducted with a definite purpose. It is ideal, for example, for teaching interviewing techniques to safety management system auditors and accident investigators. It can also be used effectively to teach people how to handle first aid situations and crisis management techniques. The trainer should make sure that all the participants have got to know one another before introducing role play exercises, otherwise the participants may feel that they will lose 'face' or prestige, because they feel that they might make a fool of themselves. As role play generates a great deal of interest as well as being highly participative, people are likely to remember about 90% of what they are taught, particularly if the setting is very realistic. The main disadvantages reside in the fact that some people may 'play to the gallery' and lose sight of the training objectives, whereas others may feel that they are under such pressure that they are unable to perform.

Case studies.   The object of a case study is to present trainees with a realistic work-based situation by giving them a vast quantity of information which they are expected to analyse and then provide solutions to specific problems. Sometimes the information is fictitious and tailored to drive home certain points, but more often than not it is a summary of a real-life event, with the trainees being expected to explore various options until they arrive at the 'right' answer. Although it can be a very proactive introduction to safety management issues, many case studies used for safety training merely expect the trainees to learn to detect errors and correct them, rather than teaching them to question the underlying assumptions, policies and strategies or goals that created the original error. This latter point is particularly salient for the training of senior and middle managers in safety management, as it is their decision-making and the subsequent implementation of their decisions that often introduce 'pathogens' into their organisations (see Chapters 1 and 9). Despite these types of difficulty the advantages of case studies are considerable as they can provide concrete subjects for discussion, particularly if the case study reflects a real event that occurred in the organisation. Other specific advantages include the use of the participants' previous experience, which can sometimes provide an opportunity to bring a multi-disciplinary perspective to a problem; and new concepts and information provided during the training can be applied to real problems in the safety of the classroom. The only real disadvantage may be that the training provider cannot find a 'real' case study that is pertinent to his or her organisation.

Most professional trainers will be aware of the above techniques (and others) and the potential advantages and disadvantages associated with each of them in different training situations. Although each method may not be universally effective in every situation, the training planners should have sufficient knowledge and experience to ensure that the appropriate techniques and learning situations are matched to the needs of the audience.

Administrative Planning

The administration of a training course is a vital feature that is often overlooked or taken for granted until things go wrong. Features of importance include the time scale of the training course, where the training should be held, who the trainers will be, what resources are required and when, what level of training is required, what (if any) pre-course activities are necessary, and what joining instructions need to be sent.

Training time scales. The time scale of the training will be determined by a number of factors. In many instances, for example, it is impossible to provide the necessary training all at once because of production-related pressures, which means that the training activities will need to be spread out over a number of days. Sometimes it is possible to conduct the training within a week, while at other times it may only be possible to train people for one day a week over several weeks. To avoid potential problems, a systematic approach needs to be adopted that takes all these factors into account.

The main factors to consider when planning the timing of a training event are:

- When does it best suit the trainees, in relation to their workload, the availability of alternative cover for the trainees' operational duties, the amount of training, and the amount of pre-course preparation?

- When will the training provider be available to carry out the training without any other commitments so that he or she can give their undivided attention to the training?
- When will all the appropriate training facilities be available (premises, equipment, paperwork, etc.)

Consideration of these factors will also depend upon whether or not the training is to be conducted on the job or in the classroom.

Where should the training be held?. For practical reasons, on the job safety training under operational conditions is an approach commonly used in organisations (e.g. manual-handling training). Often, however, the training is simply squeezed in when a supervisor, trainer or instructor can find the time. This is not fair to the trainee, who has to stop what he or she is doing at the time, listen to and/or watch the trainer, take in the information, and is then expected to exhibit the same skills or knowledge. It is important, therefore, that any training is scheduled with sufficient time for learning and practice, and that the trainee has the trainer's undivided attention during that time. The only way that this can occur is for the trainer to liaise with line managers to ensure that the training period integrates with, and does not disrupt, normal operational activities, and that it also suits the trainee, so that uninterrupted time can be set aside. It is vital that the training conditions enhance the trainee's receptivity to what is being taught. If this cannot be guaranteed, the course provider should consider off the job training.

Off the job training is usually carried out under classroom conditions, and offers the advantage of being able to expose trainees to information, ideas and experiences away from the working environment. The trainees can then devote their full attention to learning without having operational distractions. In some instances, for example, induction training, off the job training takes place before people are allowed into the working environment, but more commonly people are released from their normal activities to attend a training course. This in itself can cause problems, particularly if the trainees are supervisors or senior managers. Although senior managers are in a better position to delegate their work to others, supervisors are often expected to be available continuously to deal with operational issues that arise. As a result they are often called upon to leave the training event while they resolve problems. This should not be allowed to happen, and can be avoided by careful planning of the training schedule, and the choice of venue. If disruptions of this nature are likely to occur, it is a good idea to hold the training event off site entirely, to ensure that the trainees are completely unavailable. Other difficulties might occur with shift employees. It is important that the planner arranges the training event around the shift schedule so that those working nights are not expected to attend a training course the following day (it happens frequently).

Who should be the trainer(s)?   Determining the skills required by the training provider is a crucial element of the planning process as it will dictate the choice of trainer. A common mistake is to assume that people with the relevant knowledge and skills are capable of teaching others, which is patently untrue. A good trainer needs to appreciate how people learn and to possess good communication and social skills. Moreover, effective trainers possess in-depth, up to date knowledge of their subject matter, and have an up-to-date approach to training. They are able to establish a rapport with their audience, irrespective of whether the trainees are employees or managers, create an atmosphere of trust, get trainees to think about familiar topics in new ways, teach new skills, coach people in the new skills, and motivate them to use the new skills on the job. In many instances it is better to use fully qualified internal expert trainers, often from the Safety, Human Resources or Training departments, as they are intimately familiar with the organisation and the way things are done. In some circumstances, however, it may be appropriate to use external training providers. This normally occurs:

- where specialised expertise is not available internally
- where internal training resources are stretched to the limit
- where training forms a part of another initiative (e.g. training in the use of a proprietary safety audit system)
- where the senior management team is seeking external verification of its intended actions before proceeding.

The use of outside trainers needs to be approached with some caution because a poor training provider can cause untold damage to a company's safety efforts. If external training providers are the preferred choice, the employing organisation should assess their effectiveness by talking to a number of other companies who have previously used their services. The assessment criteria should focus on the degree of change in people's behaviour on the job since the training was given. Any training provider who claims to be able to change people's attitudes via their training course should be asked to furnish real evidence that they have actually done so. Training providers who state that this is what the trainees have told them via an evaluation questionnaire at the end of a one-day or one-week course should be avoided, as they are making unsubstantiated claims. If the training provider proves to be credible, the employing organisation needs to brief them about their preferred style of training so that they can adapt their style to match that of the organisation. To ensure consistency, they will also need to be primed about management's philosophy in relation to safety, so that they know what can be said and what cannot be said. This also helps the training provider to build up a rapport with the organisation and its employees. One major advantage offered by the use of credible external training providers is their experience of working in a wide variety of industries and companies. The information they impart can help to broaden the view of trainees whose knowledge and experience is limited to their own organisation, by providing insights into how other organisations approach their decision-making and problem-solving. In turn, this helps the trainees to place their organisation's practices into context, particularly if they learn that their organisation is not so different from others.

What resources are required?   Good planning ensures that the necessary resources and equipment are available at the time they are needed. Obviously the types of different resource will be dependent upon what is being taught and how it is being taught. Much of the provision of resources will be to do with paperwork, pens, name badges, etc. and providing a suitable venue and training aids. If anything is missing on the day (however minor), this will cause disruptions to the learning process, and thus defeat the object of the whole exercise. People are very quick to latch on to negative features, and will tend to remember them for a long time afterwards. A typical example is where tea and coffee are supposed to be available at a certain time, but fail to arrive. This commonly becomes a cause for concern which distracts people's attention away from the learning process, and is repeatedly mentioned by the trainees throughout the remainder of the training event whenever a tea or coffee break is due, further disrupting the learning process.

Determining the level of training required.   Determining the level of training required can only be done by identifying the previous learning of trainees. This is a particularly important component of the design of a safety training course as it enables the course content to be tailored to the existing knowledge base of the participants. This avoids demotivating participants by reiterating what is already well known, or by pitching the course content at too difficult a level. Thus, identifying trainees' previous learning or knowledge serves to maximise learning by focusing the course content at the right level for a particular audience. This can be achieved by examining personnel records, or by distributing a pre-training questionnaire designed to discover potential trainees' current levels of knowledge. Consequently, it is possible to categorise trainees into groups with low, medium or high levels of knowledge and skill to ensure that the content of the course and the style of teaching are appropriate for them. Any discrepancies in levels of knowledge or skill can be addressed by asking trainees to engage in certain pre-course activities to ensure that everyone has a similar level of knowledge on which to build. For example, particular books to be read could be specified, or trainees could be asked to provide an outline of a particular safety problem they want to discuss during the training.

Joining instructions.   Good administration requires trainees to be informed of where, when and how they should attend the training, what equipment they will need to bring with them, and what will be expected of them when they attend. The effect of this information is to minimise people's anxieties while at the same time creating the impression that everything is under control. The idea is to ensure that the trainees join the event in a frame of mind that is ripe for learning, rather than being in a panic because they could not find the venue or do not know what to expect. The only practical way for this to be achieved is to issue joining instructions to each trainee. In relation to purely administrative details it is suggested that a document is devised that specifies:

- the duration of the training course in terms of the dates and times
- the venue and the actual location (e.g. room) where the training will take place
- the names of the trainers, the topic they will train, and the times that they will lead the training
- whether or not accommodation, meals, etc. are provided
- what equipment participants need to bring with them (e.g. protective personal equipment).

In addition, a document should be attached that specifies what the training aims and objectives are, the methods that will be used to achieve them, whether or not trainees will be assessed and how, and the course duration (see Figure 7.3: *Example Statement of Training Course Objectives* for an example). A personal letter welcoming people to the course should also be sent, together with a map showing the exact location of the venue and travel information. It cannot be stressed enough that careful consideration of these administrative details pays handsome dividends in terms of establishing a good rapport between the training provider and the trainees.

Conducting the Training

To ensure that the quality of the training meets the needs of the trainees and the organisation, and to create an optimal learning environment, the training

Safety Management Training Course

Aims

This training programme is designed around the concept that safety management is an important part of the process by which we achieve our production goals safely, on schedule and within budget. It sets out to provide management with an understanding of, and practice in, the important skills involved.

Objectives

More specifically, the programme will help participants to:

* manage health and safety within the context of their managerial or supervisory role
* develop an understanding of management's responsibilities and accountability for health, safety and welfare
* recognise that a safe place of work is efficient, economical and productive
* harness and use their existing knowledge and experience as a basis for further development
* formulate plans for using the skills practised in the programme in their future work

Methods

Various aspects of health and safety management will be explored informally in small groups by means of various exercises that include written work and problem-solving exercises that reflect the realities of everyday production activities.

Participants will be presented with real-life problems, and will be expected to seek solutions to the various problems by drawing upon the free exchange of group members' existing knowledge and experience, combined with their newly acquired knowledge and skills. As such, in conjunction with lectures and guest speakers, a large part of the programme is concerned with 'learning by doing'.

Each participant will be expected to attain a high level of competence throughout each element of the programme. To ensure that the course objectives are being achieved, the progress of each participant will be monitored and assessed on each individual topic. Participants' progress will be assessed against the following criteria:

* Knowledge: of certain principles
* Understanding: the effects of these principles on working practices and managerial decision-making
* Application: Implementation of these principles to formulate policies
* Innovation: Application of these principles to new or unusual situations

Participants are required to achieve a minimum 70 percent pass mark for each on-going assessment. In addition, an end of course examination will be held which requires a minimum 86 percent pass mark.

Duration

37.5 hours conducted in a block of 5 days .

Figure 7.3   Example Statement of Training Course Objectives

provider should follow certain procedures known to facilitate learning. Adhering to the practices suggested below makes the training provider's task more rewarding as the learning process becomes more of a two-way process, and also assists in facilitating the motivation, interest and attention of trainees. The practices include:

- providing a grand overview of the whole course, with the appropriate sequence of training events
- providing an overview of each specific topic, prior to exploring the subject matter in detail
- identifying and setting sub goals for trainees that specify what they should be able to do at successive stages throughout the overall training process
- providing feedback to trainees about their on-going performance.

Providing a grand overview of the whole course. Providing a grand overview of the whole course, with the appropriate sequence of training events, should occur during the initial stages of welcoming and introducing the course. The purpose of this 'induction organiser' is to enhance the motivation, interest and attention of trainees by allowing them to re-organise their thoughts around the tasks or subject matter to follow, before having to learn specific subjects. The induction should include the purpose, the approximate time, the scope of the subject matter, and the links between various topics. This both helps to clarify the learning process and establish the optimal working relationship between the training provider and participants.

Providing an advance overview for each topic. Delivered at the beginning of each specific topic before exploring the subject matter in detail, an advance overview helps to establish the specific learning context and provides a framework for the primary content. The detail of each topic should be organised and presented in a way that reflects the logical progression of the subject matter elements, and the links between them. Information should also be provided as to what course members should know, or be able to do, at the end of the topic. This may be best achieved by providing a graphical representation of the subject matter. The advantage of providing these structured overviews resides in their capacity to encourage trainees to mentally organise the training content and build the correct relationships between the various concepts. This process is known to facilitate the links between knowledge and performance, while enhancing rapid diagnoses and responses to problems.

Setting specific learning goals. In order to maximise the motivation of trainees, specific goals should be set for each successive stage of the overall training process. These goals should be specified in terms of either the level of knowledge to be attained, particular skills or a combination of both. The advantages of setting learning goals at each stage are that they provide a means through which the training provider and trainees can monitor their on-going progress. This allows training providers to identify and change particular elements of the course that are not meeting their objectives, and also allows participants to track their own individual progress in relation to the course as a whole. In practice, these goals will probably reflect those specified in the topic overviews.

Providing individual feedback.   To further assist in the creation of an optimal learning environment, training providers should adopt a policy of providing individual feedback to trainees both during the learning process and after formal assessments. Feedback makes people aware of what they are doing and how well they are doing it. The benefit of good feedback is that it increases people's ability to modify and change their behaviour, enabling them to become more effective at what they do. Feedback is known to fulfil three separate, but inter-related functions:

- Informative
- Reinforcing
- Motivational.

The informative function serves to correct any misunderstandings about what the trainees are doing, while enabling them to modify their on-going responses to the learning process. Initially, the feedback should focus on the positive aspects of the trainees' performance to maintain or enhance their motivation. Feedback related to the negative aspects of performance should always be given after the positive feedback. The feedback must be clear, accurate and specific to the knowledge, skills, or behaviours being covered. It must also be given in a friendly, non-judgemental manner and be designed to be of value to the trainee, not a release of frustration for the trainer. Trainers should provide trainees with information appropriate to their level of learning, and that concentrates on the aspects of the task that are important for overall success.

Feedback also fulfils a reinforcing function that serves to strengthen the links between the course content and the trainees' performance. Since positive rather than negative feedback results in much greater learning, and since social rewards are one of the most powerful motivators we know, reinforcers are often given in the form of praise. It is important, however, that trainers consider how much praise to give and when. The amount of praise should be appropriate to the amount of improvement. Too much praise in proportion to the level of improvement may be seen as lacking sincerity and value. Praise is best given only after the correct responses are emitted. Initially, it should be given on a fairly frequent basis, but as the learning process progresses it should be given less and less, until it only needs to be given at the end of a completed task to enhance motivation. Adopting these strategies is known to facilitate long-term retention of the course content, while also helping to avoid the trainee becoming dependent on the training provider.

Feedback also serves as a motivational function, by allowing trainees to track their learning progress against the course objectives and goals. This aspect of feedback is known to encourage greater commitment to the learning process, which in turn tends to result in better performance. Consequently, in view of the many useful functions that feedback serves, it should be provided as appropriate, either for written work or for performance during group exercises. When the feedback is part of formal assessments, it should be recorded in members' individual learning records and countersigned by them to indicate agreement.

In combination, the recommended practices described above will enhance the learning process to the mutual benefit of both course providers and participants, enabling both to reach their respective objectives.

Evaluate Training Effectiveness

Evaluating the effectiveness of a training event is one of the most important, but often neglected aspects of training. Unfortunately, apart from end of course evaluative questionnaires assessing the trainers' ability and/or trainees' satisfaction with the administrative features of the event, the same can be said of a substantial number of safety training courses. This is because most external training providers are in the business of making (substantial) profits from selling their brand of training, rather than being concerned to ensure that people actually learn and use their skills in the workplace. More often than not, training providers get away with this approach simply because managers assume that safety training is bound to be beneficial, as so many organisations and publications advocate its use. Based on the ACSNI report, the HSC, for example, even go as far as to say that the main priority for safety training is the creation of a 'safety culture', despite the available evidence which shows that much safety training has no effect on people's subsequent safety behaviour or their safety-related attitudes. As such it is difficult to imagine how the effectiveness of a safety training event can be evaluated on the basis of whether or not it has created, or helped to create, a safety culture. The effectiveness of any training event, therefore, has to be evaluated on the basis of much more concrete evidence.

Since most safety training is concerned with changing people's behaviour by imparting particular knowledge and skills, it makes sense to assess how much of this knowledge and these skills has actually been learnt and how much of it is put to good use on a daily basis. Immediate assessments of the amount of learning that has taken place can be achieved by the use of post-training tests, such as written or oral examinations, course assessments of project work, actual demonstrations of skill or a combination of all three. The next step is to assess how well the training has carried over into practice in the workplace. For motor skills this can be achieved by observing people at work at pre-determined time periods (e.g. three, six, nine and twelve months) after the training event. For training events concerned with safety management and legislative issues, the degree to which learning has been put into practice could be assessed by the use of safety management system audits at six-monthly intervals. If it turns out that the training is not being put to good effect in practice, there is a need to know why, otherwise the whole training exercise becomes a sheer waste of time, money and effort.

More often than not the reason for training not being translated into practice is the lack of a supportive organisational climate that allows and encourages trainees to explore new ideas and utilise their training knowledge. In turn this is largely due to the fact that many people's jobs are governed by clearly laid down rules, procedures and systems that have evolved over many years and that tend to restrict the trainees' opportunities to demonstrate and use their new knowledge and skills. This illustrates that if organisations are willing to send people on training events, then they also have to be equally willing to change their rules, procedures and systems to fit with the new knowledge and skills where applicable. Only in this way can safety training contribute to the creation of a positive safety culture. If they are reluctant to do this, they should not send people on training events.

In addition to the assessment methods outlined above, the organisation should also examine how well the same training event works with different groups of trainees by comparing and assessing each group's levels of skill and knowledge over a period of time. Similarly, every training event should be subjected to a cost/benefit analysis. A very good inexpensive training course that could be used as a model for others, which is known to adopt the vast majority of good practices discussed above, is that of the Construction Industry Training Board's (CITB) Site Management Safety Training Scheme (1996 edition).

8

Measuring Safety Climate

INTRODUCTION

One of the most difficult aspects of creating a positive safety culture is to win over people's hearts and minds to the safety improvement cause. The difficulties arise because hearts and minds are not under the direct control of an organisation. This is just as well, as it would be extremely unethical and unhealthy for people's well-being for it to be so. Although this lack of direct control can be frustrating people have to be *persuaded* that safety is important to the organisation and this can only occur when organisations have consistently done everything in their power to create a safe working environment. In other words, organisations must actively demonstrate that safety is being taken seriously in all its various activities, not just rely on passive propaganda attempts to persuade people that safety is important. One way for an organisation to proactively win people's hearts and minds is for the organisation to conduct a safety climate survey to identify its employees' attitudes and perceptions about the organisation's efforts to create a positive safety culture. These surveys can be of enormous benefit in identifying safety management deficiencies, although it is very important that the issues identified by the employees are addressed and actioned as soon as is possible. In this way employees can be persuaded that the organisation is very serious in its attempts to create a positive safety culture which in turn will help to win over their hearts and minds to the safety effort.

SAFETY ATTITUDES

To many safety professionals, capturing people's hearts and minds involves changing people's (poor) safety attitudes. Since they feel that they have done everything in their power to improve safety, many safety professionals give the impression that all accidents are caused by people's poor attitudes. In other words, they treat everyone in the same way and adopt a 'scatter-gun' approach to changing people's attitudes by showing everybody a film or putting everybody through a safety training course in the hope that their views and subsequent behaviour will change. Because these attempts often fail, the safety professional's view of people's poor safety attitudes is further reinforced. Perhaps because they are bereft of any further ideas, or do not know what the real problem is, they spend a lot of their time doing more of the same, trying (unsuccessfully) to change people's attitudes towards safety thereby creating a vicious circle that is inevitably doomed to failure. This begs the question 'Why do these attempts fail?

Why Attempts at Attitude Change Fail

The reasons for the failure to change people's attitudes can be many and varied. However, in the main they centre around a lack of:

- understanding about the nature of attitudes
- consistent management support for the safety effort
- understanding about the influence of the physical working environment
- knowledge about the attitudes people actually hold.

A Lack of Understanding About the Nature of Attitudes

Attempts at attitude change often fail because many people do not understand what an attitude actually is. Many view attitudes as an indicator of the way people are 'predisposed to respond in a given way in a given situation'. Often, therefore, when people talk about attitudes, they are actually referring to people's behaviour. Accordingly, it makes sense to concentrate on attempting to change people's safety behaviour, rather than their safety attitudes. As previously stated in Chapter 7, an attitude is actually a label used to describe a psychological construct: it is not a physical entity. This descriptive label is merely used to make sense of the way people *consistently* think, feel and behave towards a particular topic. For example, if a manager holds an attitude (thinks and feels) that accidents are caused by employees not paying due care and attention, rather than unsafe systems of work, he or she will direct employees to work under such a system. When an accident occurs the manager will tend to be consistent with his or her 'attitude' and apportion blame to the victim's lack of care and attention as the root cause, rather than the unsafe working system. (Indeed, research has indicated that the higher up the organisation people are, the more likely they are to blame a victim's carelessness for causing the accident, rather than the systems of work.)

A Lack of Consistent Management Support to the Safety Effort

Probably the major cause of failure to change attitudes towards safety is line managers failing to reinforce good safety on a daily basis. In those organisations where line managers are inconsistent in their approach to safety (e.g. they turn a blind eye to unsafe working practices when it suits productivity needs) the effects of the safety professional's work is continuously undermined. This is simply due to the fact that line managers transmit conflicting messages about the importance of safety. The safety professional then tries to pick up the pieces by re-educating and persuading the workforce that safety *is* important. This cycle of events tends to be repeated over and over again, causing the workforce to become less and less interested in what the safety professional has to say, simply because it makes no real difference to their daily working lives. Consequently, each time the cycle is repeated, the more remote the possibility becomes of capturing people's hearts and minds to the safety cause.

Psychologists have indicated that because we tend to internalise the views and beliefs of significant others (e.g. line managers, colleagues, work groups, etc.), attitudes are socially constructed. In practice, what this actually means is that we internalise the underlying reasons for behaving in a particular way at the same time as we learn a particular behaviour. Accordingly, when line managers turn a blind eye to unsafe behaviour to suit productivity needs, employees learn that unsafe behaviour is the correct way of behaving, because production output is more important than safety. This indicates that the best way to change safety attitudes is for managers and work colleagues to specify the reasons for behaving in a safe way, while simultaneously teaching, coaching and reinforcing particular sets of safe behaviours. However, just because people have an attitude about a particular topic, it does not automatically follow that people will consistently behave in accordance with it, as shown by the findings of one research study which showed that workers with the most favourable attitudes towards the wearing of personal protective equipment (PPE) were those least likely to use it in practice.

Lack of Understanding About the Influence of the Physical Working Environment

The immediate situation in which people find themselves will also exert a much greater effect on their behaviour than their attitudes. This can be illustrated by the case of shelf stackers in a supermarket who had to replenish the freezers with stock. The stackers collected three-sided trolleys from the warehouse, pushed them to the appropriate freezers and started unloading the product boxes from the cartons. No provision had been made for the disposal or storage of the empty cartons (situation). To avoid the possibility of creating a tripping hazard (a positive attitude), the shelf stackers placed the empty cartons on the top of the trolley, at the back (behaviour). Unfortunately, once the last remaining product carton was removed from the trolley, the additional unbalanced weight of the empty cartons caused the trolley to tip over. This aptly illustrates the point that people can only behave in accordance with their positive safety attitudes when the situation allows.

Knowing People's Attitudes

Another major reason for safety professionals failing to change people's attitudes is that they often do not actually know what attitudes people hold in regard to safety. Often they make a guess based on observations of what they *thought* someone was doing. Whether or not they are correct in their guesstimates is immaterial: they act accordingly. This can be illustrated by the example of a recently hired forklift driver who broke his lower arm in two places when it was caught between the forklift truck and a door frame in a warehouse. The initial accident investigation indicated that the driver had been fooling around because the truck had been seen driving erratically by at least four people. Because of the erratic nature of the driving the safety advisor recommended the person for disciplinary action. The cause of the accident was logged as reckless driving caused by the person's cavalier safety attitudes. When the accident victim returned to work he was duly given a written warning. The victim complained bitterly that the accident was caused by the forklift truck steering not responding in the same manner as another forklift truck that he had been driving earlier the same day. The manager who issued the written warning was surprised at the vehemence of the victim's protestations and decided to investigate further. He discovered that the wheels of each type of truck steered differently: turning the wheel to the left on one truck would steer it to the left; turning the wheel to the left on the other truck would steer it to the right. Not only were there differences in the way the brakes and accelerator worked but the first truck had servo-assisted steering. The truck being driven at the time of the accident did not. This latter investigation also revealed that the accident victim's total driving experience was only six hours. Although trained instructors were on hand in the warehouse, they were also expected to carry out their normal super-visory duties, which they were doing at the time of the incident. All the other forklift drivers had previously been trained in the same way (i.e. shown what to do, and been left to get on with it). Thus, the safety advisor had made what psychologists refer to as a fundamental 'attribution error': he attributed the cause of the accident to the person fooling around as a result of a cavalier attitude towards safety, rather than to the vehicle's steering characteristics and the lack of supervision, combined with the lack of driver training.

Attribution error.   Attribution error, therefore, concerns a tendency for people to attribute the causes of other people's behaviour to them as individuals, rather than to the situational factors that may have caused them to behave as they did. Unfortunately, attribution errors of this type are commonly found amongst safety professionals, supervisors, managers, etc., which is why terms such as human error, carelessness, lack of attention, poor safety attitude, etc. can be found on so many accident reports. The primary reason for these types of attribution error is a lack of information, that is, those making the attribution error base their perceptions about the causes of people's (unsafe) behaviour, on their *own* past experience and knowledge of the workplace, and *their* beliefs about human behaviour. These personal perceptions are then mapped onto an incident. Conversely, the person involved will base their perceptions of events on the conditions surrounding an incident (e.g. work pressure, lack of the right materials, etc.), the events leading up to the incident, and why he or she did what they did. Importantly, once people have made an attribution, it is very hard to get them to change it, even if they are wrong. This is mainly due to the fact that people seek, and hang on to, information that confirms their original attribution, while simultaneously downplaying or ignoring any facts that run counter to their beliefs. One study, for example, found that people allocated the responsibility for causes of particular fires to the victims themselves. Despite these people being confronted with a vast amount of objective evidence showing that the victims were not in a situation where they could have influenced the fire, the victims were still attributed as being the primary cause. This highlights the importance of making accurate diagnoses before making judgements about people, and before suggesting that they hold poor attitudes towards safety. Thus safety professionals must accurately identify what perceptions and attitudes people hold about safety. The best way of doing this is to measure various facets of those perceptions and attitudes by conducting some form of safety climate survey. These types of survey also identify which features of an organisation are impacting upon people's safety perceptions and attitudes. In turn, this enables the organisation to undertake highly focused remedial actions in regards to safety *per se*.

SAFETY CLIMATE

The above illustrates that information is filtered by our perceptions of what we think is important, and that these perceptions will then determine the way that we behave. In regard to safety culture, the way people *believe* that an organisation applies its safety procedures and rules will serve to construct a perceived image of risk, danger and safety. In turn this affects how people behave in relation to safety on a daily basis. Because of the dynamic nature of the reciprocal relationship between our perceptions and subsequent behaviour, this image becomes self-sustaining (i.e. the more the perceived image is confirmed, the more people will behave in accordance with it. The more people behave in accordance with this image, the more the image is confirmed, and so on). Termed 'safety climate', this perceived image is largely concerned with employees' perceptions of the importance of safety and how it is implemented within the working environment.

A good safety climate is characterised by a collective commitment of care and concern, whereby all employees share similar positive perceptions about organisational safety features. This collective climate serves as a frame of reference that shapes the attitudes and behaviours of employees. In turn, the prevailing safety climate influences the outcomes of *all* the organisation's safety improvement initiatives. Nonetheless, even though each department in an organisation is subject to the same organisational policies and procedures, it is known that different safety climates exist in different departments of the same organisation. There are a number of reasons for this including the fact that different rules and procedures apply to different departments, the risks associated with the type of work will determine the emphasis put on compliance and the way safety is actually managed on a daily basis. Because safety rules and procedures tend not to be rigidly applied in offices, for example, safety tends to be seen as much less important, resulting in the office's safety climate being much worse than that for production departments. Similarly, because senior managers, line managers, supervisors and employees operate under distinct frames of reference determined by various group factors, safety climate also differs by organisational level. Research findings such as these strongly suggest that safety climate is socially constructed by the interaction between the people, their prevailing customs and practices, the risks associated with their jobs, and their position and status within the organisation.

Core Features of Safety Climate

Since safety climate is a dynamic entity that is continuously changing, a clear understanding of the processes and attitudes that have an impact upon safety-related behaviour is necessary before it can be measured. Assessing an organisation's safety climate requires the measurement of a number of applicable contextual dimensions, each comprising different sets of questions. Almost a decade of research conducted by the author and colleagues in construction, manufacturing and local government, and by the author in the chemical and food industries, has shown that the following 11 dimensions provide the main focus for ascertaining an organisation's current safety climate. Each of these has been shown to be clearly related to an effective safety culture.

Management Commitment

A 1990 survey by the CBI highlighted the crucial importance of leadership and the commitment of the chief executive toward safety, as well as the executive safety role of line management. Other research has shown that those companies which lack strong managerial commitment are associated with high accident rates, and vice versa. All too often, however, discrepancies exist between the typical mission statement which states that 'safety is a top priority' and senior management actions. Developing a good safety climate therefore requires senior management to demonstrate visibly the strongest possible commitment on a regular basis. This can be achieved in many ways. For example:

- the status of safety officers can, and should, be enhanced by promoting them to senior levels within the organisation's hierarchy
- senior management could and should become more visibly involved with safety committees on a regular basis
- resources can be allocated to ensure that the safety committee's recommendations are publicised and rapidly implemented
- the shopfloor can be visited regularly with the express purpose of discussing safety with employees
- production pressures that cause employees to cut corners or circumvent safety regulations can be balanced so that productivity is not achieved by sacrificing safety, nor safety achieved by sacrificing productivity.

Commitment to safety from senior management not only has positive effects on safety, but also reaps cumulative business rewards in terms of quality, reliability and profitability. Conversely, where employees perceive managerial attitudes and actions toward safety to be less than adequate, problems may ensue that affect the effective functioning of the organisation as a whole, as the workforce become less committed to the organisation *per se*, simply because management are seen as unwilling to provide a safe working environment.

Management Actions

The management of safety is in many respects exactly the same as the management of productivity or other functional areas of operations. An effective manager is usually seen as an effective leader who is both caring and controlling. 'Caring' refers to ensuring the welfare of the workforce, communicating with them on a daily basis on a wide range of issues, and being friendly and available. 'Controlling' refers to the setting of targets, maintaining performance standards, ensuring clear job roles and responsibilities, and getting the workforce to follow rules and procedures by consistent encouragement. Leaders who are both caring and controlling usually adopt a 'democratic' approach and involve the workforce in the decision-making process. This management style often results in the ownership of the workgroup's goals by all concerned, leading to increases in performance. In relation to enhancing the organisation's safety climate/culture, effective leaders involve personnel in decisions affecting the safety of their jobs, discuss safety with the work group on a daily basis, ensure that all personnel are clear about their safety responsibilities, consistently encourage and reinforce them to follow safety rules and procedures, and match words with deeds (e.g. do not turn a blind eye to unsafe working practices when it suits productivity needs).

Personal Commitment to Safety

Research has shown that companies with strong, clear cultures are associated with higher levels of employee commitment. Commitment to safety is defined as 'an individual's identification with and involvement in safety activities', characterised by a strong acceptance of and belief in the organisation's safety goals and a willingness to exert effort to improve safety in the workplace. The level of personal commitment to safety is very important as it tends to determine both individuals' acceptance of company safety initiatives and their personal approach towards safety in the workplace. Research has shown that personal commitment to safety can be considerably enhanced by involving personnel in the decision-making processes that affect safety in their jobs.

Perceived Risk Levels

A department's safety climate is partly based on the perceived risk level of a particular job or task. Objective hazards exist in all types of work setting including exposure to moving machinery, asbestos, chemical fumes, poisonous gases, falling objects, etc. However, people's ability to determine the risks of perceived hazards is influenced by different factors such as the ease with which past instances can be recalled or imagined; the 'on-the-job' experience of the individual; the manner in which hazards are presented in communications; attributions of blame in accident causation; and the amount of control individuals feel they have over hazards. However, hazard detection can also be problematical, as illustrated by research findings that approximately 50% of accident victims had difficulty in detecting the hazard that caused their accidents. This finding may be due to individuals applying different criteria when assessing situations that are likely to result in minor as opposed to major, injuries. Other evidence shows that workers have little concern about dangerous situations because of misplaced trust that the environment is continuously monitored by those in authority.

Perceptions of the probability of an accident occurring due to a particular hazard are known to differ between various work groups. Although this is related to group characteristics, these differences have important influences on risk perception. For example, evidence shows supervisors to be poor sources of information about the dangers inherent in a worker's task. This is because supervisors are often too far removed from operations to make meaningful assessments and therefore tend to underestimate the risks involved when compared to workers' own risk assessments. In turn, if employees perceive the risks of a given job to be underestimated by line management, it is likely that employees' commitment and loyalty to that organisation will be undermined, as the employer will be perceived to be unwilling to provide a safe working environment. Thus, departments with positive safety climates not only involve worker representatives who have intimate knowledge of the operational processes when formal risk assessments are conducted, but they also take steps to reduce the risks as much and as quickly as possible.

Effect of the Required Work Pace

A frequently cited factor of accident causation is speed of work, commonly termed 'work pace', which is the component at the heart of the productivity and safety conflict. It is often thought that productivity can only be achieved by people working fast while simultaneously ignoring safety, while safety can only be achieved by requiring personnel to work much more slowly and methodically (which effectively reduces production output). Although this notion appears to be well established in the minds of many, the converse is actually true. This is because excessive production pressures increase job strain, unsafe behaviours and accident rates, all of which can combine to decrease performance and increase costs. For example, people commit unsafe acts because they are rewarded for doing so by managers either ignoring unsafe behaviour and/or rewarding unsafe behaviour through giving bonuses for extra production that has been achieved by cutting corners. Because unsafe behaviours are often the triggering event leading to accidents, the cost of these accidents is likely to seriously dent the organisation's competitive cost base. Accidents are very expensive. In 1993, for example, the HSE demonstrated across a wide range of industries that the ratio of insured to uninsured accident costs was approximately 1:11. In 1990, the CBI estimated that the minimum non-recoverable cost of each accident was £1,500, whether investigated or not. Reducing these costs can only add to the capital value of an organisation. However, this requires that everything possible is done to remove the safety-productivity conflict, by optimising the balance between the two, and where there is any doubt, ensuring that safety always wins out. This is a vital feature of an effective safety climate/culture, that often leads to associated increases in productivity and profits.

Beliefs About Accident Causation

Beliefs about the causes of accidents are an important element of an effective safety climate because they guide people's thinking and actions when accidents occur or when they are trying to solve safety problems. As outlined above, much research has revealed a tendency for others to attribute the cause of accidents to the victim's own behaviour, whereas the victim is more likely to attribute the cause of the accident to external circumstances. Indeed, researchers have found that attributing the causes of accidents to a lack of attention and care is linearly related to the position of personnel in the organisation's hierarchy. The more senior the position, the more likely accident causes will be attributed to the victim not paying attention, rather than poor working procedures or conditions. In reality, however, accidents are often caused by a number of organisational failings (e.g. bad management, unsafe working procedures, poor working environment, etc.) that combine and lay dormant until triggered by the victim's own behaviour. Unless these organisational failings are recognised as causation factors, and not dismissed by those with the power and influence to rectify the situation, very little will be done to improve working systems. Thus, one of the critical factors in establishing an effective safety climate is to ensure that all personnel have a greater understanding and appreciation of the potential organisational causes of accidents and their manifestation. Equally, personnel need to have a clear understanding of their own behaviour, as this will help them to avoid being the triggering event and possibly the victim.

Effect of Job-induced Stress

A well known relationship exists between accident rates and job-induced stress. Although some degree of stress is beneficial to performance, too much stress induces role strain that results in lower job performance and an increased likelihood of being involved in an accident. Personnel are particularly prone to role strain when the demands of the job are too high (work overload) or too low (work underload). Work overload not only tends to cause undue anxiety leading to coronary heart disease, but also results in lapses of memory and attention so that errors and mistakes are commonly made that can put others at risk, which in turn further increases job anxiety On the other hand, work underload induces boredom, apathy and fatigue again causing lapses in memory and attention, which leads to errors and accidents. Both work overload and work underload are causal mechanisms of impaired mental health that can result in increased accident rates and absenteeism from work as personnel seek coping mechanisms. However, a considerable amount of research has shown that role strain can be mitigated by increasing the opportunity for employees to control their work activities and events. Greater opportunity for control and involvement is also a central feature of an effective safety culture. Increasing people's opportunities for control over their work activities leads to greater acceptance of the necessity and the desirability of safety rules, which results in safety belonging to everyone. This also provides the motivation for people to conform to safety rules in spirit as well as in the letter of the law. This is not to argue that employees should be given complete freedom to do as they see fit, just that they should be given greater opportunities to be fully involved in discussions about safety management issues that affect their jobs, and be involved in the review of all types of incidents, including near misses.

Effectiveness of Safety Communications within the Organisation

Organisations with good safety climates/cultures can be characterised by a good safety communication system that flows from top to bottom, bi-directionally through both formal and informal communication channels throughout an organisation. Recognising and harnessing the informal channel has been shown to be a feature of low accident facilities, as questions about safety tend to become a part of the everyday work-related conversation. Formal and informal communications between line management and the shopfloor are one of the most crucial areas for safety information to be disseminated. Unfortunately, this communication channel is often the most neglected, as perceived work pressures result only in 'crisis communications' when a specific issue needs to be addressed. The greater visibility of management on the shopfloor discussing safety contributes enormously to a positive safety climate and morale in general. Moreover, as dialogue flows between the groups providing useful feedback, improvements in safety are likely to increase at an even greater rate. A related area of safety communications that requires careful preparation is the development of written safety procedures, so that they can be easily understood and followed by the end user. If the language is complex or unclear, or the procedure has vital steps missing, accidents are likely to ensue. A company with a strong safety culture tends to enhance all forms of safety communications by involving personnel in all aspects (see Chapter 3).

Effectiveness of Emergency Procedures

An employee who is unable to respond to an emergency is a potential hazard. However, emergencies impose a considerable demand on the effectiveness of people's responses, particularly if complex decisions are necessary. Confidently responding to an emergency necessitates that the requisite responses be thoroughly and meticulously learnt, and reinforced by frequent practice. Practice is very important as it helps to highlight potential deficiencies. For example, the physical state of emergency equipment may have deteriorated, emergency plans may need to be modified, personnel may need extra training in fire fighting, team responses may need to be improved as people's job roles change, new members of staff may not be familiar with all aspects of the plant and be unaware of the effects of an emergency shutdown, etc. A company with an effective safety climate/culture will ensure that all members of staff are highly familiar with emergency procedures, to the point where responses are well rehearsed and almost automatic, as this significantly reduces the possibility of panic behaviour.

The Importance of Safety Training

Safety training remains the principal method of promoting self-protection against workplace hazards. Most safety manuals advocate training as a means of accident prevention, while safety legislation demands the appointing and training of competent persons to carry out particularly dangerous tasks. It has been found that low accident companies with a strong safety culture have developed high quality integrated job and safety training programmes (i.e. the job training included elements of safety training that were specific and relevant to the job). This highlights a general point that the content of safety training has to be relevant to the jobs of the trainees (see Chapter 7). The safety training for managers is particularly important to ensure they are up to date with current safety practices and legal requirements. There is an implicit assumption in much safety training that it is in itself a good thing, because safety trained personnel who know what to do will automatically conduct themselves in a safe manner for extended periods of time, regardless of the consequences on the job. This assumption is inaccurate because normal everyday practice will almost inevitably negate the effects of the training unless it is reinforced by management and practised by everyone on a daily basis.

Status of Safety People and Safety Committees Within an Organisation

The role of safety representatives in promoting a positive safety climate and culture is to assist in the development and monitoring of communication links between management and the shopfloor on matters of company safety policy. Safety representatives need to be respected diplomats with enhanced status if they are to influence events in the workplace positively. The role of the safety advisor necessitates very high status within the organisation as their role is one of a facilitator or consultant. Their status can be determined by their ease of direct access to the most senior levels of management, their level of seniority and salary. Not only should they be effective and influence events positively, but they should be seen to do so by being highly visible.

The general aim of a safety committee is to involve both management and workers in the safety planning process, and it is thought to add a political dimension to safety management activity that is rarely acknowledged. The perceived effectiveness of the organisation's safety committees may be judged from varying perspectives. To some extent they can be seen as an indirect measure of the safety communication flow, the prevailing industrial relations context in which the committees function, and management commitment toward safety. In addition, safety committees are judged by how well they influence and improve health and safety in the organisation. The more rapidly their recommendations are implemented and publicised the more they will be seen to be effective and the more credibility they accrue.

Contextual Features Known to Affect Safety Climate

All the above dimensions indicate that an effective safety culture/climate is made up of many important facets. However, although the above forms the core of safety culture/climate, other features may also affect safety, some of them not normally associated with safety. This is because safety culture is not developed in a vacuum: it is a sub feature of an organisation's overall culture. Such features also need to be measured so that their effects on the prevailing safety climate can be ascertained. The particular features discussed below have been personally measured by the author in different industries, and each has been shown to exert an important influence on safety climate, in specific contexts.

Effectiveness of Standard Operating Procedures

Standard operating procedures (SOPs) are written procedural controls that reflect a particular sequence of activities for carrying out a job safely. They define a safe system of work for a particular operation. SOPs are often developed for a whole range of activities and combined into a complete safety manual for the company's operations. However, because many SOPs tend to be written by line managers rather than by those who do the job, there is a very real danger that the SOPs do not reflect every aspect of a particular job, simply because the line managers lack sufficient knowledge as a result of being too far removed from everyday operations. Again, because they are often poorly presented, the end user finds it difficult to follow them. They are therefore often seen to trivialise safety, a means of covering people's (e.g. managers) backs when things go wrong, or they are thought to slow down the job too much. Thus measuring people's perceptions about them provides an indicator of the way they are viewed and how effective they are thought to be. In the author's view, the job holders' involvement in the development of SOPs is essential if they are to be 'owned' and followed.

Responses to Breaches of Standard Operating Procedures

The frequency with which people report breaches of safety rules and procedures to those in authority, and what happens thereafter, has obvious implications for safety, particularly in high risk industries such as chemicals, offshore drilling, etc. However, people will not report such events unless there is a no blame culture in operation. In other words, the conditions have to be psychologically safe, so that people do not fear adverse implications for those concerned. The whole purpose of reporting breaches of SOPs has to be one of examining the effectiveness of the SOPs themselves, not disciplining people for non-compliance. In addition, because of extreme time pressures or competing goals, line managers are prepared to turn a blind eye when breaches of SOPs are reported. These features, therefore, not only provide an indirect measure of the organisation's prevailing industrial relations and the psychological contract, but they also complement measures of management's actions in regard to safety.

Housekeeping

Many companies use the prevailing standards of housekeeping as an indirect measure of how seriously people view safety. There is some evidence that the tidier the workplace, the more rapid production can be because people do not have to continually negotiate tripping hazards. Housekeeping issues have also been implicated in numerous accidents (e.g. people stepping on nails protruding from timbers). The author's research has indicated that, while the vast majority of people accept that housekeeping is their personal responsibility, and they therefore try to keep the workplace tidy (positive attitudes), the lack of time resulting from extreme production pressures, in combination with a lack of storage facilities (poor situation) in many organisations leads to poor housekeeping (behaviour) on a daily basis. This research has also shown that these factors lead many people to believe that poor housekeeping does not matter, simply because they work in areas with poor housekeeping standards and do not see accidents occurring very frequently as a result of the poor housekeeping. Thus instilling and maintaining a positive safety climate is heavily dependent upon the organisation creating the right conditions for people to follow the rules and procedures (for example, by providing the time and the storage locations).

Job Design Changes Related to Multi-Skilling

Many organisations are concerned to increase the efficiency of their operations by introducing multi-skilling or flexible working, for example, process workers undertaking some maintenance duties while maintenance engineers undertake some process operators' duties. In principle, although many employees do not have difficulty with the notion of multi-skilling, many are concerned that their personal safety could be negatively effected if people are not properly trained. Similarly, many feel that flexible working means that people's jobs are merely enlarged to include more of the same tasks (see Chapter 3), rather than genuinely enriched to include a variety of tasks which stretch their skills and abilities for the good of the organisation. Thus, introducing multi-skilling or flexible working without giving due consideration to these features could lead to poor motivation and increased anxiety, leading to increased levels of absenteeism, leading to an increased accident rate.

Job Design Changes related to Manual Handling

Because of the number of accidents associated with manual handling, and the duties imposed by the Manual Handling Regulations 1992, many organisations are concerned to ensure that the amount of manual handling required from their employees is significantly reduced. The introduction of mechanical lifting devices and the provision of manual handling training are obvious devices to assist in this area. Nonetheless, assessing people's perceptions in relation to the types of manual handling issues thought to be important to employees can be of enormous value. Perceptual surveys conducted by the author have helped to pinpoint which types of job would benefit from an investment in mechanical devices or automation of production processes. They have also shown where manual handling training has been lacking. A lack of concern about these issues can cause many employees to feel that management are not at all concerned about their safety. This dimension also provides an indirect measure of management's commitment to providing a safe working environment.

Role Ambiguity in light of Organisational Changes

In recent years many companies have reorganised in order to improve their competitive cost base. This has often meant redundancies at very short notice, with the workload being divided between the remaining employees. In many instances this extra workload has created confusion about what people are supposed to be doing. Termed 'role ambiguity', this can lead to job-induced stress simply because people may not know what areas of work they are suddenly responsible for, or what is actually expected of them in their new role. This may lead to people feeling that they are not in control of a situation or their own destiny. In essence, their job has become so disorganised that it proves impossible for them to devote the necessary amounts of time to all the required duties. Not only can this lead to general poor job performance, but such people could feel under such extreme pressure that they suddenly become an accident waiting to happen. Often role ambiguity is the result of a failure to spell out what the person's new role actually entails, the priority to be given to each of the new duties, or the amount of authority he or she has to make decisions or delegate to others. Unfortunately, it is often front line managers who experience role ambiguity. As they also tend to be the people responsible for the safety of others, there is an acute danger that this safety responsibility will be ignored at the expense of maintaining production levels (particularly as annual performance appraisals tend to focus on productivity issues). Thus, role ambiguity tends to lead to 'management by exception' (e.g. safety is considered only when accident rates rise), which is contrary to a good safety culture.

Perceptions About Working Under Adverse Market Conditions

Although there may be cost-benefit justifications for 'downsizing' to reduce fixed costs during adverse market conditions, much research has shown that in comparison with high accident plants, low accident plants have a policy of no-layoffs in slack times, with employees being switched to other duties (ACSNI Study Group on Human Factors, HSC, 1992). Unfortunately, many companies counter adverse trading conditions by engaging in a round of redundancies as the first rather than the last option. Even though many employees support the company's efforts to continually improve its operations, redundancies create feelings of job insecurity, which in turn creates a lack of trust between managers and employees due to the company breaking its 'psychological contract' with employees. In turn, because people's attention becomes focused primarily on production as they attempt to avoid being chosen for redundancy, safety issues tend to be ignored. Thus the level of job insecurity has serious implications for creating or maintaining a safety culture. One way to minimise feelings of job insecurity is for the company to be much more communicative about their intentions during hard times. Not only can this help to reduce uncertainty, maintain morale, and increase the loyalty and commitment of 'survivors' to the company, but it can also exert a positive effect on safety.

Effect of Reductions in Manning Levels

Measuring the effects of reduced manning levels often shows that, contrary to expectations, the efficiency of work groups does not improve as a result of 'downsizing'. Rather, as a result of increased workloads, it tends to increase feelings of job insecurity, role ambiguity and anxiety about the effects the changes are having on safety performance. This anxiety can lead to lower commitment to the organisation and increased sickness absenteeism, which in turn increases accident rates, which in turn increases the activity rate of those remaining, which in turn increases people's anxiety, and so on *ad infinitum*. The fall-out from such an exercise can actually lead to increased costs and this defeats the whole purpose of the initial cost-cutting exercise. Organisations should therefore consider reducing their costs by initially focusing on their accident, health and sickness absenteeism costs, before making wholesale changes to the number of employees.

People's Commitment to the Organisation

The extent of people's commitment to an organisation has important implications for the functioning of many aspects of organisation life, each of which exerts direct or indirect effects on safety. For example, people whose jobs include the five job characteristics outlined in Chapter 3: skill variety, task identity, task significance, autonomy and feedback, are likely to show much greater commitment to an organisation. This may be due to the fact that these five job characteristics are linked to higher motivation, and higher levels of motivation are also linked to a greater degree of organisational commitment. Leaders who communicate more with their subordinates (i.e. those who provide more accurate and timely feedback) tend to enhance the working environment, which in turn leads people to becoming more committed to the organisation. Conversely, individuals who are experiencing greater role strain (i.e. work overload and work underload) tend to show lower commitment to the organisation. Low organisational commitment is linked to greater amounts of absenteeism, which is linked to increased accident rates.

Organisational commitment, therefore, provides an indirect measure of various features affecting safety climate, such as people's levels of motivation. This not only determines the likelihood of people engaging in behaviours helpful to the company (e.g. improving safety) but it also indicates the level of motivation that people find in their jobs. The degree of organisational commitment may also provide a gross indicator of the way in which a manager's leadership behaviour is thought to be effective. Thus, low levels of organisational commitment might indicate the presence of role strain.

Effect of Quality Issues on Safety

Many companies are deeply concerned to improve the quality of their products and services. Some academic literature suggests that the best way to achieve quality is to focus on safety (see Chapter 1 for examples). Others have argued that the best way to improve safety is to focus on quality. Interestingly, when the author has examined this issue in relation to safety climate, the vast majority of people indicate that they *actually* achieve quality improvements by focusing upon safety. However, given that many companies have made changes to their working practices and systems in attempts to improve quality, it is important to examine the extent to which possible ripple effects adversely affect safety.

The contextual features discussed above can exert important influences on the development of a safety culture/climate and provide a fairly comprehensive pick and mix menu for organisations to consider when they conduct a safety survey.

Analysis of Safety Climate Measures

It is also necessary to look beyond the global safety climate of an organisation to examine the extent to which the prevailing safety climate is affected by group attributes. This enables remedial actions to be highly focused and cost-effective. For example, research has shown that accident victims tend to be more negative in their perceptions about safety, are usually more dissatisfied with their jobs and are more likely to suffer mental ill-health. Similarly, the number of years' experience in a job is closely related to hazard perception and accidents, as employees' own task experience is the deciding factor in assessing safe working conditions. Age is another factor that combines with experience of a task, as young and inexperienced people are more likely to suffer accidents than older or more experienced people. Researchers have consistently found that workers with less than five years' experience were over-represented in accident statistics. Much research has also shown that managers and supervisors underestimate the risks involved in many tasks, compared to the workers themselves and others such as safety officers, trainers and engineers. Since differences in safety climates are invariably found between departments, it also makes sense to analyse the results by department. It is also useful to compare each department's safety climate scores with that for the organisation as a whole, as a way of identifying which departments are better, or worse, than the site as a whole. Analysing safety climate by these types of grouping, therefore, allows important differences in perceptions to be identified and addressed.

Typical Results of Safety Climate Surveys

The results of safety surveys in the construction, chemicals, manufacturing and food sectors have consistently revealed that although people who are safety trained still break the rules and behave unsafely, safety training does at least tend to enhance people's personal commitment to safety. Conversely, safety training does not always emphasise the organisational features that may cause accidents, such as unsafe working systems and poorly written communications such as SOPs. Rather it tends to concentrate on people's behaviours and attitudes. The effect of this is that, as people often fail to realise the importance that the situation (working environment) exerts on people's ongoing behaviour, accident investigations tend to be superficial, with the victim's poor safety attitudes being proposed as the primary cause. Also, it has always been found that line management are inconsistent in their approach to safety management, and this has undermined the effects of any safety training received.

Another consistent finding is that all types of safety personnel tend to be invisible in the workplace, which means that they are not viewed favourably by the workforce. Safety representatives are rarely given any real authority and are often ignored by line managers. This means that safety representatives are not looked to by the workforce for help with safety issues as they are not seen as having any real influence on safety on a day-to-day basis. Similarly, because many safety advisors spend so much of their time in meetings or doing paperwork, they are not seen to be 'walking the talk' or exerting any influence on safety at the sharp end. It would also appear that safety advisors are very good at telling line managers that they cannot do something, but are not so good at telling the line manager how to get round the particular problem, i.e. 'You can't do that because it is unsafe, but don't ask me to give you a solution. It's your problem, I am merely the advisor'. Similar problems can be found with safety committees. Most people are not aware of the issues being discussed by the committees, or what the results of their deliberations might be. As a result, although those who attend safety committee meetings may well be working hard, safety committees tend to be seen as coffee drinking forums rather than locations for serious discussion about the prevailing safety issues. As a whole these findings strongly suggest that all of those involved in safety in a formal capacity need to adopt a much higher profile in organisations if they are to be seen to exert an effective influence on events.

Another consistent finding is that the vast majority of people, including line managers, often take risks at work to get the job done. In most cases the reason cited is perceived pressure of work. Given that management determine the required work pace, this may explain why line managers tend to be overly optimistic in their assessment of workplace risks compared to the workforce themselves. Indeed, these differences in perceived risk between hierarchical levels (i.e. senior managers, supervisors and employees) are so large that it raises the fundamental question of who should conduct risk assessments. It is probable that a line manager, a safety professional and

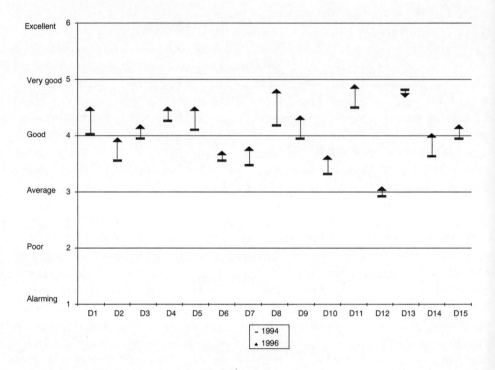

Figure 8.1 Safety Climate Graph Showing Changes. Source: Courtesy of Applied Behavioural Sciences Ltd

the person actually doing the job should be involved directly, rather than assigning the task to line managers. However, in some organisations this may not be practicable, and therefore some form of weighting may need to be applied to the figures entered into risk formulae, depending on who conducts assessments. It is conceivable that the risk perception scores obtained from a safety climate survey could be used as the weighting factor, which would offer the advantage of risk assessments taking into account the social psychological aspects involved in risk-taking behaviours.

Another consistent finding is that a behavioural safety initiative will positively impact upon people's perceptions of the prevailing safety climate. In every instance in which the author has measured safety climate before implementing a behavioural safety initiative and compared it with the prevailing safety climate as re-measured some 12 to 18 months later, there has been an improvement in people's perceptions and attitudes towards safety. Figure 8.1 provides a typical example.

The graph illustrates the fact that safety surveys are useful diagnostic tools that help companies to provide highly focused, cost-effective safety improvement initiatives. They can also be used to measure the impact of safety awareness campaigns, safety training, behavioural safety programmes and other types of safety improvement scheme.

DEVELOPING A SURVEY INSTRUMENT

The development of any type of survey involves systematic preparation and the following of a logical sequence. The basics of survey development are described below, but they are not intended to be exhaustive because they can involve relatively complex and sophisticated procedures. However, they do provide some insight into the process, enabling those considering the purchase of commercial safety climate surveys or developing their own 'in-house' surveys to appreciate what is involved.

Academics are interested in researching and modelling different theoretical relationships between various facets of safety (such as the dimensions outlined above) so that the components of an ideal safety culture can be identified. This means that they need to develop instruments that are highly reliable (i.e. they consistently measure what they are supposed to measure over many successive trials), and valid (i.e. they accurately measure what they are supposed to measure), which takes many years of painstaking work. Those organisations considering the purchase of commercially available safety climate surveys would be well advised, therefore, to seek detailed information about how the survey has been developed and tested (e.g. how many people have been sampled, and what the status and position of these people were, what industries, over what time period, etc.), and how reliable and valid it is. A number of poorly developed measures are currently being peddled by suppliers as they seek to jump on the 'bandwagon' of safety culture/climate measurement. Anyone who is still unsure about a measure's development should ask the supplier to furnish a list of companies and contact names so that the usefulness of the instrument for improving safety can be properly established. Surveys whose reliability (consistency) is below 0.70 should never be considered suitable for commercial use, nor should those that cannot differentiate between different levels of safety performance (e.g. accident rates), between different departments of an organisation or between different organisations, as their accuracy would be doubtful. Similarly, suppliers who provide feedback reports full of bar graphs showing nothing but differences in perceptions between managers and employees or between departments, and then use the results to argue that you need more of the supplier's specialist services, should also be avoided. Good suppliers provide sufficiently detailed feedback to enable organisations to follow any recommendations and make their own improvements to the deficiencies which have been identified. Only after addressing those deficiencies should the organisation make its decision as to whether or not the supplier's specialist services are of use.

Question Generation

Although high levels of reliability and validity are good to have, in reality, the same academic rigour does not usually apply to those who are developing their own 'in-house' surveys. This is because in-house surveys are used to seek clues as to what people think about safety in the organisation, or where improvements might be necessary in their safety practices, rather than developing an instrument for academic or commercial use.

Generating an Item Bank of Statements

The first step in developing a safety climate survey is to generate an item bank of statements related to a particular topic (such as management's commitment to safety), that express a wide range of views. These statements are usually obtained from the workforce via interviews, group discussions or walking round the workplace talking to people. The statements should be written in such a way that they are:

- short   — not much longer than 15 words
- simple   — focused on only one complete thought
- familiar   — using everyday language

Critical incident technique.   The critical incident technique is a particularly useful method for item generation. This involves asking people to describe two incidents: for example, one where management demonstrated their commitment to safety, and one where management failed to demonstrate their commitment to safety. It is important to ensure that each pair of statements captures both the positive and the negative aspect of the topic. Guidelines for completion could also be given, such as asking who else could or should have been involved, whether there had been other similar incidents, what the consequences were, etc. The analyst should keep asking these types of question until such time as the information being collected is continually repeated, indicating that the topic is exhausted. The exercise is then repeated for all the topics under consideration. At the end of this process the analyst is likely to have generated about 500 statements. These are then grouped under various headings (e.g. management commitment, management actions, risk taking etc.), and sorted in order of frequency and importance. They are then screened to sift out duplicates or near duplicates and awkwardly worded statements. The remaining statements can then be turned into questions or simply left as statements, and compiled into a draft survey instrument. All those involved in generating the questions or statements should be allowed to review the initial draft so that they are presented with an opportunity to modify it.

Question Writing

Survey questions must be kept as simple and clear as possible so that there can be no doubt as to the intent of the question. For example, 'I have the tools needed to do my job safely', is better than a statement worded 'All the necessary tools that I require for me to do my job safely are at my disposal whenever I require them'. The vocabulary used should be carefully aimed at the target audience and it is very important to avoid unnecessary questions. A good procedure for doing this is to go through the question bank item by item, and ask what purpose each serves. Items with two or more questions embedded in them are confusing to the respondent, and make interpretation difficult, for example, 'Everyone takes risks at home, and it's difficult to switch over at work'. This ambiguous statement asks people to agree or disagree that people take risks at home *and* whether or not they find it difficult to make the switch to working safely in the workplace. This can be overcome by dividing this statement in two, i.e. 'Everyone takes risks at home'; and 'I find it difficult to make the switch from being unsafe at home to being safe at work'.

Ensure a Good Mix of Positive and Negative Responses

It is a good idea to ensure that the survey instrument contains a good mixture of negative and positive questions or statements so that people are forced to think about the answers they give. Negatively worded questions are those where the responses indicate that something is not happening. A negative example might be 'I ignore safe working practices'. The same question positively worded would read 'I adhere to safe working practices'.

A mixture of positively worded and negatively worded questions about the same topic also provides an indicator of the respondent's truthfulness, or how carefully someone has completed the measure. For example, if both the above questions were included in a measure and the respondent answered 'agree' to both questions, that person's responses would need to be discarded from subsequent analysis as it would be difficult to identify the correct response (see Figure 8.2 for examples).

The Ideal Number of Questions

Ideally, the total number of survey questions will not exceed 100, as people may feel that it takes too long to complete if it is longer. Conversely, surveys that contain less than 50 to 60 questions may well be inadequate as they will not provide sufficient in-depth coverage of the most important facets of safety. A good rule of thumb is to use between five and ten questions per topic. It is also a good idea to give people an opportunity to express their own views on safety by including some open-ended questions, such as:

Give your answers to the questions based on your experience with Chevron and not on your experiences with other companies. Do not take long over each question, as it is usually better to indicate your first immediate response.

	highly disagree	Disagree	Not sure	Agree	highly agree
My immediate manager is well informed about safety issues.	1	2	3	4	⑤

		Highly disagree	Disagree	Not sure	Agree	Highly agree
1]	I have the right to refuse to undertake work without it adversely affecting me.	1	2	3	4	5
2]	The risks involved in my job concern me a lot.	1	2	3	4	5
3]	Operational targets are often in conflict with safety measures.	1	2	3	4	5
4]	Personally, I feel that safety issues are the most important aspect of my job.	1	2	3	4	5
5]	In my workplace, when a manager or supervisor realises that a dangerous situation has been found, he/she immediately takes corrective action.	1	2	3	4	5
*6]	The Permit to Work system is just a paper exercise	1	2	3	4	5
7]	If I make a mistake in my job, the safety of myself and others is at risk.	1	2	3	4	5
*8]	Having the Offshore Safety Division of the Health & Safety Executive, makes me feel safer.	1	2	3	4	5
9]	In my workplace, management 'turn a blind-eye' to safety issues.	1	2	3	4	5
10]	Accidents & near miss incidents are often the result of taking risks	1	2	3	4	5
11]	Retribution & blame are not seen as the purpose of investigations when things go wrong	1	2	3	4	5
12]	Sometimes it is necessary to depart from safety requirements for the sake of production.	1	2	3	4	5
13]	If I were looking for a new job, I would look for a company that places a high emphasis on safety.	1	2	3	4	5
*14]	The Permit to Work system ensures safe working.	1	2	3	4	5

*Excludes London-based employees

Figure 8.2   Sample Page of Safety Climate Questionnaire. Source: Courtesy of Applied Behavioural Sciences

- 'In your opinion what are the most important factors that adversely affect safety in your workplace?'
- 'If you could make any changes to improve the safety of your workplace what would they be?'
- 'Do you have any comments that you wish to make about safety issues?'

Scoring Formats

Since there are many ways to score an attitudinal questionnaire, an attempt should also be made to visualise how people might score each question, as this will have some bearing on the type of scoring format chosen. Although a number of scoring formats are available, from simple yes/no responses to ratings on some type of bipolar scale (usually containing a five to ten point scale, and anchored by verbal expressions), it is better to keep this as simple as possible (unless there is an occupational psychologist employed within your company who has detailed knowledge of test construction). Accordingly, most in-house surveys use a scoring scale comprised of 'agree', 'disagree' and 'don't know'. Once the questions or statements and scoring formats have been chosen, they need to be compiled into a user-friendly format with clearly written instructions and an example question, so that test users fully understand what is required to complete the survey. The developer must not assume that people have had previous experience in completing questionnaires. This means that the instructions must be clear, brief and explicit, include details about how to record a response, and what to do if the answer is not known or is not applicable to the respondent.

Demographic Information

This is also the time to consider what demographic information you need to collect to help analyse the responses (e.g. department, length of service, age, type of job, etc.). It is always a good idea to make these demographic questions anonymous by providing 'tick boxes' for various groupings (e.g. age groups = 18–25; 26-35; 36–45; 46–65) so that people do not feel that they are easy to identify. To ensure anonymity you should avoid asking for people's names or specific job titles. Figure 8.3 provides an example of some of the more common types of demographic questions.

Distributing the Survey

Once fully developed the initial measure should be tested on a random sample of employees from all levels of the organisation to ensure that the

Before completing the survey, could you please provide the following information so that Applied Behavioural Sciences Ltd can correctly analyse the responses. It must be stressed that this information does not mean that you will be personally identified. Your responses are confidential and your anonymity is guaranteed. The analysis of responses is conducted independently only by personnel from Applied Behavioural Sciences Ltd.

Please code yourself by ticking the appropriate box for each question.

1.   In which of these departments and areas do you currently work?

1.1]	Production	☐	1.2]	Maintenance	☐
1.3]	Project Engineering / Purchasing	☐	1.4]	Personnel	☐
1.5]	Research & Technology	☐	1.6]	Finance / I.T.	☐
1.7]	Safety, Health & Environment	☐	1.8]	Sales & Marketing	☐

2.   Does your job entail:

2.1]   Shiftwork? ☐   2.2]   Full -Time Days? ☐   2.3]   Other? ☐

3.   Which of these best describes your current job? (Please tick one box only).

3.1]   Process Operative ☐   3.2] Engineering ☐   3.3] Office / Clerical ☐

3.4]   Office/ Professional ☐   3.5] Scientist ☐   3.6]   Technical ☐

3.7]   Safety ☐   3.8] Other ☐

4.   Is a large part of your job concerned with:

4.1]   Managerial duties? ☐   4.2] Supervisory duties? ☐   4.3] Neither? ☐

5.   Please indicate the group which best describes the number of years you have worked on this site.

5.1]   0-5 yrs ☐   5.2] 6-15 yrs ☐   5.3] 16-25 yrs ☐   5.4] 26-45 yrs ☐

6.   Please indicate the group which best describes the number of years of experience you have had in your current job.

6.1]   0-5 yrs   6.2] 6-15 yrs ☐   6.3] 16-25 yrs ☐   6.4] 26-45 yrs ☐

7.   In which age group do you belong?

7.1]   16-25 yrs ☐   7.2] 26-35 yrs ☐   7.3] 36-45 yrs ☐   7.4] 46-65 yrs ☐

Figure 8.3   Example Demographic Page. Source: Courtesy of Applied Behavioural Sciences Ltd

questions are easily understood. This test should be carried out under the same conditions as those intended for the final version, and be accompanied by a covering letter from the chief executive endorsing the survey. The letter should:

- explain why the survey is being conducted
- ask employees to support the survey
- ask for people's honest and frank opinions
- emphasise that respondents are guaranteed anonymity and that their views are confidential
- state the time scale for completion and return (e.g. two weeks)
- stating the arrangements for personnel to return the completed surveys
- outline what the organisation will do as a result of the findings.

The survey should be distributed to those personnel chosen to test it, with the covering letter attached and a return envelope that can be sealed. One of the best types of survey return arrangement is to set up a 'post-box' in each work area so that respondents can post their completed surveys (ideally within two weeks of distribution). Although this process may seem somewhat elaborate for a trial run, it provides a useful method for assessing the practicality of the return arrangements so that any necessary modifications can be made prior to the full survey.

Return Rate

Typically, when surveys are mailed to people, the return rate is about 30%. This means that consideration should be given to the numbers of completed questionnaires that will be needed to provide confidence in the results. Under most circumstances, the return sample should be large enough to ensure that any sub group of interest does not fall below 30, although it is recognised that this may not be possible in smaller organisations or departments.

Developing the Final Version

After the trial questionnaires have been completed and returned, the next stage is concerned with analysing and sifting through the responses to eliminate unnecessary question items. An examination of each person's responses will show the percentage of question items that were attempted and the percentage of those answered correctly or in the right way. Question items that very few have attempted to answer indicate that the wording of the question may be confusing, or possibly requires specialised detailed knowledge not widely available. Once the suitability of the items has been determined, a final version is compiled. The final version can then be administered to everybody in the organisation, using the distribution procedures for the pilot survey outlined above.

Analysing the Responses

Surveys conducted solely by external suppliers tend to be analysed by them, using sophisticated statistical techniques, and interpreted in the light of the supplier's expertise. In some instances, however, external suppliers recommend that the entry of response data is conducted by a third party supplier who specialises in entering questionnaire data into computers. This data is then returned to the employing organisation for analysis. The effect of this approach is that the employing organisation is often left in the position of having to analyse the data, *and interpret the results* themselves, which is all right if the employing organisation has someone with the expertise to do so. Although suppliers will often provide a computer programme to analyse the data, they do not always furnish the means to correctly interpret the findings. This is a major failing of such software, and employing organisations should be extremely cautious about its purchase, as many of the rewards to be gained from conducting the survey could be lost. In these instances, care should be taken at the contractual stage to clarify how the survey will be interpreted and by whom.

For in-house surveys, it is sufficient in most instances for the responses to be analysed and reported as the percentage of respondents who agreed or disagreed with a particular question item. It is possible to add a further level of sophistication by placing all the questions concerned with the same topic (i.e. dimension) together under sub headings (e.g. management commitment, safety training, etc.). The scores for each of the questions in the dimension are then aggregated together to provide a summary index score for each of the dimensions measured. In this way it is possible to summarise and report the results by each topic to provide an overall view of where improvements might best be made. Open-ended questions can be categorised into themes arranged in descending order by frequency of response, i.e. the more frequently something is mentioned the more importance the theme assumes. This could be done for the organisation as a whole, or by each department. The advantage of categorising the responses by department is that a list of specific issues can be discussed and addressed by the different work groups within each department.

Providing Feedback

One of the most important (but often neglected) aspects of the survey is to provide each of the work groups with a breakdown of the survey results so that they can be discussed with a view to implementing improvements. The most useful way of doing this is to hold informal meetings with *each and every work group*. The results for the business as a whole should be presented to them, followed by detailed feedback to each of the work groups about the results for their particular department. This often provokes a thoughtful debate about the issues that leads to the identification of other issues that did not surface during the development of the survey. It is imperative, however, that any remedial actions resulting from the survey are implemented as rapidly as possible so that the organisation is seen to be genuine in its efforts to address people's concerns. It is a good idea to end these feedback sessions with the development of clear and specific action plans, with responsibility and accountability agreed by all concerned. In this way, people's hearts and minds will be won over to the safety cause. Conversely, if the results are kept from the workforce and not acted upon, the management team will lose credibility, and the importance of safety *per se* and the employee involvement process will be undermined.

9

Improving Behavioural Safety

INTRODUCTION

Many organisations spend a lot of time, money and effort trying to improve safety. This may be by installing safety management systems that include regular line management audits of unsafe acts and unsafe conditions in the workplace, supported by some safety training and the creation of various types of safety committee. Despite such efforts exerting significant downwards pressure on their lost-time accident rates, many still find that a base level of minor accidents remains that appears to be stubbornly resistant to all efforts to remove it. Although many of these accidents are attributed to people's carelessness or poor safety attitudes, a perusal of their causes shows that the vast majority are actually *triggered* by deeply ingrained unsafe behaviours. However, through proven management control techniques, formalised behavioural safety initiatives can be used to address these unsafe behaviours by proactively focusing people's attention on them. A vast amount of research evidence shows that this almost always results in a positive step change in safety performance and safety attitudes. One study conducted in a UK Cellophane manufacturing plant by the author and colleagues in 1992, for example, reduced the moving average number of accidents per 16 week period from 118 to 63. This 50% reduction saved an estimated £220,000 to £440,000 in associated accident costs inside 20 weeks. Because behavioural safety initiatives are designed to bring about continual ongoing improvements, the initiative has continued ever since. Four years on, by July 1996 the average number of accidents per 16 week period was 29. Significantly, people's perceptions and attitudes towards safety, assessed by an empirically developed safety climate measure (see Chapter 8), also improved. These are typical results which support the notion that behavioural safety initiatives are specifically designed to capture people's hearts and minds during the ultimate level of effort. They should therefore be used to complement and enhance existing safety improvement efforts, rather than to replace other initiatives such as weekly management safety inspections, etc.

It must be stressed that a behavioural safety initiative is not a 'cure all panacea' that replaces other safety efforts. Unfortunately, because they tend to be seen in this way, they are often implemented before the immediate and intermediate levels of effort have been addressed. Consequently, they often create much unnecessary resistance to safety when there is still much to do to improve the working environment and the organisation's safety systems. This is because employees believe that management are more concerned with trivial issues than with safety improvements that require capital expenditure. In turn, this leads to employees viewing behavioural safety initiatives as a convenient way for management to dodge their safety responsibilities and apportion blame to the workforce. Nonetheless, it should always be recognised that some resistance will always be present, even in the best of organisations. Once established, however, it is possible to use exactly the same behavioural management techniques to bring about production or quality-related improvements.

WHY FOCUS ON UNSAFE BEHAVIOUR?

Although difficult to control, 80% to 95% of all accidents are triggered by unsafe behaviours. Consequently, it makes good commercial sense to target unsafe behaviours if the associated human and financial costs are to be reduced. Very often, however, these behaviours interact with other negative features (termed 'resident pathogens') inherent in workflow processes or present in the working environment (see Chapter 1). In the same way as pathogens (e.g. cancer-causing cells) are present in the human body, every organisation has its fair share of accident-causing pathogens. Often inadvertently introduced into organisations during the implementation of strategic plans, these pathogens lie dormant and are relatively harmless until such time as two or more combine and are triggered by an unsafe behaviour to produce an accident. This can be illustrated by a company which installed a new production process which entailed designing and building two new mezzanine floors in an existing plant. Plant-based engineers had formulated plans that had been approved by a project team over a period of time. Once the construction work was complete, it was found that a supporting girder had been erected at a height of five feet above the second step of a staircase on both floors. This meant that two pathogens had inadvertently been introduced into the physical environment. Meanwhile, during the commissioning of the new process equipment, product blockages were frequently found to occur in the related pipework (a third pathogen) that could only be cleared by ascending to the mezzanine floors where an inspection hatch was situated. On their own these three pathogens were harmless. However, due to production pressures and a lack of adequate manpower (two further pathogens), the blockage required the operator to isolate the equipment at a lower production floor (another pathogen), and ascend the stairs to the mezzanine floors to clear the pipework. At this point all these 'harmless' pathogens combined to trigger an accident when the operator rushed up the stairs (unsafe behaviour) to clear the blockage and ran into the low girder, fracturing his skull, inflicting whiplash effects on his neck and knocking himself unconscious. This resulted in a reportable accident, lost production and associated costs.

Unsafe Behaviour is Within People's Control

In the above scenario, the potential for this type of lost-time reportable accident will always be present (representing a permanent threat to production targets) until the pathogens are addressed. However, given that it is much more difficult to address many of these resident pathogens, focusing attention on the operator's unsafe behaviour while ascending the stairs is a much easier option during the interim period. This is because the unsafe behaviour is within the operator's control, whereas the pathogens tend not to be. Since a behavioural safety initiative identifies and focuses on particular sets of critical observable unsafe behaviours, people tend to be more aware of their potential to cause harm. This then gives them the mechanism by which they can control both their own safety behaviour and that of their colleagues.

Providing a Better Index of Ongoing Safety Performance

A focus on unsafe behaviours also provides a much better index of ongoing safety performance than accident rates. The reasons for this are twofold:

- accidents tend to be the end result of a causal sequence of pathogens combining, and being triggered, by people's unsafe behaviour
- unsafe behaviours can be measured in a meaningful way on a daily basis.

Typically, companies use accident rates as the primary outcome measure of safety performance simply because they signal that something is wrong within the company's safety management system. Because of the way they are calculated, companies also use them as a benchmark to compare the effectiveness of their safety management systems against others in the same or other industries. Unfortunately, as illustrated in Figure 9.1: *Management by*

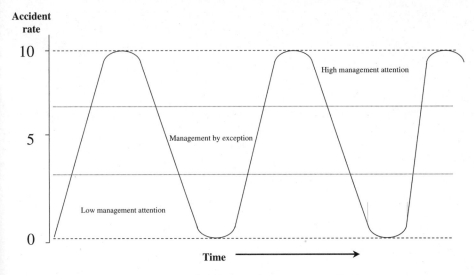

Figure 9.1 Management by Exception Cycle

Exception Cycle, this narrow focus on accident rates tends to result in 'management by exception', whereby management attention and resources are directed at safety only when accident rates rise dramatically. When the immediate problems appear to be resolved, management attention and resources are diverted to other pressing organisational issues until such time as the accident rate rises once again. Consequently, rather than being pro-active, companies which focus almost exclusively on accident rates as a measure of safety performance tend to be reactive in their approach to safety.

Measuring actual safety behaviour on a daily basis, however, allows other safety-related issues or pathogens to be identified which can be dealt with before an accident occurs. For example, a collaborative, problem-solving approach involving both management and employees has to be adopted to identify critical sets of safe and unsafe behaviours. These critical safety behaviours are then used as the unit of measurement by developing depart-mental safety performance inventories which provide the basis for personnel to systematically monitor and observe their colleagues' ongoing safety behaviour on a daily basis in an enabling atmosphere. Based on the results of this peer to peer monitoring, each work group set their own safety improve-ment target. Verbal and graphical feedback is then given on a weekly basis to allow each work group to track their progress in reaching their safety improvement target. As a result, the ongoing identification of safety prob-lems and their resolution become a normal way of life, which is why companies adopting this approach become much more proactive safety managers. In turn they are usually rewarded by fewer accidents, consistent safety management, better communications and greater involvement in

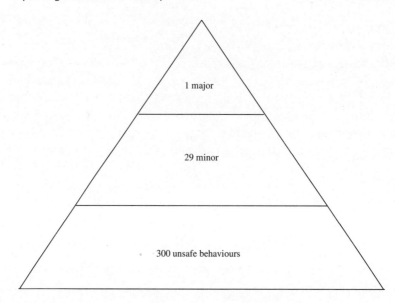

Figure 9.2   Heinrich's Triangle — Adapted from Heinrichm H.W. (1959) Industrial Accident Prevention. *New York: McGraw-Hill. Reproduced by permission*

team-working, all of which exert beneficial effects on production related issues and bottom-line profits.

WHY DO PEOPLE BEHAVE UNSAFELY?

People often behave unsafely because they have never yet been hurt while doing their job in an unsafe way: 'I've always done the job this way' being a familiar comment when asked why they behave in that way. Although, this may well be true, the potential for an accident is never far away. Heinrich's triangle (see Figure 9.2), for example, suggests that for every 330 unsafe acts, 29 will result in minor injuries and one in a major or lost-time incident.

Over an extended period of time, therefore, the lack of any injuries for those who consistently engage in unsafe behaviours is actually reinforcing the very same behaviour pattern that in all probability will eventually cause a serious injury. The principle being illustrated here is that the consequences of behaving unsafely will nearly always determine future unsafe behaviour, simply because reinforced behaviour will nearly always tend to be repeated

The Effects of Different Reinforcers

The continuation of unsafe behaviours is often supported by more than one reinforcer, some exerting stronger effects on people's behaviour than others

This is particularly true for reinforcers that are soon, certain and positive. Smokers, for example, find it hard to give up because the consequences of smoking are soon (immediate), certain (every time) and positive (a nicotine top up), whereas the negative consequences (e.g. lung cancer) are late (some years away) and uncertain (not every smoker contracts or dies from lung cancer). In exactly the same way, employees will find it hard to follow certain safety rules and procedures if they are consistently (certain) rewarded by an immediate (soon) time saving that achieves extra production (positive) by behaving unsafely. What would you do, for example, if you had to spend 10 to 15 minutes putting on the correct clothing and equipment to open a manual valve that takes only 10 seconds?

Work-Related Reinforcers

In some instances the actual workflow process also reinforces people's unsafe behaviour, simply because it may be the only way to get a job done. In one company, for example, where a particular fluid valve was continually malfunctioning, operators were forced to use a maintenance engineer's fluid valve to wash out lines conveying raw material to ensure that the next product batch was not contaminated. Unfortunately the maintenance valve was situated in an extremely awkward position, at a height of 10 feet above the floor level. To reach this valve, operators were forced to stand on a handrail, with a 30 foot drop on one side, at least 12 times per day. Because the operators' behaviour was always (certain) reinforced immediately (soon) by getting their job done (positive) to maintain production, this particular unsafe behaviour soon became part of the group 'norm'. This example implicitly illustrates that unsafe behaviour is sometimes further reinforced by line managers turning a blind eye, or actively encouraging employees to take short cuts for the sake of production. Unfortunately, this has negative knock-on effects on other areas of work activity that are not always immediately apparent, such as:

* operators learn that unsafe behaviour pays
* it wastes resources as the very behaviours that companies spend a lot of time, money and effort trying to eradicate are reinforced
* by condoning unsafe behaviour, line managers are transmitting conflicting messages that undermine employees' confidence in the whole of management's commitment to improving safety.

This can seriously undermine employees' loyalty and commitment to their organisation, as the company will be perceived to be unwilling to provide a safe working environment. This can reduce the amount and quality of production and lead to higher labour turnover and absenteeism. In the above example, if line management had halted production until such time as the original fluid valve was replaced, or provided a safe means of access (e.g. scaffolding), the establishment of an unsafe behaviour pattern would never have occurred in the first place. Possible injuries to operators, the associated accident costs and potential legal proceedings would also have been avoided. In addition, the corporate commitment to safety would have been publicly reinforced by showing how seriously the company viewed safe working practices.

HOW IS UNSAFE BEHAVIOUR PREVENTED?

Traditionally, efforts to change people's unsafe behaviour have taken the form of either altering the physical environment with engineering solutions or changing people's attitudes via safety information campaigns and safety training, or using disciplinary procedures to force them into compliance. Each of these approaches to stopping unsafe behaviour is discussed below.

Providing Engineering Solutions

Eliminating all known and potential hazards of workflow processes by engineering them out or introducing physical controls at the design stage can be an effective way of limiting the potential for unsafe behaviour. Unfortunately, the opportunity to do this is usually limited to 'greenfield' sites, or when new plant and equipment is to be installed. In practice, this means that much plant and equipment currently in use was manufactured and installed many years ago. Where this is the case, rather than replacing existing plant management often find it cheaper and easier to adapt it by, for example, installing physical guards or automatic cut-out safety devices. While successful in many instances, it does not always work, simply because people have the capacity to behave unsafely and override any engineering controls. Familiar examples include the removal or disengaging of machine guards to speed up production. A specific example involved an operator on a weekend shift who physically climbed a 10 foot high wire enclosure to reach parts of a production line that had become blocked by product bales. Unfortunately, although the operator cleared the blockage, he forgot about a swivel arm that automatically swept the raw material bales onto the production line. This swept him into the machinery, causing him to be fatally crushed between two receiving presses. Clearly, despite the fenced of enclosure and numerous warning signs the operator felt that the conse quences of behaving unsafely would be more than repaid by continued production. In the same way, many people choose to ignore or overrid arious alerting signals if they are thought to hinder production while resenting little visible risk for non-compliance. These examples illustrate the oint that because many engineering solutions are reliant on people's 'rule ollowing' behaviour, people still have the capacity to behave unsafely.

Changing People's Attitudes

is very common to find comments on accident reports that say 'Mr . . . nould take more care. With better attitudes and safety awareness, this ccident would not have happened'. This type of comment often reflects the ict that a 'blame the victim' culture exists within a company, with attempts o change unsafe behaviour based on the belief that attitudes determine ehaviour. Such companies tend to rely on information campaigns that ublicise safety and/or provide safety training to bring about changes in eople's attitudes.

Attitude and Behaviour Link

lthough positive attitudes towards safety are important and very desirable, ie link from attitude change to behaviour change is very weak. This can be eadily explained by the fact that one attitude consists of four components: a hinking' component, a 'feeling' component, an 'evaluative' component, and 'conative' component, any of which may conflict with the others (e.g. one iay think and feel positively about safety but still not behave safely). dditionally, a single attitude is usually linked with a set of other related titudes. To ensure success, therefore, logic dictates that attempts at attitude iange must target each individual component of each individual attitude, ; well as addressing the remaining set of related attitudes, for each single nployee. Obviously, simultaneously identifying and addressing all these parate components is almost impossible, particularly when we consider at many people are not even sure of their own attitudes towards many opics'. Even if this were possible, when we recognise that people hold ifferent attitudes about different 'topics' and that the perceived importance " one 'topic' will often override another in different situations we can begin see why the link from attitude change to behaviour change is so weak.

Behaviour and Attitude Link

rtunately, the link from behaviour change to attitude change is much ronger. A prime example that demonstrates this is the use of seat belts in otor vehicles. Over a period of time, various governments introduced formational safety campaigns in the media to get people to 'Clunk click every trip'. Overall, these campaigns tended to have very little effect c people's attitudes towards the use of seat belts. Approximately 90% of drive continued to ignore the message. The government of the day finally decide to change people's seat belt wearing behaviour by introducing legislation make the use of seat belts compulsory. This was initially backed up by vigorous police campaign of enforcement, until people got so used to wearir them that it became a non-issue. Were the seat belt legislation to be repeale tomorrow, most people would probably continue to use them, indicating th the vast majority of people now hold positive attitudes towards seat belt us Why should this be? Psychologists have shown that if people conscious change their behaviour for some reason, then they also tend to re-adjust the associated attitudes and belief systems to fit the new behaviour. In genera this occurs because people try to protect their psychological well being k avoiding the introduction of stressful psychological tension caused k conflicts between their behaviour and attitudes. Thus behaviour change tene to lead to new belief and attitude systems which then buttress the new set behaviours.

Effect of Peer Pressure

An additional factor that enhances attitude change by focusing on behavio in the workplace is the positive reinforcement bought about by pe pressure. Psychologists have known for some time that group membersh demands conformity to a group's behavioural and attitudinal 'norms'. If work group collectively adopts the norm that thinking and behaving safe is best for all concerned, the group as a whole will tend to apply soci sanctions to the individual who deviates from the norm. If the individu wishes to remain a part of the social fabric of the work group, he or she w soon revert back to the safety norm and behave safely. This illustrates t point that work groups will adopt a collective definition of those behaviou work practices or tasks that are considered to be risky. This fact lies at t very heart of behavioural safety initiatives, simply because the essence of ar safety improvement initiative must be to help work groups to redefi positively their own safety-related norms.

Punishing People Until they Behave Safely

The methods adopted to change group safety norms can lead to positive negative effects. Some approaches to safety management are heavily reliant c the use of authority, fear and punishment (i.e. if you do not behave in a sa manner at work you could be reprimanded, fined or even dismissed). Oft found in top-down, management-driven 'brand name' safety programme these approaches emphasise the use of discipline and punishment to discourage unsafe behaviour, while safe behaviour is largely ignored. Unfortunately, this can sometimes end in the opposite result to that intended (e.g. accident or near miss occurrences are not reported for fear of sanctions). Although the judicious use of discipline and punishment can have the intended effects, it often does not. The reasons for this are quite simple. First, the effectiveness of punishment is dependent upon its consistency. It only works if given immediately and every single time an unsafe behaviour occurs, but punishing someone every time they behave unsafely is very difficult because they will not always be seen to do so by those in authority. This means that the multitude of soon, certain and positive reinforcers gained from behaving unsafely will tend to outweigh any uncertain, late, negative reinforcers received from inconsistent punishment. Second, punishment serves more to suppress existing behaviour than to encourage new behaviour patterns. This in itself can cause considerable anxiety and resentment that surface negatively in other areas of work activity.

Praising People for Behaving Safely

Given all the problems outlined above, how can line management ensure that the reinforcers for working safely are greater than those for working unsafely? Most people tend to respond more to praise and social approval than any other factor. For instance, people usually smoke their first cigarette during the teenage years because it is seen as the 'thing' to do. Although the cigarette smoke may taste foul and also cause severe coughing, people will continue to suffer the discomfort if the cigarette-smoking behaviour meets with their peer group's approval. Similarly, some people may not use PPE at work because of their colleagues' disapproval. It makes sense, therefore, to make use of this phenomenon and praise people for behaving safely (something very rarely done) to bring about the required changes. Crucially, the effect of this is to *explicitly link the desired safe behaviour to the praise received*. Once the required behaviour pattern starts to become established, the timing and frequency of the praise and social approval can be reduced over a period of time, i.e. it doesn't need to be given immediately and every single time that someone does something well. Additional benefits include the strengthening of a positive safety culture due to increased trust and confidence between line managers and the workforce.

ACHIEVING IMPROVEMENTS IN SAFETY BEHAVIOUR

Given that attitude change will automatically tend to follow behavioural change, it must make sense to focus solely on people's safety behaviour rather than their safety attitudes in order to bring about the desired changes. Similarly, making better use of social approval and encouragement instead of discipline will bring about positive changes in a work group's safety norms. In addition, because the workforce has the most influence on any company's safety performance, they are the best people to redefine their safety norms as they control their own behaviour. It follows, therefore, that any safety improvement initiative which relies almost exclusively on line management's efforts is less likely to be as successful as one that empowers and enables the workforce itself. Accordingly, behavioural safety initiatives are very much driven and shaped by the workforce, in conjunction with line management acting as facilitators. In this way, the workforce is given responsibility and authority for identifying, defining and monitoring their own safe and unsafe behaviours, as well as setting their own safety improvement targets. As a result, work groups are able to redefine their own safety-related norms in an enabling atmosphere. Line management facilitate this process by providing the necessary resources and support to encourage employee ownership while stressing that no individual will be identified or disciplined as a result of the monitoring. In this way a blame-free pro-active safety culture is created that is so vital for long-term success.

DOES IT WORK?

Because this approach differs considerably from traditional ways of improving safety, a question commonly asked is 'Do these ideas work in practice?' Overwhelmingly, the answer is 'yes'! Psychologists from around the world have consistently reported positive changes in both safety behaviour and accident rates, regardless of the industrial sector or company size. The research includes studies conducted in metal engineering plants, bakeries, food manufacturers, shipbuilding and offshore installations. Although many of these were conducted in the USA, Scandinavia and Israel, positive results have also been obtained by the author and colleagues in the UK construction industry, polymer film manufacturers, food processing factories and chemical plants. Typical findings include:

- *Organisational features*
  - Improved levels of safety performance
  - Reductions in accident rates
  - Significant reductions in accident costs
  - Improvements in co-operation, involvement and communication between management and the workforce
  - Improvements in safety climate
  - Ongoing improvements to safety management systems.

- *Person features*
  - Greater ownership of safety by the workforce
  - Improved levels of safety behaviour and attitudes towards safety
  - Greater individual acceptance of responsibility for safety.

As these results show, focusing on specific safety behaviours leads to many positive results for both organisations and individuals. Since this approach emphasises continuous improvement it reflects many TQM principles. Indeed, because the philosophies of TQM and the behavioural safety approach are so similar, they tend to reinforce each other, with each gaining strength from the other when they are simultaneously implemented in the workplace.

HOW IS A BEHAVIOURAL SAFETY INITIATIVE PUT INTO OPERATION?

Intuitively familiar to problem-solvers, planning change involves a number of discrete steps that include:

- planning the change strategy
- identifying the problem
- implementing the change strategy
- evaluating the extent of change
- correcting any deviations from the changes required.

Planning the Change Strategy

As with any type of improvement initiative, some planning and organising will be required. Decisions about the scope of the improvement initiative (e.g. how many business units, departments or work groups will be involved) must be made before implementation, as this will affect the number of personnel required and other resources. Every person in the organisation, from the chief executive officer to the teaboy, must be seen to be involved, partly because this reduces the possibility of particular work groups feeling that they are being singled out for special attention, while the remaining departments feel left out and partly because those who push for improvements in safety performance (e.g. line managers) do not necessarily practise what they preach. This latter point has been illustrated in organisations in which production personnel were behaving safely on average 70% to 80% of the time while office personnel (consisting of line managers and clerks) were behaving safely on average only 40% of the time. One particular advantage arising from everyone's involvement is the improvements brought about in the organisation's communications systems, and the resulting benefits to other operational areas of the business. Typically, the enhancement of communications begins during the training sessions during which a whole cross-section of the workforce come together. More often than not this continues as the safety improvement initiative progresses.

Consider the Use of a Safety Climate Survey

One practical method for determining the scope and nature of the improvement initiative is to conduct a survey of the workforce's current perceptions and attitudes towards safety. A psychometric measure of safety climate can be used to provide invaluable assistance to this initial development of the overall direction of the behavioural safety initiative (see Chapter 8). The information obtained from the survey informs management about the effects that an organisation's current safety policies and practices are exerting on safety *per se*, as well as aiding the development of safety performance inventories. Moreover, the results of the survey can be used as a benchmark against which the effects of a behavioural safety initiative on people's perceptions and attitudes can later be compared (12 to 18 months). A summary of the results should *always* be communicated to the workforce as soon as is practicable.

Alternative Implementation Mechanisms—Two-Person Project Teams

Once the scope of the improvement initiative has been decided, the mechanisms to implement the project need to be established. A number of alternatives are available, each with its own advantages and disadvantages. The first takes the form of a dedicated two-person project team consisting of a senior member of management, whose role is that of project champion, and a workforce-based administrative assistant who provides a supporting role to the project champion and co-ordinates the overall effort. The main advantage resides in the fact that only two people are involved in the day-to-day running of the project. This minimises time resourcing and operational costs and leads to the project team's intimate knowledge of the overall effort. The latter point is important because it means that the project team will be fully conversant with any problem areas and will also be able to make rapid decisions to overcome them. The main disadvantage arises from the fact that if either team member is absent for any reason, the other person will bear all the responsibility for the smooth day-to-day running of the project. By way of example, it is not unknown for the senior manager designated as project champion to be so overtaken with operational duties that complete operational responsibility for the behavioural initiative is borne solely by the administrative assistant for an extended period of time. If the two-person project team approach is adopted, therefore, it may be wise to ensure that the administrative assistant possesses the necessary managerial skills to see the various stages of the project through.

Project personnel's roles—project champion. Since the project champion's role is mainly concerned with providing leadership, direction and ongoing visible support for the initiative, it is usually best that this task be given to a member of the senior management team. This is because:

- they have access to high level decision-makers
- they are able to sanction the use of various organisational resources
- they are in a position to ensure that line managers play their part in the overall initiative.

For example, plans for an engineering solution that requires capital expenditure might be proposed. The project champion's seniority will enable him or her to approve the necessary expenditure or gain the attention of colleagues. The champion can also ensure that funding is available for the provision of feedback charts and other resource items that might be required. Since senior management will be heavily involved in other aspects of the organisation's business, it is generally accepted that the project champion spends an average of only one hour per day in the champion's role, the majority of this time being taken up with talking to subordinates about the initiative and dealing with specific issues that may have arisen, such as checking on the progress of an engineering item highlighted as unsafe during the previous week. Nonetheless, a much greater time commitment will be required of the project champion when it is necessary to conduct line management and workforce briefings, observer training sessions and target-setting meetings. It may also prove useful to rotate the project champion's role amongst the senior management team each time two phases have been completed (a phase is a time period of approximately six months). In this way, senior management's commitment to the initiative is visibly demonstrated while also ensuring that the whole of the management team is intimately familiar with the overall process. At some later stage, this collective knowledge should enable the senior management team to apply the process to other areas of activity such as quality and production.

Categorically, the project champion's role should not be assigned to company safety managers/advisors—simply because they do not normally fulfil a line management function and have very little authority to implement decisions or sanction the use of funds. Nonetheless, because they provide a valuable safety knowledge resource for both the project champion and the co-ordinator, there is no good reason to exclude them from assisting in the overall process.

Project personnel's roles—project co-ordinator. The role of administrative assistant or project co-ordinator is different and more wide-ranging than that of the project champion. In the main, he or she will be concerned with the smooth day-to-day running of the initiative which consists of ensuring that:

- the work group's observers have a sufficient number of safety performance inventories available at all times
- the observers conduct their observations on a daily basis and return the scores for computation
- observers consistently adhere to collectively agreed ground rules about how to interpret and score particular unsafe behaviours
- the safety performance feedback charts are updated on a weekly basis
- the weekly behavioural safety work group briefings are being held
- all levels of the organisation are regularly informed about the project's progress
- problems are dealt with as they arise.

Other co-ordinator duties include ensuring that training rooms are booked for observer training sessions; assisting with or conducting observer training, timetabling subsequent phases; helping to develop further safety performance inventories, and analysing each week's safety performance scores so that they can be discussed and actioned at the weekly team briefings. Some organisations prefer to assign the co-ordinator's role to someone on a full time basis while others prefer to have a part-time co-ordinator. Experience has shown that a minimum of four hours per working day are needed. A practical and helpful method for minimising the time resource is to computerise the data collection and processing to allow direct data entry by observers and data analysis by the project team. The only commercially available computer program developed specifically for this purpose currently available (August 1997) is a Windows-based computer program for use on a single computer or a computer network, developed by the author as a part of his award winning 'B-Safe Programme'. This enables each work group's safety performance inventories to be stored and printed, their weekly safety performance scores to be recorded, stored and analysed, and weekly feedback reports to be generated and printed. These printed feedback reports form the basis for discussion at each work group's weekly briefing

Project personnel's roles—project observers. Since observers undertake ten minute observations of their peers' safety behaviour on a daily basis for pre-determined period of time (i.e. a phase lasting between three and six months), their role is probably the most crucial of all. Not only do they provide a communication link between the workforce and management in terms of day-to-day safety, but they are also expected to set a good example to their peers by adhering to the safe behaviours advocated on the safety performance inventories, as well as accurately recording the frequency of safe and unsafe behaviour in their workplace. They therefore bear a heavy responsibility. If they do not set a good example, or if the integrity of the observations is suspect and the safety performance scores recorded do not appear to reflect reality, the whole programme will soon lose its credibility.

Alternative Implementation Mechanisms—Plant Steering Committee

A second alternative consists of a single plant-wide steering committee comprising between five and twelve members. The main advantages offered by this approach reside in the potential site-wide representation of different work groups on the committee which can help to encourage site-wide ownership of the project. It is also easier for the work load to be shared if project personnel are absent for any reason. However, it is important to ensure that representation is balanced. At least 70% of the steering committee should be shopfloor-based, with the remainder comprising first line supervisors and line management. The disadvantages lie mainly in the diffusion of responsibility for the project's implementation. This could lead to poor project management unless the committee is very clear about its relationship with the remainder of the organisation, its agenda, its responsibilities, and the specific roles of all the different members. Similarly, because shopfloor-based personnel are not likely to be familiar with strategic decision-making or other committee functions, it may prove necessary to provide all the committee members with decision-making and communication skills training at the very outset, in order to offset any potential difficulties arising from any one person's inexperience. Although this may add considerably to the project's operational costs, this type of training could also prove beneficial to the organisation's other business activities. Similarly, it is important to recognise that the committee members also have to fulfil other job roles and will, therefore, have to be released from their normal activities. In the present economic climate and the recent downsizing of manpower in many organisations, this could mean that many committee members may find it difficult to attend all the meetings, or may only be assigned to the committee for relatively short periods.

Alternative Implementation Mechanisms—Existing Safety Committee

A third alternative is to use an organisation's existing safety committee to implement the initiative rather than set up a separate steering committee.

The main advantages are that existing members will be familiar with th
way in which committees function and the organisation's existing an
historical safety problems; they are also comprised of individuals who a
already committed to safety. Moreover, the relationships between the orga
isation and the safety committee will have already been fully establishe
The disadvantages are related to how well the organisation's safety con
mittee has performed in the past and its composition. If the committee ha
generally been regarded as ineffective, or if it is dominated by senic
management and safety professionals, its use may be inappropriate.

Project committees.   If the project is to be implemented via a steering con
mittee or the existing safety committee, the different roles of the variou
members will need to be clearly defined and properly co-ordinated to avoi
duplication of effort and confusion. A number of basic tasks fulfilled by th
committee members parallel those for the project champion and co-ordinato
Inevitably, this will involve a major time commitment from each committe
member to plan, implement and monitor the whole process.

The first step entails selecting people for the various roles, clearly definir
each person's role, and deciding on the structure of the committee. One
the first decisions to be made concerns the choice of the committee chai
person. Many may feel that this should fall to a senior manager. In som
companies this may well prove to be the case, but it is always a good idea
try and find a suitable employee from one of the work groups as th
transmits a powerful symbolic message that the initiative is truly a
employee-driven process. In turn this can make the overall implementatic
easier, as less resistance may be experienced from the work groups and fro
other committee members. Since the chairperson has several important task
to fulfil, he or she will need to possess good interpersonal, analytical an
planning skills. The chairperson's tasks include leadership, co-ordinatio:
public speaking and liaising with other organisational functions. He or sh
has the overall responsibility for ensuring that:

- the implementation effort stays on schedule
- other committee members fulfil their roles
- safety performance inventories are developed for each work group
- people are recruited and trained as observers
- target-setting sessions are held
- weekly work group briefings are held
- new implementation phases are scheduled, fully developed and impl
  mented
- problems are resolved within a reasonable time frame.

The roles of the other committee members can be clearly split into various functions. For example, one person could be given sole responsibility for recruiting and training the observers; another could be asked to develop the safety performance inventories; yet another could set up and manage the process for providing weekly feedback to the work groups, while someone else could be given responsibility for actioning and monitoring the progress of other safety issues arising from the observations. It may be useful to rotate these roles amongst the existing committee members as each phase proceeds, or indeed recruit people who have previously been work group observers to act as committee members. In this way, the committee's ongoing experience and knowledge are not lost. Additional advantages reside in avoiding the implementation effort becoming stale or the project becoming identified with only a few individuals.

Alternative Implementation Mechanisms—Summary

Although each of the above alternatives has potential problems, they are not insurmountable if the organisation is truly committed to implementing a behavioural safety improvement initiative. Whichever mechanism is adopted, the basic function of each remains the same: namely that of conducting briefings; developing safety performance inventories; identifying, recruiting, training, and supporting safety observers; and monitoring and reviewing ongoing progress. It is likely, therefore, that the choice will be determined by the size of a particular organisation, its structure, style of management and prevailing safety culture. While some organisations may find it useful to set up a steering committee and several sub-committees in their various functional departments, others may prefer to use two-person project teams, or existing safety committees. In the author's experience, irrespective of the size of the organisation, two-person project teams have generally proved to be a highly successful and cost-effective mechanism with which to implement a behavioural safety initiative.

Briefings

During the planning stages, it is important for the project team to hold briefings with both line management and the workforce as early as possible. This is particularly so in organisations in which the workforce tend to be sceptical about management's intentions. Consequently, the philosophy of the approach and the way it will be implemented should be fully explained to all concerned at the outset. Because of the particular impact that management commitment has on safety performance, great efforts have to be directed at line management to get them to buy into the process. An issue often encountered during these briefings is associated with the reasons for adopting a behavioural initiative. As such it is a good idea to outline:

- the organisation's previous efforts to improve safety
- the effects this has had on accident rates
- the costs of these accidents (e.g. compensation claims, lost production, etc.) in recent years
- the problems remaining (i.e. current accident rates)
- how the programme will complement rather than replace existing safety improvement initiatives.

It is also important to stress that, as the initiative is concerned with continuous improvement, it will continue *ad infinitum*, albeit in six-monthly phases (or other pre-determined time periods).

Management briefings.   Line management briefings are slightly different from those delivered to the workforce in that requests should be made of them to demonstrate their ongoing commitment to the process by their:

- talking to subordinates about the approach, and informing them that their co-operation will be sought
- asking for volunteer observers, or suggesting appropriate personnel
- arranging for personnel to be made available for interviewing during the initial stages
- allowing observers to conduct five to ten-minute observations during each working day/shift
- allowing all their subordinates to attend a 30-minute session to help set safety improvement targets
- attending the 30-minute sessions themselves, so as to provide visible support to the observers
- praising their subordinates who are behaving safely
- encouraging people to behave safely and not disciplining any one who does not adhere to the safety behaviours advocated on the safety performance inventories
- conducting weekly team briefings with their subordinates to explore the previous week's safety performance so as to decide on what proactive actions the work group could collectively take to improve things further

Senior management should be invited to make a point of visiting the work groups on a weekly basis, with the express aim of discussing and commenting upon progress to date. It may also prove useful to request that senior managers regularly (e.g. weekly) try and join up with an observer when an observation is taking place to show their interest and to visibly demonstrate their commitment to the process. The impact that ongoing management commitment has on safety cannot be stressed enough. The greater the commitment, the greater the beneficial effects on safety performance.

Recruiting Observers

Other activities occurring during the planning process should be directed at the recruitment of safety observers. It is essential that personnel from a wide range of job roles (e.g. line managers and operatives) are recruited as observers, so that all organisational levels are represented in the implementation effort. In practical terms this helps to demonstrate how seriously management view the improvement process, and also avoids transmitting the message to the workforce that the change of emphasis to unsafe behaviour is somehow linked to a 'blame the accident victim' approach. In fact, the majority of observers are usually drawn from the 'shopfloor'. There are two reasons for this:

- these people have first hand knowledge and experience of what actually occurs on a day-to-day basis in their workplace
- it is usually 'shopfloor' people who are involved in workplace accidents or near miss incidents.

Because of the difficulties often encountered during the first phase of implementation, progress may go more smoothly if the people recruited are known to be committed to safety (e.g. safety reps, safety committee members, etc.).

How many observers?   It is important to ensure that the minimum number of recruited observers reflects the number of locations, departments or shifts in the organisation. In some instances it may be wise to recruit extra observers from a particularly large location, so that cover is available if other observers are absent for any reason. Ideally, two observers should be recruited for each work group or work area, as this offers the advantages of a back-up if one of the observers is absent for any reason, and enables the organisation to reach a 'critical mass' of trained observers more quickly. This latter point is important, because the sooner more members of the workforce become observers, the more likely that rapid safety improvements will take place. This is partly due to the extra sets of 'eyes' in the workplace trained to focus on unsafe acts on a daily basis, and partly because the unsafe behaviours on the safety performance inventories tend to become imprinted on the observers' minds. Indeed, many observers tend to continue unofficial observations and correct their colleagues' unsafe behaviour long after they have finished their stint as an official observer.

Recruitment issues. It is essential, and courteous, to explain to potential observers that they will undergo training that will lead them to monitor the unsafe behaviour of their colleagues for a pre-determined period of time, as this helps to avoid unnecessary confusion and defensiveness. It has been known, for example, for people to attend an observer training course, thinking that they were merely attending one of a series of ongoing safety training courses provided by the company. Similarly, some observers have been known to be recruited unwillingly with a certain amount of arm-twisting. This often occurs when personnel do not wish to become involved because they are suspicious of management's intentions, or think that focusing on behaviour is trivial compared to the engineering solutions that might be needed. It must also be recognised that some people become defensive when asked to observe their colleagues, either because they lack confidence or because they are unwilling to change their own safety behaviour and set an example to others. Nonetheless, many of these recruitment problems can be overcome by explaining to people exactly what would be required of them, how it will help their colleagues avoid accidents and also help the organisation reduce accident costs, while also involving them as much as possible at every stage.

Identifying the Problem

One of the first stages in the process of changing safety behaviour involve the identification of the unsafe behaviours that are associated with the majority of accidents in a particular workplace. Initially, this is achieved by examining the company's existing accident records, near miss reports standard operating procedures and current risk assessments. Since every organisation undertakes many different types of activity, the causes of accidents are likely to vary. It makes sense, therefore, to examine and analyse all the accident-related records for the previous two years.

Historical Accident Data

Unless the computerised accident records are very comprehensive, it usually better to search through the original accident or near miss report This is so that the causes of the incident can be better categorised into behavioural or pathogenic (i.e. workflow process, plant and equipmen related) elements, or a combination of both. Once the causes have been identified they are categorised by place of work. Within each location, it is then possible to determine the extent to which a person's behaviour, the workflow process, the plant and equipment, or a combination of all three are most likely to cause an injury. This not only identifies unsafe behaviours, but also allows different types of task to be prioritised in relation to their injury potential (if not already done via risk assessments). Thereafter, the specific unsafe behaviours become the main focus of attention. For example, a near miss report may say

> 'Mr X tripped over electrical leads used by maintenance crews during repairs to the hopper in the production department. This caused a power tool to fall from overhead ducting, which narrowly missed hitting Mr X on the head.'

The unsafe behaviours presented by this scenario include people failing to tie up electrical cables on overhead ducting; failing to clear away their equipment after use; failing to place warning signs to indicate they are working overhead in the area; and failing to place barriers around a known tripping hazard.

Validating the Behaviours Identified

The frequency with which each of these unsafe behaviours appears to occur should be verified by confidentially interviewing about 15% of the workforce. These interviews also provide an opportunity to obtain information about other common unsafe behaviours or other safety issues that may not have appeared in any records. Indeed, it is possible to use interviewing techniques (see Chapter 6) with each work group as a whole to explore common unsafe behaviours, using the unsafe behaviours derived from the accident and near miss reports as a starting point. In this way the work groups will be much more closely involved in the development of the safety performance inventories, and are therefore much more likely to adopt and own them, than if developed purely by the project team, albeit with the benefit of discussions with some members of the workforce. If this course of action is adopted it is often a good idea to conduct the group sessions away from the group's workplace as the group members are likely to be much more relaxed and forthcoming.

Constructing Safety Performance Inventories

Once the frequency and extent of the unsafe behaviours have been established, safety performance inventories are constructed that focus on the most critical unsafe behaviours for each location in the workplace (e.g. production areas, maintenance, offices, etc.).

All departments. Unless the organisation is very small, it is unwise to develop one common safety performance inventory to cover the whole workplace, as each working area will have its own safety requirements. The only scenario where a single safety performance inventory might cover many work areas is in an office, although in the author's experience, even offices tend to differ from each other in many important ways.

Limits. It is usually a good idea to limit the number of unsafe behaviours for each safety performance inventory to a maximum of 25, as many more than this usually become unwieldy. Other critical unsafe behaviours can be focused upon during subsequent phases. Moreover, it may be best to leave out any mandatory behaviours such as wearing safety shoes, light eye protection, etc., as this still allows management the leeway to take disciplinary action if absolutely necessary.

Specific behaviours. The unsafe behaviours incorporated into the safety performance inventories should be written as specifically as possible. Items that reflect a number of behaviours within any one item can be confusing to measure and difficult to analyse. In turn this makes it difficult to provide detailed feedback to the work groups about the specific behaviours they are performing safely or unsafely. In some instances it may also be helpful to provide explicit instructions associated with each unsafe behaviour. The end result of this is to remove any ambiguity and ensure that people are very clear about what is required of them.

Accentuating the positive. The behavioural items should be written in such a way that they accentuate the positive, rather than represent a rule. For example,

> *'All personnel are holding the handrails when using the stairs'.*

In other words, writing them in a positive tone assumes that people are already behaving safely. The same item written as a rule would read

> *'All personnel MUST hold the handrail when using the stairs'.*

By comparing the way these two items are written it is possible to see that accentuating the positive is much more likely to engender the very behaviour that people should be engaging in.

Comments section.   It is often useful to incorporate a section for comments, as those employees who become safety observers inevitably notice other types of unsafe behaviours and the presence of hazards in the workplace. By providing the means to formally record these, it is possible to develop an item bank of unsafe behaviours that can be used to derive subsequent safety performance inventories. Any hazards identified can also be addressed in a proactive manner, before they cause any harm.

Recording Observation Scores

The format of the safety performance inventory should be such that the observers can record their observations in one of three columns: a 'safe' column; an 'unsafe' column; and a column for those items not seen (see Figure 9.3: *Example of Safety Performance Inventory*). The sum of each of the 'safe' and 'unsafe' columns is used to calculate the average percentage safe score. Each of these columns is scored in a particular way.

Recording 'safes'.   If everybody is behaving safely for an observation item, a '1' is entered in the 'safe' column, and a '0' in the corresponding 'unsafe' column. For example, if there were 10 forklift truck drivers, and all 10 of them were seen to sound their horn when going around a blind corner, they would all be scored as 'safe' by entering a '1' in the safe column and entering a '0' in the corresponding unsafe column.

Recording 'unsafes'.   If some people are behaving unsafely, a '0' is entered in the safe column, and the number of people behaving unsafely is entered in the 'unsafe' column. For example, if three of the 10 forklift truck drivers did not sound their horn when going around a blind corner '3' would be entered in the unsafe column, and a '0' in the corresponding safe column. Similarly, if eight of the forklift drivers did not sound their horn when going around a blind corner, '8' would be entered in the unsafe column and a '0' in the corresponding safe column. It is important to note that a single instance of an 'unsafe' behaviour for a safety performance inventory item always cancels out all the 'safe' instances for that item. In this way, the proportion of 'safe' to 'unsafe' behaviours can be recorded and calculated, while ensuring that the slightest improvement in safety performance is detected. In addition, because the scoring system is heavily weighted towards unsafe behaviour, any improvements in the average percentage 'safe' score should correspond with reality in the workplace.

Recording 'unseens'.   If a particular activity is not seen taking place, a '1' is entered in the 'unseen' column. For example, if the behavioural item on the

THE B-SAFE PROGRAMME ®

SAFETY PERFORMANCE INVENTORY

Group: Applied Behavioural Sciences Ltd   **Company:** Chartered Psychologists

Department: Safety   **Work Area:** Office

Team: **Date:**

Category: Office

			Safe	Unsafe	Unseen
1 0	The following are closed when not in use:				
1 1	a: Desk drawers				
1 2	b: Filing cabinet drawers				
1 3	c: Cupboard doors				
2 0	All the corridor floors are clear of files, paper, boxes, etc.				
3 0	All electrical leads have been stowed away so that they do not cause a trip hazard				
4 0	No briefcases, handbags, coats, etc., are causing a trip hazard				
5 0	Nobody is sitting in tilted chairs; all the chair legs are on the floor				
6 0	All chairs are pushed up to or under desks when not in use				
7 0	Personnel using the shredder have tucked away their ties, jewellery, etc.				

Category: Stairs

			Safe	Unsafe	Unseen
8 0	Personnel are walking up and down the stairs, one step at a time				
9 0	Personnel are holding onto the handrail when using the stairs				

Category: Shelves

			Safe	Unsafe	Unseen
10 0	No shelves above head height are overloaded				
11 0	Materials stored on shelves above head height are stored neatly and tidily				
12 0	Access to shelves is free from obstructions				
13 0	The store room is neat and tidy				

Category: Emergency Access

			Safe	Unsafe	Unseen
14 0	Access to emergency equipment is clear from obstructions				
15 0	Access to fire exits is clear of obstructions				
16 0	No fire check doors are wedged open				

% Safe = (Total Safe / (Total Safe + Total Unsafe)) * 100   **Total**

Comments

Figure 9.3   Example Safety Performance Inventory (Courtesy of Applied Behavioural Sciences Ltd)

safety performance inventory refers to forklift truck drivers sounding their horn when going around blind corners, and no-one is seen using a forklift truck, then a '1' is simply put in the 'unseen' column.

Calculating a Percentage Safe Score

To calculate the average percentage safe score, both the 'safe' and 'unsafe' columns are summed separately, i.e. all the '1's' are summed in the safe column, and the amount of 'unsafes' are summed in the unsafe column. The 'unseens' are ignored for the purposes of calculation, but are used at a later date to help develop new safety performance inventories. The next step is to add the number of 'safes' and 'unsafes' together to gain a total score. The sum of the 'safe' column is then divided by the total number of 'safes' and 'unsafes'. The product of this is multiplied by 100 to produce a percentage 'safe' score. It is important that the weekly percentage 'safe' score is derived from the summing of the observation results recorded in the 'safe' and 'unsafe' columns for each day's observations, and *not* by summing the daily average percentage 'safes', otherwise the final percentage 'safe' score will be distorted. The formulae for calculating the percentage 'safe' score is:

$$\% \text{ SAFE} = \frac{\text{Total Safe}}{\text{Total Safe} + \text{Total Unsafe}} \times 100$$

A worked example might be

$$\% \text{ SAFE} = \frac{20 \text{ Observed Safes}}{20 \text{ Observed Safes} + 20 \text{ Observed Unsafes}} \times 100$$

Equals

$$\frac{20}{40} = 0.5 \times 100 = 50\%$$

Implementing the Change Strategy

Implementation of a behavioural safety change strategy follows a basic procedure that encompasses observer training, establishing a baseline to discover current levels of safety performance, and getting the work groups to set their own safety improvement targets based on the baseline results.

Observer Training

Once the safety performance inventories have been developed it is necessary to train the observers. If there are more than 25 of them it may be prudent to allow for more than one training session, as numbers greater than this make it difficult to train them effectively. Training is sometimes conducted over two days to allow for practice observations to be undertaken on both days. However, given other organisational constraints, it may be more prudent to keep the training highly focused and limited to one day. Indeed, many trainees prefer one day's training.

The content of the training should encompass:

- the rationale for the organisation adopting a behavioural safety improvement initiative (i.e. an outline of the organisation's previous efforts to improve safety; the effects this has had on accident rates; the costs of accidents (e.g. compensation claims, lost production, etc.) in recent years; the problems remaining (i.e. current accident rate); and how the approach will complement rather than replace existing safety improvement initiatives
- the reasons for people behaving unsafely and how unsafe behaviours can be eliminated
- what being an observer means
- how the safety performance inventories were devised, and how they should be scored
- how to set safety performance targets with the trainees' peers
- how to recognise and manage resistance from others
- how to give feedback to others about their behaviour
- training room practice of observation skills by using a slide show or video of real-life examples of unsafe behaviours or conditions found in the place of work
- one hour practice observations in the workplace
- discussions about the ground rules for observations (e.g. how to interpret the scoring of unsafe behaviours or conditions)
- what they should do with the observation data (e.g. give it to project co-ordinator for calculation or enter it into a computer)
- a close-out session that summarises the training and explains how logistical and other support will be provided.

Once the observers have completed their training, they should conduct a further two weeks' practice observations in their place of work to help ensure that they are comfortable and conversant with their task. This also provides an opportunity for the safety performance inventories to be assessed in terms of their utility and practicality so that refinements can be made if interpretation of some of the behavioural items proves to be troublesome.

Establishing Baselines

Once the two-week practice period has been completed, the observers conduct daily 10 to 15-minute observations of their peers, for a four to six-week period to establish a current safety performance baseline. Each work group discovers their own baseline levels so that subsequent improvements can be compared with the baseline. The average percentage safe baseline score is used as the basis for the work group to set their own safety improvement target. In most instances, feedback about ongoing safety performance is not provided to the work group during the baseline period. This is so that the baseline observation data will reflect the true levels of current safety performance, as people will not proactively change their behaviour during this period because they will not know which specific behaviours are scoring badly. If people are suspicious about the observation process, it is often a good idea to post enlarged 'laminated' copies of the safety performance inventories on the work group's health and safety noticeboard at the beginning of the baseline period, so that they are aware of the specific behaviours being monitored and the lack of a facility to record people's names. Sometimes, however, it may prove necessary to utilise a 'moving baseline' strategy, whereby weekly feedback *is* provided during the baseline period. Although this may alter the true levels of current safety performance, it is better to do this than see the project hit large pockets of resistance which may lead to its demise before it has really got off the ground.

Target Setting

Once the baseline period has been completed, the project team calculate each work group's average safety percentage score for the baseline period. These scores are posted on specially prepared departmental 3' × 4' graphical feedback charts (see Figure 9.4). The vertical axis indicates the percentage safe score (with a range from 0% to 100%), while the horizontal axis indicates time (e.g. 52 weeks).

Each work group then holds a 30 minute target setting session that involves every member of the group. This should encompass:

- the purpose of the meeting
- the development of the work group's safety performance inventory
- how the average safety percentage score is calculated
- informing the group of their average baseline safe percentage score
- highlighting the behaviours performed safely, and where improvements can be made

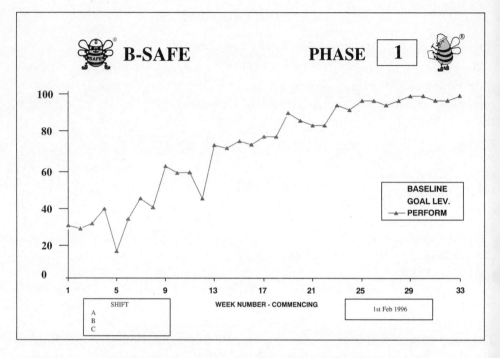

Figure 9.4   Graphical Feedback Chart. Source: Courtesy of Applied Behavioural Sciences Ltd

- setting a hard but achievable target based on the baseline safe percentage score
- stressing that no disciplinary actions will be taken if the target is not reached
- explaining that feedback about ongoing performance will be provided each week
- thanking everybody for their time and effort
- posting the work group's safety target on the graphical feedback chart at the appropriate level.

   The project champion, co-ordinator or leader of the target-setting session should take a note of each group's safety performance target as they will need to enter this information into their other records so that they will know when a work group has achieved its target. In addition, the project team should ensure that each graphical feedback chart is positioned on a wall somewhere in the work group's working area, so that it is always visible to the work groups during the working day. In this way the feedback chart acts as a permanent reminder of the safety improvement target, while also conveying the work group's ongoing progress.

Evaluating the Extent of Change

After the target-setting session, the observers continue to monitor their colleagues' behaviour each day they are at work for a further three to six-month period, depending upon how long the phase is set to last. If they wish, observers could provide verbal feedback about someone's safety behaviour at the point of observation. However, it is important to ensure that each work group is provided with feedback about their ongoing performance every week by posting the average percentage safe score on the graphical feedback chart. Group feedback should also be given via discussions at 30-minute weekly team briefings. If the feedback is not given on a weekly basis, there is a very real danger that the work group will believe that the behavioural safety initiative is not important. This could mean that the work group will start to disengage themselves from the project in the belief that it is a passing management fad. The same will be found if the weekly team briefings are not held every week to discuss the observation results.

Feedback Issues

The project team should provide a detailed breakdown of each work group's observation data so that detailed discussions can be held about their ongoing safety behaviour. This should encompass:

- the percentage increase or decrease from the previous week's average safe percentage score
- the three best and worst scoring items
- a breakdown of each individual category of a work group's safety performance inventory in terms of the number of 'safes', 'unsafes' and 'unseens' recorded
- the average safe percentage score for each category
- the percentage of observations conducted within each category.

It is *very* important for the project co-ordinator to allocate the time to this task every week. When done by hand, it takes approximately four hours per eight workgroups. This is why it is better to try and use computerised methods of calculation, as the results can be analysed and printed in a matter of minutes, thereby significantly reducing the ongoing costs of the behavioural safety initiative.

Correcting any Deviations from the Changes Required

At a strategic level, the observation data is further analysed by the project team to ensure that everything is running smoothly. The data is analysed in various ways so that any deviations can be spotted and addressed. This usually means monitoring:

• trends
• the data, to see if discrepancies in the average safety percentage scores exist between shifts working in the same area, etc.
• the data with a view to developing new safety performance inventories for the next phase
• the levels of ongoing support the observers receive from management.

Monitoring Trends

It is inevitable that people's ongoing safety behaviour will be affected by other organisational activities (e.g. increases in sales or production, new plant and equipment coming on stream, maintenance shutdowns, etc.). The project team can monitor trends in the safety observation data to ascertain which of these other activities are affecting people's ongoing safety behaviour. If, for example, the observation scores for a particular work area dipped unexpectedly, the project team would want to know why. They could talk to the work group concerned to discover whether this was caused by people disengaging themselves from the project or whether the activities that were taking place during that week were thought to be responsible. The project team could then either address the concerns of those who might have disengaged themselves, or peruse the appropriate activity records and compare the two sets of data to discover the magnitude of the relationship (if any). By using this latter method it is possible to discover which of the organisation's activities adversely affect safety. This information can then be used to good effect at the times these activities take place. For example, the work group's observers could be asked to increase the frequency of their observations to twice a day, and line management could be asked to be on hand to encourage people to work safely when these activities take place.

Monitoring the Observation Data for Each Shift

If a particular working area is run on a shift basis, it is always a good idea to compare each shift's observation data for large discrepancies. Although it is not unusual to find small differences between shift groups working in the same area, large discrepancies in the observation data could indicate problems in the interpretation of some or all of the behavioural items. Something is amiss, for example, if two shift observers consistently indicate housekeeping problems such as spills and leaks, and another shift observer indicates that there are no problems with spills and leaks. Large differences such as this could signal the need for the project team to undertake a 'double monitoring' observation period with each of the shift observers to ensure that the interpretative ground rules are being adhered to. In this way it is possible to discover and address any discrepancies between observers to ensure that the observation data accurately reflects reality in the workplace.

Monitoring the Frequency of Observations

It is also important for the project team to monitor the frequency of observations for each work group, as a lack of observations would indicate problems. For example, an observer may be finding it difficult to conduct daily observations because of the pressure of work, because of a lack of cover of the observer's normal job by a colleague, because the observer's line managers will not allow him or her to conduct observations, or because the observer has withdrawn from the project. It is only by monitoring the frequency of observations that the project team can apply the appropriate solutions to the problems identified.

Developing New Safety Performance Inventories

The data can and should be analysed to help develop new safety performance inventories. This is achieved by looking for safety performance inventory items that are, or were, consistently scored as 'safe', 'unsafe, or 'unseen' by the observers. Items consistently recorded as 'unseen' would be excluded from the new safety performance inventory. However, it is always worth checking why the item is never seen, as it may simply be due to the timing of each 10-minute observation period. Items consistently scoring 'safe' could indicate that the safety behaviour has improved to such an extent that it is no longer a problem. If this is the case it would not appear on the new safety performance inventory but be replaced with a new behavioural item. Items consistently scoring as 'unsafe' would remain on the new safety performance inventory until such time as they consistently scored as 'safe'. Analysing the data in this way helps to ensure that the development of new safety performance inventories is truly evolutionary.

Monitoring the Levels of Visible Ongoing Support

To ensure that everything is running smoothly, it is important to monitor the weekly levels of visible ongoing support received by the observers from their line managers, as well as the project champion and co-ordinator. Each work group's line manager should accompany an observer during an observation period at least once a week, and either conduct the weekly briefings or support the observers when they conduct the briefings. Both the project champion and co-ordinator should also make a point of contacting each work group's observer during the week to make sure they are not experiencing any problems. Ongoing visible support inventories should be compiled before the project is implemented. These should be completed once a week by each work group observer to provide an indication of the levels of support they have received. In this way any organisational problems can be quickly identified and addressed, before they affect the viability of the project.

A Final Word

The above provides a strategic overview of the major elements to implementing a behavioural initiative. It must be recognised that although a successful implementation will take a great deal of time and effort on everybody's part, the rewards (e.g. reductions in accidents and their associated human and financial costs) far outweigh any problems that might arise. This strategic overview has been derived from extensive scientific field trials in the construction, chemicals and manufacturing sectors personally conducted by the author. Recognising that many companies are exerting downward pressures on their competitive cost base, this implementation strategy has been deliberately structured to keep operational costs to the absolute minimum by including only the essentials. Therefore it is recommended that *none* of the key elements should be left out during the process of implementation. Indeed, it may be possible to add value to the programme (e.g. publicising progress via in-house journals, training observers over two days rather than one, etc.).

It is also vital to ensure that the organisation's management play a strong proactive supportive role in the day-to-day running of the programme, as this can make or break the project in the longer term. This means involving them as much as possible at each stage, so that they 'buy in' to the process. It is certainly worthwhile keeping everybody informed of progress on a regular basis. In the same vein, it is very important to ensure that the work groups are fully involved at every stage in the project's development, as it is important that the project team do not find themselves developing the programme in a vacuum and then trying to impose it on the work groups by dictat. If this occurs, resistance will be met at all levels of the organisation which may well lead to the demise of the project before it has got off the ground. Similarly, do not allow a bureaucratic nightmare to be created, as this will demotivate many of the people who should be involved. The value of the programme resides in the observation process and the feedback this provides, simply because it focuses people's attention on their ongoing safety behaviour. Although some records will need to be kept to aid in the development of new phases and safety performance inventories, these are mainly concerned with keeping a box file of memos, completed safety performance inventories, and copies of the work group's weekly feedback reports. Thus bureaucracy can be kept to a minimum.

Finally, it is inevitable that those implementing the programme will meet resistance, obstacles and problems, especially during the early phases. It can sometimes appear that they are going forwards two steps, and one step backwards. However, these problems present learning opportunities that will help them to continually improve their safety efforts and reduce their company's accident rates. As such, it is in their colleagues' interests that they keep persevering and do not give up. They should aim for zero accidents, and when they achieve that, strive to maintain their safety performance at that level of excellence.

Additional Readings

For readers who want more information about improving safety culture, the author recommends the following books:

Arnold, J., Robertson, I. T. and Cooper, C. L. *Work Psychology: Understanding Human Behaviour in the Workplace*, 2nd edition, Pitman, London, 1995.

Atkinson, P. E. *Creating Culture Change: The key to Successful Total Quality Management*, Kempston, IFS, 1990.

Bandura, A., *Social Learning Theory*. Englewood Cliffs, N. J.: Prentice Hall, 1986.

Bryman, A., *Leadership and Organizations*, Routledge & Kegan Paul, London, 1986.

CBI, *Developing a Safety Culture*, London, 1990.

Child, J., *Organization: A Guide to Problems and Practice*, 2nd edition, Harper & Row Ltd, London, 1987.

Combs, M. R., *Information Systems for Business Management*, Pitman, London, 1995.

Cooper, M. D., *The B-Safe Programme*, Applied Behavioural Sciences, Hull, 1996.

Cooper, M. D. and Robertson, I. T., *The Psychology of Personnel Selection: A Quality Approach*, Routledge, London, 1995.

Cotton, J. L., *Employee Involvement: Methods for Improving Performance and Work Attitudes*, Sage, London, 1993.

Douglas, M., *Risk and Blame: Essays in Cultural Theory*, Routledge, London, 1992.

Glendon, A. I. and McKenna, E. F., *Human Safety and Risk Management*, Chapman & Hall, London, 1995.

Grandjean, E., *Fitting the Task to the Man: An Ergonomics Approach*, Taylor & Francis, London, 1980.

Hackman, J. R. and Oldham, G. R., *Work Redesign*, Addison Wesley, Reading, Ma., 1980.

Hannagan, T., *Management: Concepts and Practices*, Pitman, London, 1995.

Harry, M., *Information Systems in Business*, Pitman, London, 1994.

HSC, *Management of Health and Safety at Work Regulations*, HMSO: London, 1992.

HSC, *Third Report: Organising for Safety*, ACSNI Study Group on Human Factors, HMSO: London, 1992.

HSE, *Successful Health and Safety Management*, 2nd edition, Health and Safety Series booklet HS(G) 65, HMSO: London, 1992.

HSE, *Human Factors in Industrial Safety*, HS(G) 48, HMSO, London, 1989.

HSE, *The Costs of Accidents at Work*, HMSO: London, 1993.

Ishikawa, K., *What is Total Quality Control? The Japanese Way*, Prentice-Hall, Englewood Cliffs, 1985.

Karasek, R. and Theorell, T., *Healthy Work: Stress, Productivity and the Reconstruction of Working Life*, Basic Books, New York, 1992.

Kirwan B. and Ainsworth, L. K., *A Guide to Task Analysis*, Taylor & Francis, London, 1992.

Mathews, R. H., (ed.), *Reliability, 91*, Elsevier, Amsterdam, 1991.

Perrow, C., *Normal Accidents: Living with high risk technologies*, New York: Basic Books, 1984.

Rasmussen, J., Learning from Experience? How? Some Research Issues in Industrial Risk Management, In B. Wilpert and T. Qvale (Eds). *Reliability and Safety in Hazardous Work Systems*. Lawrence Earlbaum Associates: Hove, Sussex, 1993.

Reason, J., *Human Error*, NY: Cambridge University Press, 1990.

Robertson, I. T., Smith, J. M. and Cooper, M. D., *Motivation: Strategies, Theory and Practice*, IPM: London, 1992.

Rousseau, D. M., The Construction of Climate in Organisational Research, In C. L. Cooper and I. T. Robertson (Eds). *International Review of Industrial and Organisational Psychology*, Wiley: Chichester, Vol 3, 139–58, 1988.

Singleton, W. T. and Hovden, J., *Risk and Decisions*, J. Wiley & Sons, Chichester, 1994.

Waring, A., *Safety Management Systems*, Chapman & Hall, London, 1996.

Warr, P., *Psychology at Work*, 2nd edition, Penguin Books, Harmandsworth, 1978.

Warr, P., *Psychology at Work*, 3rd edition, Penguin Books, Harmandsworth, 1987.

Yates, J. F., *Risk-taking Behaviour*, Wiley Series in Human Performance and Cognition. J. Wiley & Sons, Chichester, 1992.

Index